SCHOLASTIC

Research-Based Reading Lessons

Grades 4-6

LATE

MAUREEN McLAUGHLIN

AMY HOMEYER

JENNIFER SASSAMAN

New York • Toronto • London • Auckland • Sydney
Mexico City • New Delhi • Hong Kong • Buenos Aires

Teaching *Resources*

Acknowledgments

As always, there are many people to thank for their assistance in producing
this book. We thank them now for their patience and encouragement.
We offer special gratitude to the following:

ALEXANDRIA GIBB, East Stroudsburg University of Pennsylvania

JANE SASSAMAN, Ironia Elementary School, Randolph, New Jersey

TEACHERS & ADMINISTRATORS, Lincoln-Roosevelt School, Roxbury, New Jersey

KATHRYN O'BRIEN, John J. Marshall Elementary and
John F. Kennedy Elementary, Scranton, Pennsylvania

DANIELLE BEVILACQUA, East Stroudsburg University of Pennsylvania

LYNN WARD, East Stroudsburg University of Pennsylvania

MARLA MOYER, Palmer Elementary School, Easton Area School District,
Easton, Pennsylvania

HEATHER GARRISON, East Stroudsburg University of Pennsylvania

JOANNA DAVIS-SWING, Editorial Director, Scholastic Teaching Resources

SUSAN KOLWICZ, Senior Marketing Manager, Scholastic Teaching Resources

Cover and interior design by Maria Lilja
Cover photograph © Comstock Images
ISBN-13: 978-0-439-84381-2 • ISBN-10: 0-439-84381-2

2 3 4 5 6 7 8 9 10   40   11 10 09 08 07 06

Contents

Introduction

As reading teachers, we strive to meet our students' needs. We do this by keeping informed of developments in research and best practices. These, in turn, become the basis of our professional development and our teaching. This book focuses on the current emphases for teaching reading in the intermediate grades: word study, fluency, vocabulary, and comprehension.

Each of these components of literacy contributes to readers' understanding of text. Word study, or examining how words are structured, provides a deeper understanding of our language and how it works. Fluency, or reading with expression, helps the reader to move beyond word-by-word reading and comprehend the text as a whole. Vocabulary, or understanding what words mean, is an essential component of comprehension, the process through which the reader constructs meaning. Research shows that word study, fluency, vocabulary, and comprehension can and should be taught.

We wrote this book as a practical guide for teaching these literacy components in Grades 4–6. We begin with a research-based discussion of current trends in teaching reading. Then, in Chapters 2 through 5, we examine each of the four building blocks of literacy— word study, fluency, vocabulary, and comprehension—by explaining the component, delineating its research base, presenting a sound instructional format, providing practical ideas for teaching, describing numerous classroom-tested lessons, and offering suggestions for further reading. The lessons in these chapters follow six classic intermediate-grade themes: Mystery, Survival, Biography, Fantasy, the Holocaust, and Poetry. In the conclusion we discuss the challenges of teaching from a strategy-based perspective. The book ends with numerous appendices that include resources such as teaching ideas, annotated book lists and Web site lists, detailed descriptions of comprehension strategies and related blackline masters, and guidelines for using literature circles and creating literacy centers.

If you are an intermediate-grade teacher, reading specialist, reading coach, curriculum specialist, school administrator, preservice teacher, or teacher educator, this is the volume that will take you beyond the activity books and provide you with a clear understanding of the research base for the building blocks of literacy as well as a strong instructional framework and classroom-tested lessons. In the final analysis, the teaching of reading is not about the federal government's emphases; it's about our continuing quest to become excellent reading teachers—educators who won't settle for anything less than having all our students achieve their greatest possible potential.

CHAPTER 1

Teaching Research-Based Reading in Grades 4–6

As teachers of reading, we know all too well the need to keep pace with developments in literacy. Like you, we want to know which components of the reading process should be emphasized in instruction and how best to teach them. Word study, vocabulary, fluency, and comprehension are the current research emphases in the intermediate grades, and these elements are the focus of this book.

In this volume, we focus on three aspects of teaching these building blocks of literacy: (1) reporting what the research has to say; (2) providing a well-established instructional framework for teaching; and (3) presenting classroom-taught lessons that feature teacher think-alouds and examples of student work.

The research base and lessons differ for each component and, consequently, are presented separately in Chapters 2, 3, 4, and 5, each of which addresses a specific element. The teaching framework and its theoretical underpinnings, which provide the instructional foundation of all the lessons, are detailed in the next section.

The Guided Comprehension Model for the Intermediate Grades

The instructional framework used to create the lessons in this volume is the Guided Comprehension Model for the Intermediate Grades (McLaughlin & Allen, 2002a). The Model is underpinned by numerous current beliefs about literacy. These include the following:

• Good readers are active and strategic (Askew & Fountas, 1998).

• Motivation and engagement are essential to the reading process (Gambrell, 1996; Guthrie & Wigfield, 2000).

• Reading comprehension skills and strategies can and should be taught— beginning in the primary grades (Hilden & Pressley, 2002; McLaughlin, 2003).

• Multiple types and levels of texts should be read daily.

• Assessment is a dynamic process.

The Guided Comprehension Model for the Intermediate Grades is a three-stage process focused on direct and guided instruction, application, and reflection (see Figure 1-1). The Model progresses in the following sequence:

STAGE ONE: Teacher-directed whole-group instruction

STAGE TWO: Comprehension strategy practice in teacher-guided small groups and student-facilitated comprehension centers and routines

STAGE THREE: Teacher-facilitated whole-group reflection and goal setting

FIGURE 1-1

Overview of Guided Comprehension Instruction

(adapted from McLaughlin & Allen, 2002a)

STAGE 1

Teacher-Directed Whole-Group Instruction:
Teaching a comprehension strategy using easy, instructional, or challenging text.

EXPLAIN the strategy of the day and how it relates to the class goal.

DEMONSTRATE the strategy using a think-aloud and a read-aloud.

GUIDE student practice by reading additional sections of text aloud and having students apply the strategy with support. Monitor students' application.

PRACTICE by having students apply the strategy to another section of text you have read, providing minimal support. Application can occur in small groups or pairs.

REFLECT by having students think about what they know and how they can use this strategy on their own.

STAGE 2

Students apply the comprehension strategies in teacher-guided small groups and student-facilitated comprehension centers and routines. In these settings, students work with varying levels of support and use appropriate instructional- and independent-level texts.

Teacher-Guided Small-Group Instruction:
Applying comprehension strategies with teacher guidance using instructional-level texts and dynamic grouping (4 to 6 students).

REVIEW previously taught strategies and focus on strategy of the day.

GUIDE students to apply the strategy of the day as well as previously taught strategies as they read a section of the instructional-level text. Prompt students to construct and share personal meanings. Scaffold as necessary, gradually releasing support as students become more proficient. Encourage discussion and repeat with other sections of text.

PRACTICE by having students work in pairs or individually to apply the strategy. Encourage discussion. Have students record their strategy applications in their Guided Comprehension Journals and share them with the class during Stage 3.

REFLECT by having students engage in a second reading of the text, retell what they have read, and share ways in which the strategy helped them to understand the text. Talk about ways in which students can apply the strategy in comprehension centers and routines.

Student-Facilitated Comprehension Centers and Routines:
Applying comprehension strategies individually, in pairs, or in small groups using independent-level texts.

COMPREHENSION CENTERS are purposeful, authentic, independent settings that provide opportunities to practice strategy application and extend understanding.

COMPREHENSION ROUTINES are procedures that foster habits of thinking and processing that aid in comprehension of text such as cross-age reading experiences and literature circles.

STAGE 3

Teacher-Facilitated Whole-Group Reflection and Goal Setting:
Reflecting on performance, sharing experiences, and setting new goals.

SHARE performances from Stage 2.

REFLECT on ability to use the strategy.

SET NEW GOALS or extend existing ones.

Assessment Options: *Use authentic measures in all stages.*

STAGE ONE

The structure of the Model supports scaffolded teaching and learning. It begins with explicit whole-group instruction during Stage One. In this stage, the teacher provides a great deal of support, including read-alouds and think-alouds, during the Explain and Demonstrate steps. This support gradually decreases as the students work in small groups or pairs in the Guide step and may lessen to an even greater degree in the Practice step, when students may progress from working in small groups to pairs, or from pairs to individually. In the Reflect step, the teacher and students openly discuss what has been learned.

The texts used in Stage One vary and may include chapter books (narrative or informational), picture books (narrative or informational), informational articles, and poetry. During Stage One, the teacher reads the text.

STAGE TWO

In Stage Two, students experience three settings: small-group guided instruction with the teacher; independent practice with a partner or individually in the comprehension centers; and independent practice in pairs or small groups in comprehension routines, such as Literature Circles and Cross-Age Reading Experiences. Detailed descriptions of each aspect of Stage Two follow.

Teacher-Guided Small-Group Instruction

Teacher-Guided Small-Group Instruction consists of guided reading. Students are assessed—usually by using running records. Then, students are initially organized into small groups based on similarities in their instructional level; as they progress, they are placed in more advanced groups. Therefore, the structure of guided reading groups is dynamic and changes frequently to accommodate students' progress.

Texts used in this setting, which may include chapter books, picture books, informational articles, and poetry, accommodate students' instructional levels. In reading, there are three levels: independent, instructional, and frustration. Students can read books at the independent, or easy, level with little or no assistance. Consequently, this is the level of text students read when they are working independently. Students can read books at the instructional, or just-right, level with some help from the teacher. This is the level of text used in guided reading, because the teacher works with the small group and is able to provide support as necessary. The final level of reading, the frustration level, is the level at which students may encounter difficulty when reading. Books at this level are too challenging for students to read on their own, so they are often shared through books on tape, teacher read-alouds, or Cross-Age Reading Experiences. Students should be exposed to all three levels of text every day.

When teaching guided reading, we follow four steps: Review, Guide, Practice, Reflect. To *review*, we usually introduce the book, remind students which strategy and teaching idea we will be focusing on, and have a brief discussion. If we are beginning a new chapter book, we may read the opening chapter to help students make connections. Next, we *guide* the students as they begin reading a set amount of text. For example, we may offer a prompt, such as "As you're reading, remember to stop periodically to make connections [or use whatever strategy the students will be practicing]." While reading, students apply their reading comprehension strategies. When the students finish reading the designated segment of text, we discuss as a class our strategy applications as they pertain to the text. Then the students continue to read and *practice* their comprehension strategies. When that segment is read, we discuss again. Finally, we *reflect* on what we have learned about the text and strategy use. Each guided reading group lasts about 20 minutes.

Because the books used during guided reading are at the students' instructional levels, they are not used for homework. Students read easier, independent-level, theme-related texts at home.

To learn more about Guided Reading, consider reading

- Fountas, I. C., & Pinnell, G. S. (1996). *Guided reading: Good first teaching for all children.* Portsmouth, NH: Heinemann.

- McLaughlin, M., & Allen, M. B. (2002a). *Guided Comprehension: A teaching model for grades 3–8.* Newark, DE: International Reading Association.

Comprehension-Based Literacy Centers

Comprehension centers provide purposeful, authentic settings for students to independently integrate and apply their comprehension strategies. Students may work in small groups, pairs, or individually at the centers.

Center activities should accommodate a variety of learning levels and be open-ended and capable of being completed independently—in small groups, pairs, or individually. The activities should be purposeful, address a variety of interests and intelligences, and help students to think critically and creatively. They should also be engaging, foster discussion, extend learning, and promote decision-making and student ownership of learning.

The centers are usually located around the perimeter of the classroom and away from teacher-guided small-group instruction. The centers vary in appearance from tabletop displays to pizza boxes and gift bags. It is important to remember that the content of the center is more important than its physical appearance.

Although there are many activities that can be completed at literacy centers, it is important to remember that in Guided Comprehension, center activities are designed to promote the students' development and application of comprehension skills and strategies. Examples of centers, including the Theme Center, Listening Center, Poetry Center, Word Study Center, and Writing Center, are featured in the lessons in Chapters 2, 3, 4, and 5.

To learn more about Comprehension-Based Literacy Centers, consider reading

- Ford, M. P., & Opitz, M. F. (2002). Using centers to engage children during guided reading time: Intensifying learning experiences away from the teacher. *The Reading Teacher, 55*, 710–717.

- McLaughlin, M., & Allen, M. B. (2002a). *Guided Comprehension: A teaching model for grades 3–8.* Newark, DE: International Reading Association.

Literature Circles

If you've ever read a great book, chances are you couldn't wait to discuss it with a friend. Literature Circles offer this opportunity to students by providing time to converse about texts in meaningful, personal, and thoughtful ways (Brabham & Villaume, 2000).

To implement Literature Circles, explicitly teach the concept and engage in active demonstration. We use the five steps in Stage One of Guided Comprehension: Explain, Demonstrate, Guide, Practice, and Reflect.

Begin by explaining that Literature Circles are informal gatherings in which groups of students who are reading the same book meet to discuss various aspects of the text. Also explain that the books read in Literature Circles are not assigned; they are chosen by the students. Our favorite ways to facilitate the students' choices are the Book Sell and the Book Pass. In the Book Sell, the teacher holds up a book, shares the title and author, and reads the first few pages. Then students jot down the title if it interests them. This procedure is repeated five or six times—depending on the number of Literature Circles being organized. In the Book Pass, one copy of each of five or six titles is placed on a table. Then the students gather at the table and individual students examine each title for three to five minutes. The students read the title, examine the cover illustration, and read a few pages. If they have interest in a book, they jot down the title. After they have examined the book, they pass it to the person next to them. This continues until all of the students have reviewed all of the titles. In both the Book Sell and the Book Pass, the Literature Circles are formed based on students' book selections. For example, if one of the texts on the Holocaust theme was *The Diary of Anne Frank* and five or six students chose it, those students would become members of the same Literature Circle. We like to share theme-related books because it extends the theme and motivates students to take a more active role in theme-related activities. We also share books at different reading levels to accommodate all of our learners. Appendix F (page 208) features lists of titles related to the themes presented in this book: Mystery, Survival, Biography, Fantasy, the Holocaust, and Poetry.

In the second step of Stage One, the teacher demonstrates how Literature Circles work. To begin, the teacher reads aloud a short text that will be the focus of the Literature Circle. Next, the teacher invites several students to become part of a Literature Circle that can serve as a model for the class. The teacher explains that each student performs a particular role, but the roles change every time the Literature Circles meet. So, for example, if Roberto were Discussion Director today, he may be the Word Finder tomorrow. That is why it is important to teach all of the roles to all of the students.

The teacher can decide which roles will be used, but common roles include the following:

- Discussion Director

- Word Finder

- Connector

- Illustrator

- Summarizer

The Discussion Director is responsible for keeping the conversation focused and asking meaningful questions. The Word Finder chooses a vocabulary word or two that the whole circle discusses. The Connector makes text-to-self, text-to-text, and text-to-world connections. The Illustrator sketches a scene from the text that will inspire discussion. The Summarizer reiterates the important points of the discussion and may also briefly summarize the pages read for that day's meeting. Roles are generally used to prompt ideas until the students can actively engage in discussion about their books without them.

The teacher usually proposes parameters about the time frame, suggesting how frequently the circles will meet, how long each circle session will last (usually 20 minutes), and how many pages or chapters may be read for each meeting; but it is the students who make the final decisions.

In the third step of direct instruction, the teacher *guides* other students in the class to contribute ideas to the model Literature Circle. Next, the teacher invites the remaining students to form Literature Circles and *practice* various roles. Finally, the class *reflects* on what it knows about Literature Circles and how to engage in them.

Because the teacher does not participate in Literature Circles, it's especially important for the students to engage in self-assessment. Students reflecting on and responding to questions, such as those raised in the Literature Circle Student Self-Assessment blackline (see page 209), is one way teachers can assess how well students perform while in the circles. Other assessments may include students' completed strategy applications (see blacklines in Appendices C and D) and the group Literature Circle Extension Project List. (See Appendix E for project suggestions.)

Literature Circles offer students opportunities to engage in the social construction of meaning through discussion. This helps students understand that we all have ideas about what we read and that sharing them is an illuminating and rewarding experience. Daniels (1994) and Tompkins (2001) suggest ten guiding principles for using Literature Circles:

- Students self-select the books they will read.
- Each group reads something different.
- Groups meet on a regular basis, according to predetermined schedules.
- Students use writings or drawings to guide their conversations.
- Students determine the topics for discussions and lead the conversations.
- The teacher acts as a facilitator, not an instructor or leader.
- Teachers assess students by observing conversations within groups and engaging students in self-evaluation.
- Students are actively involved in reading and discussing books.
- After reading the books, the students share with their classmates, choose new books to read, and begin the cycle anew.

To learn more about Literature Circles, consider reading

- Daniels, H. (1994). *Literature circles: Voice and choice in the student-centered classroom.* York, ME: Stenhouse.

- Day, J. P., Spiegel, D. L., McLellan, J., & Brown, V. B. (2002). *Moving forward with literature circles.* New York: Scholastic.

- McLaughlin, M., & Allen, M. B. (2002a). *Guided Comprehension: A teaching model for grades 3–8.* Newark, DE: International Reading Association.

Cross-Age Reading Experiences

Cross-Age Reading Experiences usually involve younger students working on a specific literacy task with students who are usually at least two years older for a particular period of time. In Guided Comprehension, Cross-Age Reading Experiences—one of the routines students use to apply and transfer comprehension skills and strategies—involve text exploration and the construction of personal meaning. The resulting learning experiences are meaningful and memorable for all involved.

Cross-age activities can vary, but in Guided Comprehension they usually focus on classroom visits, in which the older students read to the younger students and practice related comprehension strategies. Other activities may include but are not limited to Cross-Age Journals, in which younger and older students write about their favorite hobbies, books, and experiences and exchange their journals weekly, and Helper Days, in which older students visit the classrooms of younger students and serve as scribes for their stories or interest inventories.

When planning these experiences, begin by identifying the cross-age partners. Students from upper grades, community volunteers, and classroom aides are among those who may volunteer for this position. Once the partners are selected, a few informal training sessions should be held. These meetings may focus on modeling read-alouds, reviewing comprehension strategies, demonstrating upcoming teaching ideas, introducing texts, and discussing the role of the partner in the cross-age experience. It is important that the partners understand that Cross-Age Reading Experiences are designed to help students practice and transfer comprehension strategies.

This is also a good time to think about scheduling. The partners will need to be available during the reading/language arts block. Although community volunteers and classroom aides may be able to work with students on a more frequent basis, upper-grade students may be available only once a week for a limited amount of time. Still, all have much to offer as cross-age partners.

The texts used in the Cross-Age Reading Experiences can be narrative or informational and vary by genre according to the theme of study. It's important to remember that they should be easy-level texts, so the students can read them without teacher assistance.

There are several ways to assess students' participation in Cross-Age Reading Experiences. Students can engage in self-reflection by thinking about and responding to questions, such as those raised in the Cross-Age Reading Experience Student Self-Assessment blackline (see page 205). Other assessments may include students' completed strategy applications (see blacklines in Appendices C and D) or tape-recorded Cross-Age Fluency Experiences (see Appendix B for ideas to teach fluency).

Cross-Age Reading Experiences are rewarding for all participants. Younger students benefit because their partners are more fluent readers who have a greater knowledge of reading strategies. Older students reinforce their knowledge by providing fluent reading models and practicing reading strategies with the younger children. Of course, the social nature of this routine is a reward in itself. Examples of Cross-Age Reading Experiences can be found in the lessons featured in Chapters 2 through 5.

Organizing for Stage Two

Having three different settings operating during Stage Two may seem challenging from an organizational standpoint, but it is reasonably easy to manage when you have an organizational plan. Figure 1-2 shows what we believe is the best way to organize when multiple settings are operating in the same classroom. This chart, which can be hung on the classroom wall, shows where everyone in the class should be during Stage Two. It is important to teach all of the students how to read the chart and use it every day to know their scheduled locations.

The students move from whole-class instruction into one of three settings: small-group teacher-guided instruction (guided reading), comprehension-based centers, or comprehension-based routines, such as Literature Circles and Cross-Age Reading Experiences. The organizational chart shows where every student should be in every phase of Stage Two. The chart is based on having three different sessions in Stage Two, so each student's name will appear once in each section every day. For example, as seen in Figure 1-2, Cristin would begin Stage Two in the Vocabulary Center. After 20 minutes, she would move to the Teacher-Guided Small Group. Twenty minutes later, she would move to Cross-Age Reading Experiences. Similarly, Manuel may look for his name and learn that he should report to Cross-Age Reading Experiences first. For the second session, he would go to the Teacher-Guided Small Group. For the third, he would go to the Theme Center. Students quickly learn to look for their names and understand where they should be at what time. Students move when a guided reading group concludes. Because guided small groups generally last for about 20 minutes, the students change locations approximately every 20 minutes.

STAGE THREE

After completing their work in Stage Two, the students put their work—completed strategy applications and self-assessments—into their literacy portfolios or folders. In Stage Three, another whole-group setting, students share the work they completed in Stage Two. Then the teacher and students reflect on what they have learned and decide whether to extend the current goal or create a new one.

FIGURE 1-2

Organizing and Managing Stage 2

	Session 1	Session 2	Session 3
CENTERS			
Drama Center			
Listening Center			
Vocabulary Center	Cristin		
Theme Center			Manuel
Writing Center			
ROUTINES			
Cross-Age Reading Experiences	Manuel		Cristin
Literature Circles			
TEACHER-GUIDED SMALL GROUPS		Cristin Manuel	

Adapted from McLaughlin & Allen, 2002.

Integrating Guided Comprehension and Thematic Instruction

Because most intermediate-grade language arts curricula are organized thematically, the lessons featured in chapters 2 through 5 represent six themes: Mystery, Survival, Biography, Fantasy, the Holocaust, and Poetry. As seen in Figure 1-3, each lesson is based on a text that was used for direct instruction in that particular theme (Mystery: *The Westing Game*; Survival: *Hatchet*; Biography: *You Want Women to Vote, Lizzie Stanton?*; Fantasy: *Tuck Everlasting*; the Holocaust: *Lily's Crossing*; Poetry: various titles). For example, in the Holocaust unit from which the theme-based lessons were extracted, *Lily's Crossing* was the focus novel for whole-group direct instruction. It was just one of many novels that could have been used for that purpose. In Appendix F, an extensive list of other novels and Web sites is provided for each of the six themes. The books listed may be used as the focus text, in guided reading, or in Literature Circles. They may also be used at the Theme Center.

The lessons in each chapter are appropriate for all types of learners. In our classrooms we may have students who speak English as a second language, struggling readers, and students with special needs. To accommodate these learners, the lessons include the use of multiple modalities (singing, sketching, etc.), working with partners, books on tape, cross-age experiences, and extra guided instruction for students who struggle. It's important to note that although the lessons featured in each chapter are taught at particular grade levels, they can be adapted to accommodate other levels and needs. Students develop at their own rates, and their needs for different skills and strategies vary. To adapt the lessons to accommodate English-language learners (ELL), struggling readers, and special needs students, consider: changing the level of the texts, adding more modeling and demonstration, providing more examples or focusing on fewer examples, providing time for more guided instruction or independent practice, and changing the level of word choice or questioning. Most of the lessons address skills and strategies that develop over time and need reinforcement.

For further ideas on adapting the lessons, see the Assessment Options section of each lesson and the final thoughts at the end of each chapter.

Note that in Stage Two in Teacher-Guided Small Groups, the level of text varies to accommodate the reading level of each group.

FIGURE 1-3

Lesson Overview of Chapters 2–5

Chapter 2: Word Study

THEME	TEACHING IDEA	STAGE ONE TEXT	STAGE TWO GUIDED READING TEXT
Mystery	Root Mapping	*The Westing Game*	*Encyclopedia Brown Takes the Cake*
Survival	Parts of Speech, Cinquain—Synonyms	*Hatchet*	*Call It Courage*
Biography	Homonyms	*You Want Women to Vote, Lizzie Stanton?*	*Beethoven Lives Upstairs*
Fantasy	Suffixes	*Tuck Everlasting*	*Harry Potter and the Chamber of Secrets*
The Holocaust	Parts of Speech, Diamante—Antonyms	*Lily's Crossing*	*Twenty and Ten*
Poetry	Prefixes	Student-authored poems	Student-authored poems

Chapter 3: Fluency

THEME	TEACHING IDEA	STAGE ONE TEXT	STAGE TWO GUIDED READING TEXT
Mystery	Readers Theater	*The Westing Game*	*The Soccer Shoe Clue*
Survival	Patterned Partner Reading	*Hatchet*	*Brian's Winter*
Biography	Repeated Readings	*You Want Women to Vote, Lizzie Stanton?*	*Dear Benjamin Banneker*
Fantasy	Radio Reading	*Tuck Everlasting*	*The Lion, the Witch, and the Wardrobe*
The Holocaust	The Fluent Reading Model	*The Yellow Star, Lily's Crossing,* "Holocaust"	*Number the Stars*
Poetry	Choral Reading	"Stopping by Woods on a Snowy Evening"	"America the Beautiful"

FIGURE 1-3 *continued*

Chapter 4: Vocabulary

THEME	TEACHING IDEA	STAGE ONE TEXT	STAGE TWO GUIDED READING TEXT
Mystery	Probable Passages	*The Westing Game*	*The Ghost of Lizard Light*
Survival	Context Clues	*Hatchet*	*Julie of the Wolves*
Biography	Semantic Question Map	*You Want Women to Vote, Lizzie Stanton?*	*Rosa Parks*
Fantasy	Semantic Map	*Tuck Everlasting*	*Harry Potter and the Sorcerer's Stone*
The Holocaust	Concepts of Definition Map	*Lily's Crossing*	*The Devil's Arithmetic*
Poetry	Vocabulary Bookmark Technique	"California Ghost Town," "Washington, D.C."	"Islands in Boston Harbor"

Chapter 5: Comprehension

THEME	TEACHING IDEA	STAGE ONE TEXT	STAGE TWO GUIDED READING TEXT
Mystery	Self-Questioning, "I Wonder" Statements	*The Westing Game*	*From the Mixed-Up Files of Mrs. Basil E. Frankweiler*
Survival	Bookmark Technique, Monitoring	*Hatchet*	*Island of the Blue Dolphins*
Biography	Summarizing, Bio-Pyramid	*You Want Women to Vote, Lizzie Stanton?*	*What's the Big Idea, Ben Franklin?*
Fantasy	Making Connections, Connection Stems	*Tuck Everlasting*	*Harry Potter and the Prisoner of Azkaban*
The Holocaust	Previewing, Story Impressions	*Lily's Crossing*	*The Butterfly*
Poetry	Visualization, Draw and Label Visualizations	"The Raven"	"My Shadow"

One of the essential aspects of theme-based instruction is the opportunity for students to experience teaching, guidance, and practice within the theme (Shanahan, 1997). Guided Comprehension readily accommodates this. It provides a viable means of integrating both direct and guided strategy-based reading instruction. It also uses multiple types of theme-related texts written at a variety of levels and provides many opportunities for students to practice in a variety of settings. Guided Comprehension enhances theme-based teaching by providing a framework for strategy integration.

Assessment During Guided Comprehension Lessons

In addition to providing a framework for teaching, the Guided Comprehension Model for the Intermediate Grades offers numerous opportunities for informal assessment. For example, in Stage One we can use observation of student responses (oral, written, dramatized, sketched) and work habits to assess. In Stage Two's Teacher-Guided Small Groups, we can ask the students to whisper-read, so we can assess their fluency. We can also do running records in this setting. When the students are working independently in the centers and routines, we can assess their completed work and review their self-assessments. The results of these assessments provide direction for our teaching. For example, the results of a running record may indicate a need to move a student to a higher guided reading group.

Observation is one technique that can be used in every stage of the lesson. As teachers, we sometimes wonder how often we should observe individual students, what we should be observing, and how to take and manage observational notes. It's important to note that there is no magic number when it comes to observations. Although it is valuable to have several observations of each student per marking period, we suggest that teachers seek their own comfort level in terms of timing. For example, if you observe every student once a week, you would have about eight observations per student per marking period. This isn't as complex and time-consuming as it sounds, because in every guided reading session, we have the opportunity to observe all the students in the group while they are reading. As noted earlier, this is the perfect setting to invite individual students to whisper-read as you listen to their fluency.

When we think about what to observe, our literacy classrooms provide plenty of possibilities. Here are a few examples of what we may choose to observe and how we might phrase our observational notes:

1. During Teacher-Directed Whole-Group Instruction, we can observe a student contributing a meaningful response. For example, if we were teaching summarizing, using the Bio-Pyramid, and Alex made meaningful contributions to the pyramid we were creating, we may write:

    > During whole-group instruction, Alex paid close attention to today's lesson and contributed several ideas to our Bio-Pyramid.

2. During a Teacher-Guided Small Group, we can observe students' fluency by listening as individual students whisper-read during guided reading. For example, we may write:

    > As Timmy whisper-read in guided reading, he was more aware of punctuation and read different characters' parts with greater expression.

3. When teaching summarizing using retellings in a Teacher-Guided Small Group, we may comment on a student's ability to retell. For example, we might write:

    > In guided reading, when Danielle retold a story today, she used greater detail when describing the problem and solution and remembered to include the ending.

4. When observing students working in small groups, we may describe students' ability to work with others. For example, we may write:

    > David demonstrated that he has become more understanding of other students' opinions. He let other members of his group speak and made connections between their comments and his.

5. Discussion of text also provides possibilities for observing students. For example, we may write:

    > Dashawn made significant contributions during small-group discussion. Her ideas clearly reflected what she read and were more detailed and more focused on the specific discussion topic—the Holocaust.

6. We can also assess students' abilities to stay focused, transition efficiently between instructional settings, and use time effectively. For example, we may write:

    > Nicole was able to read independently with little distraction today. She was also able to move from guided reading to her Literature Circle group without wasting time or disturbing other students' activities.

Each observational note should include

- the student's name,

- the date,

- the setting,

- meaningful information about the student's literacy development.

Of course, when observing, we need an organizational plan. We suggest using a clipboard on which all the students' names appear. The names may be on mailing labels or sticky-notes; we prefer the labels. This greatly facilitates recording the notes and keeping them organized. While observing a student, we can write our observation directly on the label. After we have written the observation, we peel that label off the clipboard and place it, chronologically, on a piece of paper that we keep in that student's assessment folder (manila folders that we store alphabetically in our desk drawers). That way, at the end of the marking period, we have several observations for each student.

Students' skill and strategy applications and self-assessments are other examples of measures that help teachers assess student progress. These are stored either in students' Literacy Portfolios, goal-based collections of student work over time, or reading folders. The teacher records and stores the results of running records and similar assessments.

Final Thoughts on This Chapter

This chapter provides an overview of our text and shared essential beliefs about the research-based Guided Comprehension Model for the Intermediate Grades, which serves as the instructional framework for the lessons featured in Chapters 2 through 5.

In the next chapter, we begin our exploration of the essential components of literacy by examining how to teach word study through the six themes that permeate lessons in this volume: Mystery, Survival, Biography, Fantasy, the Holocaust, and Poetry. We begin by presenting research-based information about word study and then introduce six lessons that demonstrate how to teach it. It is important to note that the lessons that are featured in Chapters 2, 3, 4, and 5 were authored and taught by a group of intermediate-grade teachers, including coauthors Amy Homeyer and Jennifer Sassaman. Consequently, the teachers identify themselves as "I" when relating their personal experiences.

CHAPTER 2

Word Study

Word study provides readers with insight into how words work. It helps us to identify which parts of speech they are, to analyze their structure (prefixes, roots, suffixes), and to spell them. These skills enable us to comprehend words and recognize them more quickly when we read text.

To study a word's part of speech, we often use clues that appear in the text to make connections between what we know about grammar and how the word is used in the sentence. For example, if we can put *a*, *an*, or *the* before a word, then we know it is a noun. If a word names a person, place, or thing, we know it is a noun. If a word begins with a capital letter, we know it is likely to be a proper noun. Similarly, we know that if a word shows action, it is a verb. If it describes a noun, it is an adjective, and if it modifies a verb or adjective, it is an adverb. We use these clues to help us determine the word's meaning.

Structural analysis is an important aspect of word study in the intermediate grades. Long ago, the Romans and Greeks developed words by beginning with word roots and then adding affixes (prefixes and suffixes) to change the roots' meanings. Today we analyze the words by breaking them down into roots, prefixes, and suffixes. Once we establish the meanings of the word parts, we put them together to try to determine the word's meaning.

Spelling is another essential component of word study. Knowing how the word root is spelled can help us in determining the word's structure.

Spelling knowledge is also critical when we are forming plurals, working with homonyms such as *to*, *two*, and *too*, and using words that have multiple meanings.

It's clear that we cannot comprehend what we read unless we know words' meanings. Word study helps us to meet that goal by allowing us to examine the inner workings of words. Consider this sentence: *They transported the package to the United States.* Through word study, we would determine that in the word *transported*, *port* is the word root, which comes from Latin and means "to carry." That makes sense because if we examined the part of speech, we would discover that *transported* is an action word or verb. Next, we would study the prefix *trans* and learn that it means "across." Coupled with the word root *port*, we would figure out that *transport* means to "carry across." Finally, we would examine the suffix *ed* and discover that it is often used to indicate the past tense of a verb. Then we would know that *transported* means "carried across." So, our basic conclusion would be that the package was "carried across" or sent to the United States.

In this chapter, we focus on teaching word study in Grades 4 through 6.

Part One: Research Base

What is word study?

Word study is essential to learning. According to *The Literacy Dictionary* (Harris & Hodges, 1995), word study includes practice in word identification—as in structural analysis (examining roots, prefixes, and suffixes), spelling, and vocabulary building. Bloodgood and Pacifici (2004) further note that "upper-level word study focuses on the structure and meaning of words by drawing students' attention to spelling patterns and word roots" (p. 250). Examples of word knowledge include roots, affixes (prefixes and suffixes), homonyms (homophones and homographs), and other vocabulary, spelling, or grammatical features.

What does the research tell us?

Word study is an active process for examining words. It "provides a method for including vocabulary and grammar with spelling instruction, exercises multiple components of word knowledge, and carries over to reading and writing development" (Bloodgood & Pacifici, 2004, p. 262).

In a study conducted by Bloodgood and Pacifici (2004), teachers and students found word study to be engaging and informative. They learned about word origins, spelling-meaning relationships, and grammar. Using hands-on activities, logic, and critical thinking helped the participants expand their vocabularies and personal understandings of how written language works.

Part Two: Lesson Overview

In this section we put research into practice by presenting six lessons that focus on various aspects of word study. As seen in the chart below, the lessons are theme-based and feature a variety of teaching ideas. The texts also vary. In Stage One, the teacher reads, so the text level may be easy, just right, or more challenging. In the guided reading groups, texts are at students' instructional levels, and at the centers and in the literacy routines, independent level texts are used. Appendix A contains additional resources for teaching word study. Appendix F features other texts and Web sites that can be used when teaching these themes.

THEME	TEACHING IDEA	STAGE ONE TEXT	STAGE TWO GUIDED READING TEXT
Mystery	Root Mapping	*The Westing Game*	*Encyclopedia Brown Takes the Cake*
Survival	Parts of Speech, Cinquain—Synonyms	*Hatchet*	*Call It Courage*
Biography	Homonyms	*You Want Women to Vote, Lizzie Stanton?*	*Beethoven Lives Upstairs*
Fantasy	Suffixes	*Tuck Everlasting*	*Harry Potter and the Chamber of Secrets*
The Holocaust	Parts of Speech, Diamante—Antonyms	*Lily's Crossing*	*Twenty and Ten*
Poetry	Prefixes	Student-authored poems	Student-authored poems

Word Study Lessons

LESSON 1 Root Mapping
Theme: Mystery

STAGE 1 Teacher-Directed Whole-Group Instruction

TEXT: *The Westing Game* (Raskin, 1978)

EXPLAIN: I began by asking students to tell me what *root* means when we are engaged in word study. Daniela said, "It is part of a word." Carlo said, "It is the part of the word that is left when all the prefixes and suffixes are taken off." I said: "Both of your answers are correct. Today we are going to be learning about word roots that come from the Latin and Greek languages. Long ago, the Romans (who used the Latin language) and Greeks came up with a system for creating words by putting together smaller word parts: prefixes, suffixes, and roots. We are going to focus only on the root, the part of the word that remains when we remove prefixes and suffixes. We need to know word roots and their meanings because that will help us to figure out the meanings of longer, more complicated words." I continued by explaining to students, "Today we will be working on improving our understanding of words and their meanings by studying different word roots. Then it will be our job to think of as many words as possible that are formed using the word roots we learn. Finally, we will define the words we think of and study them to see if we can find a common theme among their meanings."

DEMONSTRATE: I demonstrated by using a think-aloud, a read-aloud, and an oversize sheet of poster paper. I began by reading aloud Chapter 10 of *The Westing Game* by Ellen Raskin. I explained to the students that I had selected a word from the chapter that had a Latin root, and that we were going to create a Root Map for that root (see Figure 2-1). I used a think-aloud and the chart paper and said, "Our root is the Latin root *-j-e-c-t*, so I will write that in the center of our map. I have chosen that root because on page 70 of our text there is a sentence that reads, 'It's much harder to judge reactions when I have to bring up the subject myself.' Underneath *-ject* I will write its meaning, which is 'to throw.' Now we need to brainstorm words that have *-ject* as a root. I know that *subject* is one, because that is where we got our root, so I will write that as a branch on our Root Map. Under *subject*, I will write its meaning, which we will say is 'a basic theme or topic.' Another word with the Latin root *-ject* is *eject*, so I will write that on our map, too. Underneath the word *eject* I will write its meaning, which is 'to throw or force out.'" I continued thinking aloud and adding words such as *project*, *object*, *interject*, and *reject* as branches on our Root Map.

GUIDE: To guide the students, I explained that we would be taking our Root Map a step further and adding branches off the words I had just listed. I provided the students with dictionaries and invited them to work with partners. Then I asked, "What words can we make out of the word *subject*?" One response was *subjective*, so we added a branch off the word *subject* and wrote *subjective* and its meaning on our map. The students worked in pairs to discover more words related to *subject* that they could add to the map. Their responses included *subjectivity* and *subjection*. We added a branch off *subject* for each word. Then we added the definitions: *subjective* (particular to a given person); *subjectivity* (judgment based on individual opinions rather than external facts); and *subjection* (forced submission to control others).

PRACTICE: Students practiced by searching for more words to add to the map. As they found words to branch off our first set of words they recorded both the word and its definition. Some of the words and definitions they came up with were *interjection* (a sudden, short utterance), *rejection* (the refusal to accept an offer), and *objective* (not influenced by emotions or prejudice). Students then shared what they had found with the class, and we added all the new words and definitions to our class Root Map. Then we examined their definitions to see if we could find a common theme. Students agreed that we could find the meaning "to throw" in all of the words. For example, Jill said, "To *interject* something is kind of like throwing a comment into a conversation, and *ejection* is when someone gets thrown out of a place." Paige added, "When you *reject* something you are kind of throwing it out too, because you don't want it, and even *objective* can be seen as throwing something out because you are not being influenced by your emotions, so you are throwing them away." We left our completed Root Map hanging on the wall, so the students could easily use the words in their reading, writing, and speaking, and pairs of students took turns creating sentences using the words on our Root Map. (See Figure 2-1 for our completed Root Map.)

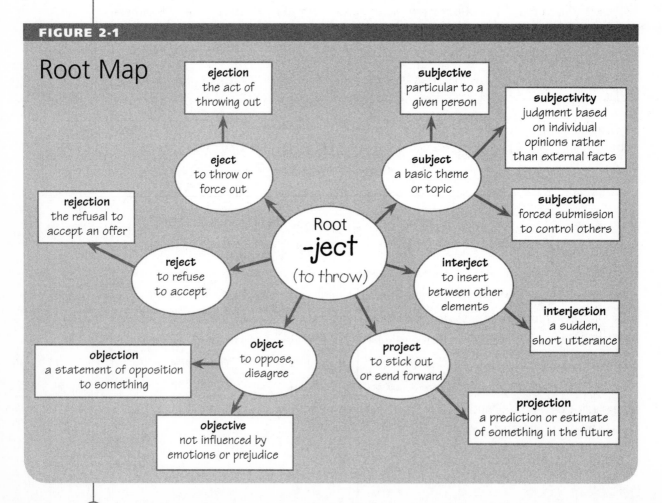

FIGURE 2-1

Root Map

REFLECT: As a class we reflected on how knowing the meaning of the root helped us to better understand the meaning of the word. Kyle said, "Now I know that if I see a word with the root *-ject* in it, it probably has something to do with throwing. Then I might be able to figure out what the word means."

STAGE 2 Teacher-Guided Small-Group Instruction

TEXT: *Encyclopedia Brown Takes the Cake* (Sobol, 1982)
(Texts varied according to the students' abilities.)

REVIEW: To review, we discussed how knowing the meaning of a root helps us to figure out the meaning of that word. I explained that we would be continuing to study roots by making Root Maps for words found in the first chapter of our text, *Encyclopedia Brown Takes the Cake*, by Donald J. Sobol.

GUIDE: I guided students to partner-read Chapter 1, "The Case of the Missing Garlic Bread." After we discussed the story, I turned the students' attention to the root *auto-* on page 3. I explained that this was a Greek root meaning "self." I placed *auto-* in the center of our map and wrote its meaning, "self," below. Then I guided the students to brainstorm words made from the root *auto-*. Responses included *automobile*, *autobiography*, *automatic*, and *autograph*. We listed these responses, as well as their meanings, on the map.

PRACTICE: To practice, the students continued to add words and their meanings to the map. I reminded the students that they could branch related words off those we had already listed. One student branched *autobiographical* off *autobiography*. I provided students with dictionaries to help them discover words and their meanings. While they worked, I circulated, providing assistance as needed. Once the map was completed, students volunteered to use the words in sentences to further show their understanding of the words and their meanings.

REFLECT: To reflect, we discussed how we can use Root Maps to help us learn new words and meanings from words we already know. We agreed that all of the words we found had meanings that relate to the word *self*. Jada said, "*Autobiography* is a biography about oneself, and an *autograph* is your own signature." The students were excited to see the connections among all of the words and how many new words they were able to discover.

> Cody, Alison, and Miguel were working on a science _project_ and they needed to choose a _subject_ to research. Cody said that they should research _astronauts_ and outer space, but the others wanted to research geology and learn things about Earth. After talking about it more, they all agreed to research _geology_.

FIGURE 2-2

Student-Facilitated Comprehension Centers

THEME CENTER: Students self-selected texts from the Theme Center, where I had left numerous theme-related texts at a variety of reading levels. I had also provided a limited list of Latin and Greek roots at the center. After reading, students went back to find words formed from those roots. Then they created Root Maps of their own.

WORD STUDY CENTER: Students used either a Latin or a Greek root and worked in pairs to create Root Maps of their own.

WRITING CENTER: Students wrote stories and included at least three words from our various Root Maps. Figure 2-2 features a story written by Kevin and Carlos.

Student-Facilitated Comprehension Routines

CROSS-AGE READING EXPERIENCES: Students read with cross-age partners. Then they selected a Latin or Greek root that appeared in their text and created a Root Map together.

(STAGE 3) Teacher-Facilitated Whole-Group Reflection and Goal Setting

SHARE: In small groups, students shared the Root Maps they created during Stage Two. After sharing in small groups, some students then volunteered to share with the whole group.

REFLECT: The students reflected on how creating Root Maps helped to increase their vocabulary and to discover new words' meanings. Michele said, "I can't believe how many new words I learned!" David said, "I never thought of words being related like that." We all agreed that knowing the meanings of different roots can help us discover the meanings of unfamiliar words.

SET NEW GOALS: We decided that we wanted to continue to learn more roots and their meanings and would continue making and using Root Maps as we read.

Assessment Options

I used observation, students' completed Root Maps, and student self-reflections as assessments. When working with special education students, I was careful to provide individual assistance to complete the task. I also assessed them on smaller components and their ability to complete them. When working with ELL students, I also allowed extra time for more specific and individualized instruction. I assessed their performance both orally and in written format.

LESSON 2 Parts of Speech
Theme: Survival

STAGE 1 Teacher-Directed Whole-Group Instruction

TEXT: *Hatchet* (Paulsen, 1987)

EXPLAIN: I began by asking students to brainstorm different parts of speech. We created a list on the board that included nouns, verbs, adjectives, adverbs, prepositions, and participles. Then the students defined and gave examples of each part of speech, and I recorded their responses on the board. Next, I explained to the students that we would be writing cinquains, a type of form poem that required using different parts of speech (see Appendix A, page 167, for a fuller explanation of cinquains). I said, "Today we will be creating cinquains." I wrote "*c-i-n-q-u-a-i-n*" on the board and said, "This is how cinquain is spelled, but it is pronounced 'sin-kane.' Cinquains are a type of form poem that requires us to write specific parts of speech for each line. Cinquains also help us to understand how to use synonyms, words that have the same or nearly the same meaning."

I showed an enlarged copy of the Cinquain blackline (see page 169) and began to explain the cinquain format. I said, "The first line asks for a noun. On our Grammar Wall, it says that a noun names a person, place, or thing. It also says that *teacher*, *school*, and *book* are some examples of nouns. So, when we're choosing a noun for line one, we're really choosing the topic of our cinquain, and we will also need a synonym for the word we choose, because we will need to write that on the last line. For example, if we chose *book* as our focus

Cinquain
one word – noun
two adjectives describing line one
three -ing words telling actions of line one
four-word phrase describing a feeling related to line one
one word – synonym or reference to line one

word for line one, we could use *text* as its synonym." Students suggested other synonyms for *book*, including *novel* and *paperback*.

"The second line asks for two adjectives that describe the noun," I continued. On our Grammar Wall, it says that adjectives describe nouns. Examples of adjectives and the nouns they describe include *green* (light), *happy* (family), and *deserted* (house). So, for line two, we will need to write two adjectives that describe the noun we chose for line one. The third line asks for three *-ing* words that describe the action of the noun on line one. Our Grammar Wall says that participles end in *-ing* and can describe nouns. Our examples of participles and the nouns they describe include (man) *running*, (football) *flying*, and (dancer) *leaping*. The fourth line is a four-word phrase that describes a feeling related to line one. In our cinquains we can write any kind of phrase, as long as it describes a feeling relating to the noun we write in line one."

Next, I said, "The fifth and final line is a one-word synonym for the noun on line one. We know that synonyms are words that mean the same or nearly the same thing, so this word must be a synonym for the word we write on line one." I continued to explain, "Let's notice that the first line requires that we write a noun, and the last line requires that we write its synonym. So, a cinquain is a form poem about synonyms. There are many ways to approach writing a cinquain, but it is sometimes easiest to write this form poem by completing the first and last lines before completing the others."

DEMONSTRATE: To demonstrate, I used a read-aloud, a think-aloud, and the Cinquain blackline. I began by reading aloud Chapter 9 of *Hatchet* by Gary Paulsen. I explained to students that I would choose the noun that would be the topic of our cinquain from this chapter. Then I used a think-aloud as I began writing the cinquain. I said, "This chapter is about Brian trying to start a fire, so I'm going to make fire the topic of our cinquain. I am going to write *fire* on the first line, where it says 'noun,' because that is the subject of my poem and I know that a subject is always a noun. Next, I need two adjectives for *fire*. Who can remind us what an adjective does?" Benjamin responded, "It describes a noun." Then I said, "Right. The first word that I'm thinking of to describe *fire* is *hot*, so I will write that on the first blank. Another word I'm thinking of to describe *fire* is *bright*, so I will write that on the second blank. So, the two adjectives I wrote on line two are *hot* and *bright*. Now, I need to think about the third line. I need to write three *-ing* words that describe the action of *fire*. What part of speech are *-ing* words?" Julianne said, "They are participles." I said, "Yes. A participle that comes to mind is *flaming*, so I will write that on the first blank on line three."

GUIDE: Next, I guided the students to work in pairs to complete the next two blanks on line three. The partners offered their suggestions and I wrote *sparking* and *crackling* on blanks two and three on line three.

PRACTICE: Students practiced by completing lines four and five of the cinquain poem with their partners. Then they shared their responses with the class. We selected responses to complete our cinquain, and then we read our completed poem. (The cinquain the students and I wrote is featured in Figure 2-3.)

REFLECT: We reviewed the different parts of speech and then reflected on how we can use the cinquain form to review certain parts of speech and summarize a concept. The students thought it was fun to

Cinquain

fire
one word – noun

hot   bright
two adjectives describing line one

flaming   sparking   crackling
three -ing words telling actions of line one

warmth on cold nights
four-word phrase describing a feeling related to line one

flame
one word – synonym or reference to line one

FIGURE 2-3

manipulate the parts of speech to make them fit onto the necessary lines and number of spaces. For example, Jeffrey said, "I knew that a fire made sparks, so I changed *sparks* into *sparking* in order to use the word on line three."

STAGE 2) Teacher-Guided Small-Group Instruction

TEXT: *Call It Courage* (Sperry, 1940) (Texts varied according to the students' abilities.)

REVIEW: To review, we revisited the cinquain form. We also briefly discussed the parts of speech we had listed in Stage One and gave examples of each. I explained that we would be continuing to use the cinquain to practice using these parts of speech and that we would choose the topic for our cinquain after reading the first chapter of our text, *Call It Courage*, by Armstrong Sperry. Then I distributed Cinquain blacklines (see page 169) to the students.

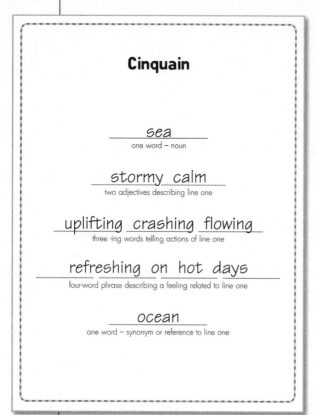

Cinquain

__sea__
one word – noun

__stormy calm__
two adjectives describing line one

__uplifting crashing flowing__
three -ing words telling actions of line one

__refreshing on hot days__
four-word phrase describing a feeling related to line one

__ocean__
one word – synonym or reference to line one

FIGURE 2-4

GUIDE: I guided students to partner-read Chapter 1, prompting as necessary. After we discussed the events of the chapter, I asked students to think of a noun that could be the topic of our cinquain. As a group, we decided on the word *sea* because that is the focus of the first chapter. After writing the word *sea* on the first line, the students worked together to think of adjectives to describe the sea. I suggested that they close their eyes, visualize the sea, and think of words to describe it. Liza asked if they could use words from the chapter, and I told her that was a great idea. The group chose *stormy* and *calm* because those were words that described the sea at different times.

PRACTICE: To practice, I had the students work in pairs to complete the remaining lines of the cinquain. When the cinquains were completed, each pair shared its poem with the rest of the group. Ann and Liza's cinquain is featured in Figure 2-4.

REFLECT: The students explained that they thought using the cinquain form was a fun way to practice using parts of speech correctly. They also thought it was a great way to write poetry. Silvio said, "I like writing form poems. They tell us what kinds of words to put where they need to be. This makes poem writing easier and more fun for me."

Student-Facilitated Comprehension Centers

MAKE-A-BOOK CENTER: Students wrote and illustrated cinquains on theme-related topics as pages for our class book of cinquains. Computers were available and most students chose to use them to create their pages.

THEME CENTER: Students self-selected texts from numerous titles at varying reading levels that I had placed at this center. Then they wrote cinquains using theme-related topics as their focus words.

Student-Facilitated Comprehension Routines

LITERATURE CIRCLES: We adapted the Literature Circle, enabling the students to write cinquains as an extension activity. They based their cinquains on the novels they were reading and shared them with the other members of their group.

CROSS-AGE READING EXPERIENCES: Students read with cross-age partners and wrote and illustrated cinquains together.

(STAGE 3) Teacher-Facilitated Whole-Group Reflection and Goal Setting

SHARE: In small groups, students shared their cinquains from Stage Two. After sharing in small groups, some students volunteered to share with the whole group.

REFLECT: The students reflected on how writing cinquains helped them to practice using different parts of speech correctly. They all agreed that this was a fun way to write poetry and review and practice parts of speech.

SET NEW GOALS: We decided that we were comfortable using the cinquain poetry form and wanted to learn to write other types of form poetry such as diamantes (see page 167).

Assessment Options

I used observation, students' completed cinquains, and student self-reflections as assessments during this lesson. When working with special education students, I was careful to put a different-colored dot at the start of each line of the cinquain, so I could easily draw students' attention to a particular line. In guided settings, I assigned a volunteer "scribe" to each student, so after special education students expressed an idea to add to their cinquain, the scribe recorded it for them. In practice settings, I enlarged the Cinquain blackline so the students could more easily record their responses. When working with ELL students, I allowed extra time for more specific and individualized instruction. I assessed their performance both orally and in written format. I also paid close attention to their illustrations, checking for a poem-picture match.

LESSON 3 Homonyms
Theme: Biography

STAGE 1 Teacher-Directed Whole-Group Instruction

TEXT: *You Want Women to Vote, Lizzie Stanton?* (Fritz, 1995)

EXPLAIN: I began by explaining to students that today we would be continuing our word study to include homonyms, words that sound the same but have different meanings. (For a list of homonyms, see page 171.) I said, "We need to understand and be able to use homonyms to help us understand what we are reading and writing." I said that our specific focus would be the homonyms *there*, *their*, and *they're*. I wrote the three words on the board and began explaining the meanings of each. I pointed to the word *there* and said, "*There*, spelled *t-h-e-r-e*, is a place. For example, if I say, 'Where is the book? It is there. Is it here? No, it is there,' then I am using *t-h-e-r-e*. One way to remember that *t-h-e-r-e* means place is to remember that the word *here*, also a place, is inside of the word *there*."

Next, I pointed to the word *their*. "Our next homonym is *their*, spelled *t-h-e-i-r*," I said. "It is plural and possessive. Who will tell me what *plural* means?" Jake responded, "More than one." "Okay, good. Who will tell me what *possessive* means?" Emily said, "It belongs to someone. It shows ownership." "Yes," I replied. "*Their*, spelled *t-h-e-i-r*, shows ownership by more than one." To help students better understand this concept, I asked Richard to hold up his book. Next, I asked Elizabeth to hold up her book. Then I asked all of the students to hold up *their* books.

I continued by pointing to the word *they're* and saying, "The last *they're* that we will talk about is *t-h-e-y-'-r-e*, which is the contraction for *they are*. What part of speech is the word *they*?" Christopher responded, "It's a pronoun." I then wrote the words *they are* next to the contraction *they're* on the board. I asked the class, "Who will tell me what letter has been replaced by the apostrophe in *they're*?" Nicole said, "The *a* has been replaced." I reminded students that when we have a contraction, we have a combination of two words, and the apostrophe takes the place of one or two letters that have been deleted. In this case the apostrophe had taken the place of the *a* in the word *are* when we formed the contraction *they're*. "'They're going to school' is an example of how we can use this contraction," I said. I explained that today we would be practicing using these homonyms correctly by examining them in the context of the book we have been reading.

DEMONSTRATE: To demonstrate, I used a think-aloud and sentences from our text, *You Want Women to Vote, Lizzie Stanton?* I began by displaying a sentence from the book on the overhead projector. I said, "This is a sentence from our text. In the blanks, I need to decide which word—*there, their,* or *they're*—is correct. The sentence reads, 'If you had been around then, you might have seen three little girls, _____ hands over _____ heads, dodging the trees, racing for home.'" I thought aloud, "I know that the sentence is talking about the three girls' hands and heads, which means that the hands and heads *belong* to people. That means ownership. I also know that there is more than one, because *heads* is plural and the sentence also mentions three little girls. If the word is plural and shows ownership, it is the word *their,* spelled *t-h-e-i-r.* I will write *their* in both blanks." So the sentence read, "If you had been around then, you might have seen three little girls, their hands over their heads, dodging the trees, racing for home." Next I wrote the sentence "Elizabeth liked to go _____ and visit her father." I thought aloud, "Elizabeth liked to go where? Since it must be a *place* she liked to go to, the word must be *there,* spelled *t-h-e-r-e,* that fits in the blank." I completed the sentence, so it read, "Elizabeth liked to go there and visit her father."

GUIDE: I passed out three paper strips to each pair of students and invited them to write each of the three words, *there, their,* and *they're,* on a strip of paper. I explained that they would use these papers to show me which one of the homonyms they would use in the following sentences from our text. Then I placed this sentence on the overhead, "The clergymen were the most violent in _____ opposition to the women." I told students to discuss with their partner which of the words they should use, and that once they had made a decision, they should hold up the correct paper strip. Once the strips were all up, I asked a volunteer to explain his or her choice. Kari said, "I chose *t-h-e-i-r* because it was describing someone's opposition, so it was the opposition belonging to someone. The 'someone' was the clergymen, which is plural, so it has to be *t-h-e-i-r.*" The next sentence I put up was "_____ so busy talking." Again, I had students work in pairs to decide which word would correctly fill in the blank and to hold up their answer once they had finished. This time Nicolas said, "We chose *t-h-e-y-'-r-e* because we can replace the blank with the words *they are.* Since *t-h-e-y-'-r-e* is a contraction for *they are,* we know that's the answer."

PRACTICE: Students continued to practice filling in the blanks for the remaining sentences, explaining their choices by using the definitions for each of the words.

REFLECT: As a class we reviewed the different meanings of the homonyms *there, their,* and *they're.* We decided that we would continue to practice using these words correctly with our texts in Stage Two.

STAGE 2) Teacher-Guided Small-Group Instruction

TEXT: *Beethoven Lives Upstairs* (Nichol, 1994) (Texts varied according to the students' abilities.)

REVIEW: To review, we defined *there, their,* and *they're* and used each word correctly in sentences. I explained that we would be continuing to practice using these homonyms correctly. I said that we would be looking at sentences from our text, *Beethoven Lives Upstairs*, by Barbara Nichol, and deciding which of the three words is the correct one to use in each case.

GUIDE: I introduced *Beethoven Lives Upstairs*, and the students read the book silently. After a brief discussion, we resumed our study of the homonyms *there, their,* and *they're*. The students brought their paper strips marked *there, their,* and *they're* with them. I showed them the first sentence, "_____ like the sounds of an injured beast." I asked the students to read the sentence to themselves and then asked for a volunteer to read the sentence aloud. Next, I asked the students to discuss with their partner which spelling of the word would be correct in the sentence. Once they had decided, they held up their answers. I asked James to explain his response. He said, "I chose *t-h-e-y-'-r-e* because when I tried the words *they are* it made sense in the sentence. Plus, it isn't a place and it doesn't belong to anyone so it can't be either of the other two spellings." I told him that was correct and happily noted that everyone in the group had displayed the same response.

PRACTICE: To practice, I had the students continue to work in pairs to complete the following sentences with *there, their,* or *they're*.

_____ was Mr. Beethoven, staring at a sheet of music.

_____ were beads of water collecting on the ceiling above my head.

He reads _____ messages and answers them out loud.

Uncle, _____ is no hour of the day when I forget that Mr. Beethoven is in the house.

It seems his family is well remembered _____.

People who lived near _____ house remember hearing music coming from the attic late at night.

Mr. Beethoven has not returned _____ kindness.

_____ called sopranos because _____ singers who can sing very high.

Once the students had finished, we discussed their responses and verified their choices by referring to the definitions.

REFLECT: The students said that they felt more comfortable using the three forms of this homonym. They said that referring to the definitions helped them, and that the more times they practiced using the words, the less they had to look back at the board to remember the definitions. They also liked the clues, such as the one explaining that the word *here* is inside *there*.

Student-Facilitated Comprehension Centers

WORD STUDY CENTER: Students worked in small groups and played Homonym Rummy. The game is similar to regular rummy, except that instead of finding cards with pairs or triplets of like numbers, students search for pairs or triplets of homonyms. They earned points for each pair or trio they made. The object was to discard all of the cards in your hand, while accumulating the most pairs or triplets. When the game was over, the students used the homonym cards remaining in players' hands in sentences.

WRITING CENTER: Pairs of students wrote imaginary character biographies using *there*, *their*, and *they're* correctly. When finished, they hung their work in our Biography Theme Corner.

Student-Facilitated Comprehension Routines

LITERATURE CIRCLES: We adapted the Literature Circle so that students could practice using *there*, *their*, and *they're* correctly. We created the role of Homonym Finder. This person's job was to find six sentences using *there*, *their*, or *they're*, write them on sentence strips, leaving blanks where the homonyms should be, and share them with the group. The group then figured out which form of the word should complete the sentence.

(STAGE 3) Teacher-Facilitated Whole-Group Reflection and Goal Setting

SHARE: In small groups, students shared their experiences using *there*, *their*, and *they're* during Stage Two. After sharing in small groups, some students then volunteered to share with the whole group. The class visited the Biography Theme Corner, and pairs of students read the imaginary character biographies they had authored.

REFLECT: The students reflected on how understanding the meaning of *there*, *their*, and *they're* helped them to determine the correct spelling for a given situation. Scott said, "The more I thought about the meanings and spellings of each of the three words, the easier it was to remember when to use each one. Now I feel I really know them!"

SET NEW GOALS: We decided that we still wanted to practice using *there*, *their*, and *they're* correctly, but we were also ready to practice other homonyms that are confusing to spell, including *to*, *too*, and *two*.

Assessment Options

I used observation, students' completed sentences and stories, and student self-reflections as assessments. When working with special education students, I was careful to limit the number of sentences they were required to complete. I was also sure to allot more time and provide individual assistance to complete the task, as necessary per individual student. When working with ELL students, I also limited the number of sentences they were required to complete and allowed extra time for more specific and individualized instruction. I assessed their performance both orally and in written format.

LESSON 4 Suffixes
Theme: Fantasy

STAGE 1 Teacher-Directed Whole-Group Instruction

TEXT: *Tuck Everlasting* (Babbitt, 1975)

EXPLAIN: I explained to the students that we would be focusing on how words work by examining the suffixes of various words related to our novel, *Tuck Everlasting*. I explained that we were going to concentrate on words with the endings *-er*, *-or*, and *-ar*. I told my students that words with these endings are generally nouns that have Greek or Latin roots.

I also explained that many of the words in our language are derived from Greek and Latin. I noted that by understanding words with these endings we could increase our vocabulary and build our spelling skills. Then I added, "It's important to remember that the words we will be working with are nouns, but not all words that end in the letters *-er*, *-or*, or *-ar* are nouns. For example, *for* and *far* are not nouns."

DEMONSTRATE: To demonstrate, I used a think-aloud, chart paper, and the chalkboard. To begin, I asked students, "Will someone tell me what a suffix is?" Bobbie offered, "A suffix is a group of letters you add to the end of a word to change the word and its meaning or part of speech." The class agreed, and we decided this was the definition we had learned. Then I turned to a large poster page on which I had previously written three words and said, "We will be looking at words such as *runner*, *scholar*, and *dictator*. Let's notice the ending of each of these words and think about what the root word is and how the suffix changes the meaning."

Next, I made a three-columned chart on the board. At the top of the columns I wrote *-er*, *-ar*, and *-or*. I used a think-aloud to begin writing words with these endings. I said, "I am going to write words that end in the suffix *-er*. Some words that I know that end in the suffix *-er* are *racer*, *driver*, *sweeper*, *reporter*, *gardener*, and *trainer*." Then I wrote the words on the chart paper and underlined the root and suffix in each of my examples. I said, "Based on the words I am using as examples, I think that the definition of the suffix *-er* is 'a person or thing that does something.' For example, a driver is one who drives and a reporter is one who reports." After reviewing the roots and suffixes, we discussed the meaning of the words, noted they were all nouns, and used them in sentences. For example, I said, "A racer could be one who races cars or bicycles." Then pairs of students provided sentences for the other words. Examples included "My mother is a reporter for our local newspaper" and "Our gardener planted new flowers near the front door." Next I said, "Now I am going to write some nouns that end in the suffix -ar. Some nouns that I know that end in the suffix -ar are scholar, beggar, and liar. I wrote these words on our chart and asked the students to work with their partner to discuss what the meaning of each word with the suffix -ar might be. Following a brief sharing of ideas, the students settled on "one who has knowledge, one who begs, and one who lies." Then the pairs of students wrote sentences using each noun.

GUIDE: Next, I wrote the following words under the -or column: professor, creator, inspector, editor, negotiator, and director. Again, I read the words aloud and underlined the root and the suffix. I invited the students to join me in determining the meaning of the suffix -or in these words. Jillian said, "I think it means 'one who'—just like -er and -ar did in the other lists of words. So, creator is 'one who creates' and editor is 'one who edits.'" We discussed the fact that some suffixes have more than one meaning, but for the nouns on our lists, -er, -ar, and -or meant "one who." At the end of our discussion, I showed the students a new section of our Word Study Wall. It was titled "Roots, Prefixes, and Suffixes." I explained that we could use this section of our wall to help us remember different word parts, what they mean, and what some examples are. Then the students copied the definition of suffix and a few example -er, -ar, and -or words from our list into their Word Study Journals.

PRACTICE: To practice, the students worked with a partner to make a chart of -er, -ar, -or nouns that related to the novel Tuck Everlasting. Amy and Tulio's chart included the following: kidnapper, character, teacher, author, illustrator, and burglar. After the chart was complete they read each word aloud and took turns underlining the root word and suffix. The students also wrote their nouns in their Word Study Journals as I added them to our Word Study Wall. Next, the students wrote a novel-related sentence for each word and underlined the nouns that had -er, -ar, and -or word endings. Following are some examples of their sentences:

> Jesse acted as a <u>kidnapper</u> in the story because he helped his family take Winnie away from her home.

> Mae is a <u>character</u> in the story, and she is very kind and loving.

> Winnie would have been a good <u>teacher</u> because she was so patient.

> Natalie Babbitt is the <u>author</u> of Tuck Everlasting.

The <u>illustrator</u> did a great job on the cover.

The <u>burglar</u> stole the family's horse in the story.

REFLECT: We reflected on the fact that knowing how words work can help build our vocabulary and increase our understanding of our language. Sarah said, "This was fun because I never knew there were nouns that had different suffixes that meant 'one who.'" The students said they also liked looking for nouns with -er, -ar, and -or endings that meant "one who" and that were related to the story, because it was a challenging task. Wendy said, "It sounds like it will be easy to find the nouns, but it's not. You can find lots of words that end in -er, -ar, or -or that aren't nouns and that have endings that don't mean 'one who,' like the word *circular*. It's not a noun, but it ends in -ar."

STAGE 2   Teacher-Guided Small-Group Instruction

TEXT: *Harry Potter and the Chamber of Secrets* (Rowling, 1999) (Texts varied according to the students' abilities.)

REVIEW: I reminded the students that we were working to increase our knowledge of how words work. I reviewed that we were looking for nouns that had -er, -ar, and -or suffixes that meant "one who."

GUIDE: I guided the students by asking them if they could think of any nouns ending in -er, -ar, and -or in which the suffix meant "one who" and that related to our new novel, *Harry Potter and the Chamber of Secrets*. The students noticed instantly that the word *Potter* ended in -er. Maria said, "Since we know that nouns ending in -er can mean 'one who does something,' I think that Potter must mean 'one who pots.'" Then the students discussed the idea that Harry's great-grandparents may have been gardeners who used pots, because some of the students themselves also had family names that related to professions. For example, one student's last name was Baker. He explained that his family had ancestors who were bakers. When we concluded our discussion about family names, we made a three-column word-endings chart and the students brainstormed with a partner to find possible words related to the Harry Potter novel. The students' ideas included *professor*, *author*, *illustrator*, *character*, and *teacher*. After we filled in the chart, pairs of students used each word in a sentence relating to the novel.

PRACTICE: To practice, the students worked with a partner to whisper-read the first two chapters of *Harry Potter and the Chamber of Secrets* and record any nouns that had -er, -ar, and -or endings that meant "one who." The following nouns are from the list John and Michaela created from Chapters 1 and 2:

Potter	sorcerer
player	builder
mother	brother
sister	professor

Then the pairs met in small groups. They shared their lists and the pairs took on the challenge of using each word they found in a sentence relating to the text. John and Michaela's sentences follow:

1. Harry <u>Potter</u> does not like living with his aunt and uncle.
2. The Dursleys don't think Harry is a team <u>player</u>.
3. Harry's <u>mother</u> died trying to protect him from Voldemort.
4. Harry thinks of Hermione like a <u>sister</u>.
5. One day Harry will be a great <u>sorcerer</u>.
6. The <u>builder</u> in town thought he could build Harry a new trunk.
7. Harry thinks of Ron like a <u>brother</u>.
8. <u>Professor</u> Dumbledore is very important to Harry.

REFLECT: The students thought the more they practiced, the easier it was to recognize nouns that would be appropriate for our list. Even though they were reading *Harry Potter*, the students were able to locate the words pretty quickly. The students thought they would be able to find many other nouns of this type as they continued to read.

Student-Facilitated Comprehension Centers

ART CENTER: At this center, the students created a page for our class book of nouns. They worked on the section titled "One Who." On their page they wrote a word and underlined its -er, -ar, or -or suffix meaning "one who." Then they used the word in a sentence and illustrated their page. Students had the option of using a computer to complete their pages.

WORD STUDY CENTER: Students worked with a partner to read theme-related texts at various levels that I had left at this center. As they read, they noted and discussed nouns similar to those we had been studying. When they encountered a noun from this category that was not already in their Word Study Journal, they added it and used it in a sentence about the text they were reading.

WRITING CENTER: The students wrote stories using the fantasy genre. They used their Word Study Journals to include at least ten nouns that ended in -er, -ar, and -or and meant "one who." When they finished writing, they underlined the words that contained these endings, shared their story with a classmate, and hung their work in our Authors' Corner.

(STAGE 3) Teacher-Facilitated Whole-Group Reflection and Goal Setting

SHARE: The students shared their -er, -ar, and -or charts and sentences from Stage Two in small groups. Then students shared their stories and their pages for the book of nouns.

REFLECT: We talked about the importance of knowing how words work. We also talked about how different suffixes change the meaning of words and how useful it was to know what suffixes mean. Shauna said, "I was happy to find out that most words that end in -er, -ar, or -or are nouns. That will help me when I read if I come across a word I don't know. The first thing I will do is try to find the root and see if 'one who' might be the meaning of the suffix."

SET NEW GOALS: The students decided that they felt comfortable using these suffixes with narrative text, but they wanted to learn how to use them with informational text.

Assessment Options

I observed the students as they brainstormed words with the class as well as with their partners. I also reviewed the students' charts and sentences, pages for the book of nouns, and fantasy stories. When working with special education students, I provided them with previously prepared charts and encouraged them to share their sentences orally. They seemed to especially enjoy making their pages for our class book. When working with ELLs, I carefully monitored their progress and provided individual assistance as needed. During paired settings, I ensured that both my special education and ELL students worked with a stronger reader to provide extra support.

LESSON 5 Antonyms
Theme: The Holocaust

STAGE 1 Teacher-Directed Whole-Group Instruction

TEXT: *Lily's Crossing* (Giff, 1997)

EXPLAIN: I explained to the students the importance of knowing how words work and focused on antonyms and using diamantes. First, I asked students if they could explain what an antonym is. Tulio said, "An antonym is a word that is the opposite of another word." The class agreed and said that they had used antonyms before in their writing. Then I said, "A diamante is a seven-line form poem shaped like a diamond. It is based on a word and its opposite, or antonym. The first three lines are about the original word, and the last three lines are about the antonym." (For more on diamantes, see Appendix A, page 167.) As I said this, I pointed to the enlarged Diamante blackline (page 170). I showed students that line four is the pivotal point, in which the focus of the poem changes, and the remainder of the poem is about the antonym. I said, "The first and last lines of the diamante are

nouns. I know nouns are persons, places, or things. The second and sixth lines require adjectives. I know adjectives describe nouns, so I will need to write adjectives that describe the first word and the last word in those spaces. The third and fifth lines require -*ing* words. These are called participles. Participles are words like *swimming* and *running*. They are based on verbs, but they can be used as adjectives. The middle line of the poem needs four nouns—two relating to the first subject and two relating to the second subject. When we write our diamantes we must choose our words carefully and make sure we are using the correct part of speech."

DEMONSTRATE: I demonstrated by using a think-aloud, a poster-size copy of the Diamante blackline, and a read-aloud. I pointed to the blackline and selected a pair of antonyms, *peace* and *war*, that related to our novel, *Lily's Crossing*. I thought aloud and said, "I know *peace* and *war* are opposites and I know they are nouns, so these words meet the requirements for the first and last lines of the diamante." Then I wrote *peace* on the first line of the blackline and I wrote *war* on the last line. I read the description of information needed to write the next line: two adjectives that describe the subject. I said, "I need to think of two adjectives for *peace*. As I think about what peace is like, *calm* and *quiet* come to mind. I'm going to write these words in the blanks that require adjectives, because I can describe *peace* as 'calm' and 'quiet.'"

GUIDE: I guided students to work with a partner to help me complete line three, which required three participles (*-ing* words) that tell about the original word. I said, "I know that we have studied participles, so we know that participles are based on verbs, end in *-ing*, and work like adjectives. So, we need to think of three words that end in *-ing* that describe peace." I waited a few moments to give the partners time to think and then I asked the students which participles (*-ing* words) come to mind when they think about peace. Caitlin and Brittany suggested peace was "freeing." David and Diane suggested peace was "caring." Alyssa and Javier suggested peace was "unifying." I recorded their suggestions on our blackline. Then I reviewed what we had written about peace so far. Next, I noticed that line four required two nouns related to peace and two nouns related to war. I said, "What person, place, or thing do you and your partner think of when you hear the word *peace*?" I waited a few moments and then asked the students to volunteer responses. Maria and Carmen said that doves reminded them of peaceful times. Felicia and Duane suggested *treaties*, because when wars are over, there are peace treaties. We reread the peace section of the diamante as a class before we began our work on the half that related to the antonym, *war*.

I then guided the students to work with their partners to complete the remainder of line four, which required two nouns related to war, and line five, which required three participles. I monitored the students as they discussed possible responses. When they had finished thinking about the words we needed, most of the students suggested war-related nouns such as *tanks* and *guns*, so we added them to our diamante. For war-related participles, students suggested *hurting*, *bombing*, and *killing*, so we added those to our diamante.

PRACTICE: To practice, the students worked with a partner to suggest two adjectives to complete the poem. After listening to the responses, they suggested we added *senseless* and *horrible* to our poem. We read our completed diamante and then discussed how powerful it sounded when we contrasted two words in one poem. This is our completed diamante:

Peace

Calm, quiet

Freeing, unifying, caring

Doves, treaties, tanks, guns

Hurting, bombing, killing

Senseless, horrible

War

REFLECT: We discussed how the diamante allows us to examine antonyms and demonstrate our knowledge of parts of speech. Students discussed how much they liked the format of the diamante, saying that although it seemed easy to use because it was a form poem, it really made us think about different parts of speech. The students noticed that this would be a good form poem to use in any school subject because all they needed to get started was a pair of antonyms.

STAGE 2) Teacher-Guided Small-Group Instruction

TEXT: *Twenty and Ten* (Bishop, 1952) (Texts varied according to the students' abilities.)

REVIEW: I reviewed strategies good readers use and focused on Knowing How Words Work using antonyms. We also reviewed the form we used to complete the Diamante.

GUIDE: I guided students to read Chapter 4 from the novel *Twenty and Ten*. Then I asked the students to think of two antonyms in this section of text that we could use to begin our diamante. They decided on *soldier* and *child*. I guided the students through the first three lines of the poem as they offered suggestions to complete each line. For the second line we decided on the adjectives *mean* and *Nazi*.

PRACTICE: The students practiced in pairs to work on completing the rest of the diamante. The pairs wrote their choices on Diamante blacklines and then shared with the group. This is Brian and Melissa's completed diamante, which we began as a group but they completed as partners:

Soldier

Mean, Nazi

Commanding, shooting, fighting

Guns, helmets, recess, toys

Jumping, skipping, laughing

Innocent, playful

Child

REFLECT: We reflected on how fun it was to write poetry using antonyms and what we learned from writing them. The students said they liked working together to try to figure out the parts of speech that were required for the diamante.

Student-Facilitated Comprehension Centers

ART CENTER: The students created pages for our class book of Holocaust diamantes. The students used a variety of materials to create their pages. When it was completed, the book was copied and distributed to parents. Copies were also kept in our school and classroom libraries.

THEME CENTER: I left many theme-related texts at various levels at this center. The students worked in pairs to read a text and complete a diamante using antonyms they found in their Holocaust-related readings. If time permitted, they also illustrated their diamantes. The students hung their completed work in our Poetry Corner. They shared their poems in Stage Three and at our Poetry Night, which we developed to share our writing with our families.

Student-Facilitated Comprehension Routines

LITERATURE CIRCLES: Students met in their circles and discussed their readings. Then they wrote diamantes as an extension activity and shared them with their group.

(STAGE 3) Teacher-Facilitated Whole-Group Reflection and Goal Setting

SHARE: Students shared their diamantes from Stage Two in small groups. The class also visited the Poetry Corner, so students could share the theme-related diamantes they had posted there. We also reviewed our completed diamante class book. The students shared their thoughts and feelings about using the diamantes and commented on how they could use this type of poetry in other subject areas.

REFLECT: We discussed how the format of the diamante helped us to complete the poem, use different parts of speech, and feel more confident about our abilities as writers.

SET NEW GOALS: The students felt that they had a good understanding of how to use different parts of speech to create diamantes and wanted to learn about other aspects of words. So we decided to investigate synonyms using cinquains.

Assessment Options

I observed the students in all stages of this lesson and reviewed students' self-assessments. I also read and commented on their completed diamantes, book pages, and illustrations. When working with special education students, I provided completed diamantes and wrote a sample word in each line of the diamantes they wrote to provide a model response. The students took great pride in completing their diamantes—especially their pages for our class book. When working with ELLs, I made sure they had enough time to complete their diamantes and encouraged them to use our Spanish-English theme-related word wall.

LESSON 6 Prefixes
Theme: Poetry

(STAGE 1) Teacher-Directed Whole-Group Instruction

TEXTS: Student-authored poems

EXPLAIN: I explained to the students that in our lesson we would be focusing on prefixes. "Learning about prefixes will help us analyze words we don't know. We will be able to take the word apart by finding its root and seeing what prefixes and suffixes may have been added. Because we will know the meaning of all the parts of the word, we will be able to figure out its definition. Today we are going to concentrate on prefixes that indicate direction: *circum* (around), *inter* (between), *intro* (within), *sub* (under), and *trans* (across). We're going to learn what these prefixes mean and when they are used. This will help increase our vocabulary and build our spelling skills."

To begin, I asked the students, "Will someone tell me what a prefix is?" Marzene answered, "A prefix is a letter or letters you add to the beginning of a word root to change the word and its meaning or part of speech." Everyone agreed, and we decided this was the definition we had all learned and remembered. I briefly reviewed our work on word roots, which the students seemed to remember very well.

DEMONSTRATE: To demonstrate, I used a think-aloud, chart paper, and the chalkboard. To begin, I turned to a large poster page on which I had previously written the prefixes and their meanings and said, "We will be looking at words such as *circumference*, *intertwine*, *introduce*, *subway*, and *transatlantic*. Let's look at the beginning of each of these words and think about what the root word is and how the prefix alters the meaning." Next, I made a five-column chart on the board. At the top of the columns, I wrote *circum-*, *inter-*, *intro-*, *sub-*, and *trans-*. I used a think-aloud to begin writing words that included these prefixes. I said, "I am going to write words that begin with the prefix *circum-*. Does anyone know what *circum-* means?" Danny said, "I know this from math. *Circum-* means around. *Circumference* means the distance around a circle."

Next, I asked student pairs to think of words that begin with *circum-*. Carole and Edward offered *circumnavigate*, and Beth and Richard suggested *circumstance*. I wrote these words on the chart paper and underlined the root and prefix in each example. I said: "We know that the prefix *circum-* means 'around.' And Danny has already reminded us that we know *circumference* from math, and it means the distance around a circle. Let's look at other examples. *Circumnavigate* is next on our list. If *circum-* means around, what does *circumnavigate* mean?" Mary said, "I think it means 'to sail completely around.' So, to circumnavigate an island would mean to sail all the way around it." Next, we discussed *circumstance*. Tammy said, "A circumstance is like a setting—a place and time where things happen. It's a certain situation. I could say, 'I would have done what you did in that circumstance,' meaning where you were, at a certain time, and with whoever you were with."

After this brief discussion, I encouraged the pairs of students to use the words in sentences. For example, I said, "Ferdinand Magellan *circumnavigated* the world." Then I asked students if my example was correct. Jamie said, "Yes, because Magellan sailed around the world." The pairs of students provided sentences for the other words. Examples included "Finding the *circumference* of a circle is like finding the perimeter of a square" and "I couldn't concentrate on my homework, because I was distracted by the *circumstance*." The examples worked well, so I moved on to the other prefixes on our chart.

GUIDE: For each prefix, I wrote two or three words on the board containing that prefix and asked students to join me in determining the prefix's meaning. When our discussion concluded, I referred the students to the section of our Word Study Wall titled "Roots, Prefixes, and Suffixes." I explained that we would use this section of our wall to help us remember different word parts, what they mean, and what some examples are. Then the students copied the definition of *prefix* and a few example *circum-*, *inter-*, *intro-*, *sub-*, and *trans-* words from our chart into their Word Study Journals.

PRACTICE: To practice, the students worked with a partner to create a chart of *circum-*, *inter-*, *intro-*, *sub-*, and *trans-* words found within various poems we had read in our Poetry unit. Jackson and Monique's chart included the following words: *circumvent*, *intermediate*,

Circle
Circumference, circumnavigate
Rounding, shaping, boxing
Intersect, interlock
Square

Joe wanted to take the subway,
But he couldn't find his way.
This was quite a circumstance,
So he jumped up and did a dance,
Joe started getting frantic,
And decided to go transatlantic.

FIGURE 2-5

interlock, introductory, subtotal, and transparent. After the chart was finished, they read each word aloud, defined it, took turns underlining the root word and prefix, and used the words in sentences. The students also wrote their words in their Word Study Journals while I added them to our Word Study Wall. Next, the students worked with partners to write poems, using some words from their prefix charts. Some students wrote form poems and others wrote free verse. Carl and Elaine wrote the following cinquain. The topic they chose to write about was prefixes.

Prefixes
Short, beginning
Interviewing, introducing, transmitting
Changing words and meanings
Affixes

Other student-authored poems are featured in Figure 2-5.

REFLECT: We reflected on the fact that knowing how words work can help build our vocabulary and increase our understanding of our language. Kayla said, "I liked learning what each of the prefixes meant. Now I will be able to tell what other words mean if they have these prefixes." We also reflected on using the prefix example words in our writing. The students were pleased that they knew what the words meant and how to use them. They enjoyed using them when writing their poems. Suzanne said, "I like it when we use new words in our writing. It helps me to remember what they mean."

STAGE 2   Teacher-Guided Small-Group Instruction

TEXTS: Student-authored poems

REVIEW: I reminded the students that we were working to increase our knowledge of how words work. I reviewed the prefixes we were working with: *circum-, inter-, intro-, sub-,* and *trans-*. We also reviewed the definition of each of the prefixes and agreed that all of the prefixes showed direction or position.

GUIDE: I guided the students by asking them to work with a partner to invent new words using *circum-, inter-, intro-, sub-,* or *trans-*. I explained that the goal was to invent at least one new word for each prefix. "The words you create will need to show direction or position, but for each word, you will also need to explain what part of speech it is and what it means. In addition, you will need to use each word in a sentence. Finally, you will illustrate one of the words you invent." We began with *circum-* and *inter-*. I provided a few minutes for the partners to develop one new word for each prefix. Then I invited the students to share their new words. Janelle and Caroline shared *circumdrive*. They explained it was a verb and meant "to drive around something." Their sentence was "We are going to circumdrive the town to see if any stores are open." Tom and Carla's example for *inter-* was *interlunch*. They said it was a verb and it meant "to eat lunch while sitting between friends." Their sentence was "Yesterday I had pizza when I interlunched with Dave and Julianna."

PRACTICE: The students very much enjoyed this activity, so they practiced by working with the prefixes *intro-*, *sub-*, and *trans-*. Words they invented included *subauto*, an adjective meaning "under a car"; *transwave*, a verb meaning "to surf across several waves"; and *introsing*, a verb meaning "to sing inside yourself." After all the students in the small groups shared their ideas, we talked about why inventing words was so much fun. Melissa suggested, "It's fun because we know the meaning of the prefix and we pair it up with another word we know to invent a new word." Josh said, "Yes, and because we invent the new words, they're really easy to remember, we know how to spell them, and their definitions help us to remember what the prefixes mean."

It was clear the students enjoyed inventing words. Finally, they chose their favorite invented word, illustrated its meaning, and shared their work with their groups. Examples of students' illustrations are featured in Figure 2-6.

FIGURE 2-6

REFLECT: The students decided that the more they practiced, the easier it was to know and use prefixes that show direction or position. Crystal said, "Knowing the meaning of the prefixes helped me to invent my words." The students were excited about the words they had invented. They decided that they were ready to learn more prefixes.

Student-Facilitated Comprehension Centers

ART CENTER: At this center, the students formatted and illustrated one of their prefix poems for our class book of poetry. They also contributed to a book chart that listed each prefix used in the book, as well as its part of speech and meaning. Students had the option of using a computer to complete their pages.

WORD STUDY CENTER: Students worked with a partner to read theme-related texts at various levels that I had left at this center. As they read, they noted and discussed words that had the prefixes *circum-*, *inter-*, *intro-*, *sub-*, and *trans-*. When they encountered a word that included one of these prefixes that was not in their Word Study Journals, they added it and used it in a sentence about the text they were reading.

WRITING CENTER: The students wrote poems about various topics. They used their Word Study Journals to include at least six words with directional or positional prefixes. When they finished writing, they underlined the words that contained the prefixes, shared their poem with a classmate, and hung their work in our Poetry Corner.

(STAGE 3) Teacher-Facilitated Whole-Group Reflection and Goal Setting

SHARE: Students met in small groups to share their *circum-*, *inter-*, *intro-*, *sub-*, or *trans-* charts and sentences, as well as their invented words and poems. They were absolutely enthusiastic as they did so. It was wonderful to see all of them so excited about language learning.

REFLECT: We reflected on the importance of knowing how words work. We also talked about how different prefixes change the meaning of words and how useful it is to know what prefixes mean. Randy said, "I was happy to find out that the words that start with *circum-*, *inter-*, *intro-*, *sub-*, or *trans-* all have something to do with direction or position. That will help a lot when I read if I come across a word I don't know. The first thing I'll do is try to find the root. Then I will check out the prefixes and suffixes to see if I can figure out the meaning of the word."

SET NEW GOALS: The students decided that they would like to learn the meanings of other prefixes, so they could increase their vocabulary even more.

Assessment Options

I observed the students as they brainstormed words with the class as well as with their partners. I also reviewed the students' charts and sentences and pages for the book of poetry. When working with special education students, I provided them with previously prepared charts and encouraged them to share their sentences orally. They seemed to especially enjoy making their pages for our class book. When working with ELLs, I carefully monitored their progress and provided individual assistance as needed. During paired settings, I ensured that both my special education and my ELL students worked with stronger readers to provide extra support.

Final Thoughts on This Chapter

The lessons in this chapter focused on various aspects of word study. It's important to remember that word study builds on students' knowledge of language, including grammar and phonics. These are skills and strategies that develop over time and need to be nurtured and reinforced. In the next chapter, we examine the role of fluency in the reading process. We begin by addressing its theoretical underpinnings and then present a variety of lessons focused on teaching fluency in the intermediate grades.

What can we read to learn more about teaching word study?

Bear, D. R., Invernizzi, M., Templeton, S., & Johnston, F. (2003). *Words their way: Word study for phonics, vocabulary, and spelling* (3rd ed.). Upper Saddle River, NJ: Merrill/Prentice Hall.

Blevins, W. (2003). *Teaching phonics and word study in the intermediate grades.* New York: Scholastic.

CHAPTER 3

Fluency

After years of being all but ignored in texts on the teaching of reading, fluency is now a focus of literacy instruction. And it should be. Reading fluently eliminates word-by-word reading and helps students to better comprehend what they read. Although many people think that fluency is a topic studied only in the primary grades, we now know that fluency is taught through high school.

To become fluent readers, students need to have good models, access to text, and time to read. To practice fluency, students engage in techniques such as choral reading, rereading of familiar texts, and Readers Theater. To do this independently, they need to have access to text that is easy to read. One of the many benefits of having leveled texts in classrooms is that students can read them to improve fluency. As Hudson, Lane, and Pullen (2005) and Griffith and Rasinski (2004) observe, there are many techniques for teaching fluency and it is time for us to focus our attention on them. Helping our students to become fluent readers is the focus of this chapter.

Part One: Research Base

What is fluency?

According to *The Literacy Dictionary*, fluency is

> (1) the clear, easy written or spoken expression of ideas; (2) freedom
> from word-identification problems that might hinder comprehension in
> silent reading or the expression of ideas in oral reading; (3) automaticity.
> (Harris & Hodges, 1995, p. 85)

Rasinski (2003) agrees, stating, "Reading fluency is the ability to read accurately, quickly, effortlessly, and with appropriate expression and meaning." Pikulski and Chard (2005) suggest that a comprehensive definition would include both *The Literacy Dictionary* and the report of the National Reading Panel (2000) definitions:

> Reading fluency refers to efficient, effective word-recognition skills that
> permit a reader to construct the meaning of text. Fluency is manifested
> in accurate, rapid, expressive oral reading and is applied during, and
> makes possible, silent reading comprehension. (p. 510)

What does the research tell us?

According to Rasinski (2004), fluency builds a bridge to comprehension. The structure consists of accuracy in word decoding (sounding out words with minimal errors), automatic processing (using as little mental energy as possible to decode, so the energy can be used to comprehend), and prosodic reading (parsing the text into appropriate syntactic and semantic units). Samuels (2002) concurs, noting that becoming a fluent reader is challenging because components of reading, such as word recognition, determining the meaning of words, grouping words into grammatical units, generating inferences, and constructing meaning must be coordinated to happen simultaneously.

Fluency is also directly related to motivation. Oakley (2003) reports that fluent readers are more likely to read more and learn more and, consequently, become even more fluent. In addition, Rasinski and Padak (2000) note that fluent readers have a more positive attitude toward reading and a more positive concept of themselves as readers. It is generally agreed that fluency is an outcome of reading practice. Good reading models, teacher feedback, and methods such as repeated reading foster fluency, as do low-risk environments where students are comfortable and willing to read (Nathan & Stanovich, 1991).

Part Two: Lesson Overview

In this section we put research into practice by presenting six lessons that focus on various ways to teach oral reading fluency. As seen in the chart below, the lessons are theme-based and feature a variety of teaching ideas. The texts also vary. In Stage One, the teacher reads, so the text level may be easy, just right, or more challenging. In the guided reading groups, texts are at students' instructional levels, and at the centers and in the routines, independent-level texts are used. Appendix B contains additional resources for teaching fluency. Appendix F features other texts and Web sites that can be used when teaching these themes.

THEME	TEACHING IDEA	STAGE ONE TEXT	STAGE TWO GUIDED READING TEXT
Mystery	Readers Theater	*The Westing Game*	*The Soccer Shoe Clue*
Survival	Patterned Partner Reading	*Hatchet*	*Brian's Winter*
Biography	Repeated Readings	*You Want Women to Vote, Lizzie Stanton?*	*Dear Benjamin Banneker*
Fantasy	Radio Reading	*Tuck Everlasting*	*The Lion, the Witch, and the Wardrobe*
The Holocaust	The Fluent Reading Model	*Lily's Crossing, The Yellow Star,* "Holocaust"	*Number the Stars*
Poetry	Choral Reading	"Stopping by Woods on a Snowy Evening"	"America the Beautiful"

Fluency Lessons

LESSON 1   Readers Theater
Theme: Mystery

STAGE 1   Teacher-Directed Whole-Group Instruction

TEXT: *The Westing Game* (Raskin, 1978)

EXPLAIN: I began by asking students what makes a reader interesting to listen to. Andre replied, "They don't make any mistakes." Kim Lynn said, "They make it sound interesting, like you do when you read aloud and change your voice for different characters." Kara added, "They change their voices at different parts in the story—like faster or slower when you know something important is going to happen. The reading doesn't all just sound the same." I said, "You have all just given great explanations of what makes a reader interesting to listen to. We say that someone who reads with the characteristics you have just described is a *fluent* reader." I explained to the students that we would be learning about an interesting approach to reading called Readers Theater. I also explained that this approach was designed to help us become more fluent readers. In Readers Theater, the story is written in the form of a script, so it is similar to a play. Students do not dress up or use props to perform it, though. Instead, they use their voices to help bring the characters to life. I told students, "Our voices will be the tools we use to convey different characters' emotions. Practicing our reading by reading scripts will improve our fluency, which in turn will improve our comprehension."

DEMONSTRATE: To demonstrate, I invited students to help me create a short dialogue between a student and teacher called "The Case of the Missing Homework." When we finished writing, students read the script to me using a lot of expression. (See Figure 3-1.) I asked students to close their eyes and listen to the dialogue to see if they could visualize what was happening. I explained that by using a lot of expression in our voices, we could create a picture of what was happening without using any props.

FIGURE 3-1

The Case of the Missing Homework

MRS. COOKIECRUMB:	Freddy, where is your homework?
FREDDY:	I don't know! I really did do my homework. It was in my locker before gym.
MRS. COOKIECRUMB:	So it disappeared during gym?
FREDDY:	I don't know. It's just not in my locker.
MRS. COOKIECRUMB:	Are you sure you looked through all of your papers?
FREDDY:	Yes, I'm sure I did.
MRS. COOKIECRUMB:	Well, maybe it got stuck in a folder or under a book. Why don't you go check again?
FREDDY:	Okay, I'll check again. [*pauses to check his locker*] Mrs. Cookiecrumb! You were right! It was stuck under my math book. I must have put the book on top of it before I went to the gym!
MRS. COOKIECRUMB:	Well, I am glad that you found it, but next time make sure that you put your homework inside of a folder or other safe place so you don't lose it.
FREDDY:	Don't worry, Mrs. Cookiecrumb, I will!

GUIDE: To guide students I explained that we would be using Readers Theater to read the next chapter in the book *The Westing Game* by Ellen Raskin. "I have gone through part of this chapter and turned the text into a dialogue for us to 'act out' with our voices," I said. It is important to remember what we know about the characters so far, so that you can use the proper tone and expression in your voice to help bring them to life. The characters in this script are the narrator, Angela Wexler, Mrs. Wexler, Flora Baumbach, and Turtle Wexler. Before we decide who will read each role, let's review what we already know about each of these characters." We proceeded to have a short discussion reviewing the characters' traits. Then I showed students a Character Map, which I had begun on chart paper earlier in the day. As students commented on each character, I wrote the traits they suggested underneath that character's name on the map. Then students met in groups of five and decided who would read which part in their Readers Theater. (See Figure 3-2 for our completed Character Map.)

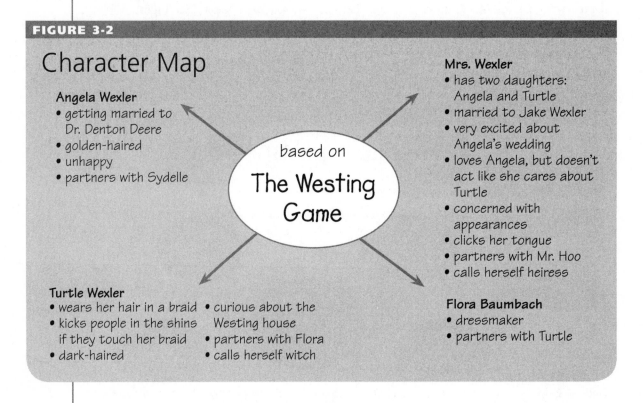

FIGURE 3-2

Character Map

based on
The Westing Game

Angela Wexler
- getting married to Dr. Denton Deere
- golden-haired
- unhappy
- partners with Sydelle

Mrs. Wexler
- has two daughters: Angela and Turtle
- married to Jake Wexler
- very excited about Angela's wedding
- loves Angela, but doesn't act like she cares about Turtle
- concerned with appearances
- clicks her tongue
- partners with Mr. Hoo
- calls herself heiress

Turtle Wexler
- wears her hair in a braid
- kicks people in the shins if they touch her braid
- dark-haired
- curious about the Westing house
- partners with Flora
- calls herself witch

Flora Baumbach
- dressmaker
- partners with Turtle

PRACTICE: The small groups of students practiced their scripts, focusing on using their voices to bring the characters to life. The script they were reading was adapted from Chapter 3, pages 11–13, of *The Westing Game* by Ellen Raskin. (See Figure 3-3.) Following their practice sessions, each group read the script for the class, and we offered positive feedback.

FIGURE 3-3

Readers Theater Script for *The Westing Game*

NARRATOR: Upstairs in 3D, Angela Wexler stood on a hassock as still and blank-faced pretty as a store-window dummy. Her pale blue eyes stared unblinkingly at the lake.

FLORA: Turn, dear.

ANGELA: Oh!

NARRATOR: Startled by the small cry, Flora Baumbach dropped the pin from her pudgy fingers and almost swallowed the three in her mouth.

MRS. WEXLER: Please be careful, Mrs. Baumbach; my Angela has very delicate skin.

ANGELA: Mrs. Baumbach didn't prick me, Mother. I was just surprised to see smoke coming from the Westing house chimney.

NARRATOR: Crawling with slow caution on her hands and knees, Flora Baumbach paused in the search for the dropped pin to peer up through her straight gray bangs. Mrs. Wexler set her coffee cup on the driftwood coffee table and craned her neck for a better view.

MRS. WEXLER: We must have new neighbors. I'll have to drive up there with a housewarming gift; they may need some decorating advice.

TURTLE: Hey, look! There's smoke coming from the Westing house!

MRS. WEXLER: Oh, it's you.

TURTLE: Otis Amber says that old man Westing's stinking corpse is rotting on an Oriental rug.

FLORA: My, oh my!

TURTLE: Mrs. Baumbach, could you hem my witch's costume? I need it for tonight.

MRS. WEXLER: Can't you see she's busy with Angela's wedding dress? And why must you wear a silly costume like that? Really, Turtle, I don't know why you insist on making yourself ugly.

TURTLE: It's no sillier than a wedding dress. Besides, nobody gets married anymore, and if they do, they don't wear silly wedding dresses. Besides, who would want to marry that stuck-up-know-it-all-marshmallow-face-doctor-denton . . . ?

MRS. WEXLER: That's enough of your smart mouth! Doctor Deere is a brilliant young man. Angela will soon be Angela Deere; isn't that a precious name? And then we'll have two doctors in the family. Now where do you think you're going?

TURTLE: Downstairs to tell Daddy about the smoke coming from the Westing house.

MRS. WEXLER: Come back this instant. You know your father operates in the afternoon; why don't you go to your room and work on stock market reports or whatever you do in there.

TURTLE: Some room, it's even too small for a closet.

ANGELA: I'll hem your witch's costume, Turtle.

MRS. WEXLER: Angela, what an angel.

Adapted from Chapter 3

REFLECT: To reflect, we discussed Readers Theater and continued to comment on the characters' traits. We also talked about what we did to help bring the characters to life and thought about how we might be able to do that even better in our Readers Theater. Cathy suggested that it would be a good idea to have some sign or prop to distinguish each of the characters they were portraying. I said that may be something they would enjoy creating when they visited the Art Center in Stage Two. They were excited about performing the script and wanted to perform this Readers Theater for the other classes in our grade.

(STAGE 2) Teacher-Guided Small-Group Instruction

TEXT: *The Soccer Shoe Clue* (Keene, 1995) (Texts varied according to the students' abilities.)

REVIEW: To review, I asked students to explain what Readers Theater is and how it helps us become more fluent readers. Micah responded, "It's like putting on a play but without costumes, or acting, or props." Kelly added that "we use our voices as a way to bring the characters alive."

GUIDE: To guide students, I invited them to read the first chapter of *The Soccer Shoe Clue* by Carolyn Keene. Next, I shared the script that I had adapted from the chapter and assigned parts to students. The characters were Nancy Drew, Amara Shane, Narrator 1, Narrator 2, Erin Kelly, Coach Santos, and Lindsay Mitchell. Since our guided reading groups had only five students each, two students read the parts of two characters—Amara Shane and Lindsay Mitchell, and Erin Kelly and Coach Santos.

PRACTICE: The students practiced the script a few times and then shared their interpretation of the Readers Theater script. The script (see Figure 3-4) is adapted from Chapter 1, pages 1–5, of *The Soccer Shoe Clue* by Carolyn Keene. When the reading was finished, we discussed how effective it was and what we might do to make it better next time. Ideas students shared included working on the rate at which they read certain lines and reading some of the parts describing the goo in the shoe with even more expression.

FIGURE 3-4

Readers Theater Script for *The Soccer Shoe Clue*

AMARA SHANE: Eewww . . . yuck!

NANCY DREW: What's wrong?

AMARA: There's something yucky in my soccer shoe. Something sticky. It's gross!

NARRATOR 1:   Nancy looked around for her friend George Fayne. George was the captain of the soccer team. She would help Amara. But George was not in the locker room. All the other girls watched as Nancy got up and walked over to Amara.

NANCY: Let me see.

AMARA: I don't want to touch it.

NANCY: I can't see anything. You'll have to take off your shoe.

NARRATOR 2:   Amara wrinkled up her nose and made a face. But she took her shoe off. She used only two fingers of each hand, so she wouldn't have to touch it much.

GIRLS IN THE ROOM: Eewww! Gross!

NARRATOR 1:   Amara's knee sock was covered with something slimy. Something dark red and slimy. Nancy bent down to take a closer look. It was really gross.

NARRATOR 2:   All the other girls crowded around Amara. All except Carrie Rodis. She kept putting on her own soccer shoes.

NARRATOR 1:   Carrie was new at Carl Sandburg Elementary School. She had just moved into Nancy's neighborhood. She had joined the Tigers team the week before.

NANCY: That's the third mean trick someone has played on us this week.

ERIN KELLY: I'll help you clean it up.

AMARA: Thanks.

COACH SANTOS: Girls? Are you ready to practice?

NARRATOR 2:   Coach Santos was Julie Santos's mother. Both Julia and her mother were very good soccer players. They were from Brazil, and soccer was a big sport there.

NANCY: We're not quite ready. Someone put something icky in Amara's shoe.

COACH SANTOS: Oh no! Not another prank.

AMARA: I can't play goalie with my shoe all slimy.

COACH SANTOS: Well, clean it up. Put on a clean sock, too. And everyone else, hurry up. It looks as if it's going to rain. Let's get practice started.

NANCY (*whispering to herself*): Where is George?

NARRATOR 1:   Nancy wanted to go look for her friend. But Coach Santos was watching her.

continued on the next page

FIGURE 3-4 continued

COACH SANTOS:	Come on, Tigers. The sky is getting cloudier all the time. Let's get outside while we still can play.
LINDSAY MITCHELL (*whispering to Nancy*):	This is creepy. On Wednesday someone tied big knots in the laces of my soccer shoes.
NANCY:	I know. Someone let the air out of Julia's ball on Friday, too.
LINDSAY:	You're a detective. Maybe you can figure out who's doing this—and who put the icky stuff in Amara's shoe.
NANCY:	Maybe I can. At least I can try.
NARRATOR 2:	Nancy saw Carrie Rodis walking ahead of them, all by herself. She had noticed that Carrie had ignored Amara. She hadn't seemed to care about the goo in Amara's shoe.
NANCY (*thinking aloud*):	Is Carrie the one trying to hurt the team? There is no way to know for sure. But someone had been playing tricks on the soccer team. And Carrie has a good reason to do it.
NARRATOR 1:	Before she had moved, Carrie had played for the Lions. They were another elementary school team. And they were the Tigers' biggest rivals!

REFLECT: We discussed how Readers Theater helped us to improve our fluency. Sarah said, "Readers Theater makes me want to read, so I don't mind practicing. I like that we all have different parts to read and that we can read like we think the characters would." Cliff said, "I like that we are putting on a play by using our voices. I don't mind practicing, because it's fun to read it over when everyone in the group has a part." When we finished sharing our reflections, we reread the script as a whole class. This final reading proved to be a lot of fun, because all of the students who had been assigned a particular part read it chorally.

Student-Facilitated Comprehension Centers

ART CENTER: Students worked on creating hats or signs depicting their character's name to use when practicing their Readers Theater scripts. We decided to make generic signs, so we could add different names as we read various scripts.

READERS THEATER CENTER: The students worked in small groups to perform additional Readers Theater scripts. The scripts that I had available at the center were found on the Web site www.fictionteachers.com/classroomtheater.html. Other good sources for Readers Theater scripts are www.aaronshep.com/rt/RTE.html, which contains legends and folktales from all around the world, and www.teachingheart.net/readerstheater.htm.

Student-Facilitated Comprehension Routines

LITERATURE CIRCLES: We adapted the Literature Circle to include Readers Theater scripts created by the students for the chapters they had been reading. Students worked together to write the scripts and then tape-recorded them and shared them with the class in Stage Three.

(STAGE 3) Teacher-Facilitated Whole-Group Reflection and Goal Setting

SHARE: We began our sharing by listening to the Literature Circle Readers Theaters on tape. This was enjoyable for everyone, but especially for the readers, who liked hearing their very expressive voices on tape. Then, in small groups, students reflected on how Readers Theater helped them to become more fluent readers and what they enjoyed most about the experience. Later, in whole-class sharing, they all agreed that having the right amount of expression for each character was an important part of bringing the characters to life, but they also said that practicing the script was helpful. Kate said, "The better we know our parts, the better our Readers Theater is."

REFLECT: The students reflected on how each time they practiced the lines, they added more expression to their voice and became more comfortable with the part they were reading. They also felt that they knew exactly how the character would say the lines. All of them agreed that it was a fun way to read a story. Kyle said, "It was fun because I felt like I was a part of the story!"

SET NEW GOALS: We decided that we would continue to use Readers Theater to help improve our fluency and that we would perform our scripts for other classes.

Assessment Options

I used observation, the audiotapes, and student self-reflections to assess. When working with special education students, I was careful to ensure they took active roles in Readers Theater, but I limited the amount of dialogue they needed to perform. I also provided individual assistance as needed. The Readers Theater scripts were available on tape to provide fluent models and to help students bring their lines to life. The tapes were also available for use at home, so students could practice their fluent reading. I assessed these students on smaller components and their ability to complete them. It was a joy to see them participate in Readers Theater. They thoroughly enjoyed it and their small groups were very supportive.

When working with ELL students, I limited the amount of dialogue (if necessary) and provided more specific, individualized instruction. The scripts on tape were used as needed in the classroom and were available for students to take home to practice their fluency. I assessed their performance through observation, as well as oral and written formats.

LESSON 2 Pattern Partner Reading
Theme: Survival

STAGE 1 Teacher-Directed Whole-Group Instruction

TEXT: *Hatchet* (Paulsen, 1987)

EXPLAIN: I began by asking students to recall things that make readers sound more fluent. Responses included, "They don't just read all the words all the same," "Their reading isn't too fast or too slow, it's just right," and "The reader doesn't make any mistakes." I agreed that those were all characteristics of fluent readers and explained that we were going to use an idea called Pattern Partner Reading (McLaughlin & Allen, 2002a) to help us become more fluent readers and to help us monitor or pay attention to what we are reading. I said, "Pattern Partner Reading provides a structure for reading interactively and strategically with one another. It involves partner reading, but it is different from what we usually do because it uses patterns such as Read–Pause–Retell, Read–Pause–Question, and Read–Pause–Sketch. In these patterns one partner reads, then both partners pause, and the partner that didn't read retells what was read or both partners ask each other questions, or both sketch and share with each other. There are many patterns that we can use when we are using Pattern Partner Reading [see page 175]. Partner reading gives us an opportunity to practice our fluency. Using a pattern helps keep our reading focused and gives us a chance to practice our strategies. There are many patterns we can use for Pattern Partner Reading, but today we will focus on just one—Read–Pause–Say Something."

Next I explained the activity. "When we do this type of partner reading, one partner reads a page aloud while the other partner listens and follows along. When you or your partner finishes reading a page, you will both pause and then each say something. You may choose to 'say something' about what a character did or about something that happened that surprised you. What you say about what you read is up to you. After you say something about the text, you're going to both say something about the reader's fluency.

For example, you may say, 'I liked the way your voice changed when you read the parts of different characters' or 'You read so fast, it was hard to understand what you were reading. Maybe you could read a little slower next time.' Whatever you decide to say about your partner's fluency, remember to say it nicely—either as a compliment or as a helpful suggestion. Once each partner has had a chance to say something, the other partner takes a turn reading. You and your partner continue using this pattern until you finish the selection."

DEMONSTRATE: I demonstrated how to use Pattern Partner Reading by using a read-aloud of the book *Hatchet* by Gary Paulsen. I asked for a volunteer to be my partner, and Tori raised her hand. We began by reading Chapter 5. We had decided that I would read a page while Tori followed along, and then Tori would read the next page while I followed along. After I read the first page, it was time for each of us to say something about what I had read. I prompted, "Now it's time for each of us to say something about what we just read. I'll go first. I feel badly for Brian! First we found out that he had to crash-land the plane he was on, and now he is badly sunburned and his face feels like it is on fire from sleeping in the sun. Along with that, he is really thirsty!" Then I told the class, "Now it's Tori's turn to say something." Tori said, "When you read how thirsty Brian was, I remembered once being almost as thirsty as he was. I was at soccer practice on a really, really hot day and I ran out of water, but I still don't know if I would have gotten a drink from the lake!" Then we exchanged comments on my fluency. I said, "I tried to read fluently, but it was a little difficult, because I hadn't practiced reading this section." Tori said, "I think your reading was fluent, but you hesitated a few times, so practice would probably help you with that." Of course, I had read *Hatchet* many times and was very familiar with the book, but I deliberately hesitated when pronouncing two words, hoping that Tori would notice and make a suggestion.

GUIDE: I guided students as they Pattern Partner Read the next two pages in the chapter. We decided that while we were learning this new technique it would be best for readers to switch after reading just one page. (Later you may want to increase the amount each partner read before stopping to say something.) I reminded them to be good listeners while their partner was reading, to follow along, and to be thinking of things they may want to say. I circulated as the partners read, listened to their comments, and provided feedback and suggestions as necessary. When Jerry and Alisa first paused to say something, Jerry said, "I wonder how Brian is going to get more water since he got sick on the lake water. I wouldn't drink that again if I were him!" and Alisa said, "It's disgusting that Brian drank the lake water in the first place. I have been to the lake by my house and would never drink out of it! There are bugs and other things in it!" Jerry had read this page, so

Alisa said, "Your reading was fluent and you paid attention to the text and changed your voice to read different sections. I liked how you sounded when you read that the water had made Brian sick. It sounded almost as if you had drunk some of the lake water." Jerry said, "It's interesting that you commented on that section. I drank lake water once when I was camping and it tasted terrible. I was thinking about that when I was reading about Brian."

PRACTICE: To practice, I had students continue to Pattern Partner Read Chapter 5 using the Read–Pause–Say Something pattern that included a special comment on fluency. In some cases, to provide fluent models, I paired a more able reader with a less able one.

REFLECT: To reflect, students discussed how Pattern Partner Reading and the Read–Pause–Say Something pattern helped them to really think about what they were reading. Raj said, "I was trying hard to come up with something interesting to tell my partner, so I was really listening, following along, and thinking about Brian." They also thought that reading with a partner helped them to improve their fluency. Mallory commented, "Since I was reading for someone else, I was focusing on reading fluently. I remembered what we had learned about using expression, paying attention to punctuation, and reading at a good pace." We all agreed that this technique helped us to think about how and what we were reading. Patterned Partner Reading helped us to focus on improving our fluency and to think about what we were reading, so we could say something meaningful about the text.

(STAGE 2) Teacher-Guided Small-Group Instruction

TEXT: *Brian's Winter* (Paulsen, 1996) (Texts varied according to the students' abilities.)

REVIEW: To review, I asked students to describe the characteristics of fluent reading. Their responses included using expression, using punctuation clues, and not reading too fast or too slow. Then I asked students to explain what Pattern Partner Reading is. John said, "It is when you take turns reading with a partner and after each of us reads, we stop to say something about what we read. Then we say something about the reader's fluency." I acknowledged that John was correct, but I reminded students that even though we would be using the Read–Pause–Say Something Pattern, many different patterns could be used. Next I introduced our text, *Brian's Winter* by Gary Paulsen. After a brief discussion about the title and Brian, students began to read the book.

GUIDE: To guide students, I reminded them that each partner would read and then they would both pause and say something about the text that had been read. I reminded them to focus not only on what they were reading but also how fluently they were reading it. After one partner had read a page, they paused and each said something about what they had just heard. After they commented on the text, they discussed the reader's fluency. Then they switched roles. As the pairs read, I made observations about their reading and their discussions about the text and fluency. After several pages were read, we discussed the text and their ideas about fluency.

PRACTICE: To practice, students continued to Pattern Partner Read *Brian's Winter*, using the Read–Pause–Say Something pattern to comment on the text and the reader's fluency.

REFLECT: To reflect, we discussed how reading aloud with a partner helped us to practice our fluency and how stopping after a few pages to say something helped us to really pay attention to what we were reading and how the reader was reading. Frankie said that he liked reading with a partner because "if I got stuck on a word or something, my partner helped me." Angela said that she liked having to say something about what she and her partner had just read. "It helped me to think about what was happening and make connections to things I know about." They all seemed to enjoy commenting on each other's fluency. Rob said, "I liked when Mike reminded me to read with more expression. If someone reminds me, I can fix it right away. If we didn't talk about it, I might have read all my pages without expression."

Student-Facilitated Comprehension Centers

THEME CENTER: I had placed a variety of theme-related titles at various levels at this center. Students used the Read–Pause–Say Something pattern as they selected and read books or articles. First they commented on the text, then on the reader's fluency.

Student-Facilitated Comprehension Routines

CROSS-AGE READING EXPERIENCES: Students read with cross-age partners and engaged in the Pattern Partner Reading technique using the Read–Pause–Say Something pattern.

SHARE: In small groups, students shared their experiences using the Read–Pause–Say Something pattern during Stage Two. They discussed what they enjoyed about partner reading using a pattern to comment on the text and the reader's fluency.

REFLECT: The students reflected on how the Read–Pause–Say Something pattern helped them to better understand what they had read. They also commented on how it was helpful to have a partner share ideas about the text and their fluency. Susannah said, "I liked listening to my partner because I was paying attention to the things he did that made him sound more fluent, like using expression. Then I made sure that I did the same thing when it was my turn to read."

SET NEW GOALS: We decided that we would continue to use Pattern Partner Reading to improve our fluency and comprehension. We all felt comfortable using Read–Pause–Say Something, so we decided to learn how to use more patterns.

Assessment Options

I used observation and student self-reflections to assess. When working with special education students, I was careful to partner them with more capable readers. I also had available the book on tape for them to listen to, so they could follow along. When working with ELL students, I limited the amount of text they were required to read at a given time and allowed extra time for more specific and individualized instruction. Books on tape were also used when needed. I assessed the students' performance both orally and in written format.

LESSON 3   Repeated Readings
Theme: Biography

STAGE 1   Teacher-Directed Whole-Group Instruction

TEXT: *You Want Women to Vote, Lizzie Stanton?* (Fritz, 1995)

EXPLAIN: I began by explaining to the students that we would be using a strategy called Repeated Readings to help us improve our fluency. I reminded students that fluency is the ability to read a passage with expression, clearly, at a good pace, without making any errors. I said, "When we read fluently, we read with expression and the thoughts and ideas that we are reading about are easy to understand." I explained that Repeated Readings is a technique that will help us to become familiar with words in a passage so we can read the passage more fluently.

I read a short poem to the class—first, word by word, then fluently. I asked students which reading was easier to understand, and they all said the second reading was. Emma said, "The first time you read the poem I was paying attention to one word at a time. The second time you read it, it flowed better, so I paid attention to the poem. It made sense the second time." I agreed with Emma and said, "Today we will be doing Repeated Readings using a passage from a book we have already read, *You Want Women to Vote, Lizzie Stanton?* The more times we practice reading a passage, the more fluently we will read it and be able to comprehend it. When we engage in Repeated Readings, I will read a passage aloud, and then we will read it together chorally. Finally, you will read the passage to a partner three times and your partner will give you feedback about how you read. Then you and your partner will switch roles and your partner will read the passage three times and you will offer feedback. So we will be reading the same passage several times. We'll also be listening to our partners read the passage."

I reminded students that it's important to provide positive feedback to their partners: "Let's think about how we offer feedback on one another's writing. We say one good thing and make one suggestion. That means that when we offer feedback during Repeated Readings, we will say one good thing about our partner's fluency and make one suggestion to improve it."

DEMONSTRATE: To demonstrate, I used the overhead projector to display a copy of a page from the text.

> Margaret was younger than two years old when Elizabeth was asked by the women's association in New York to address the New York State Legislature in Albany. For once the women wanted to speak directly to the men who made the laws. And who could present their case better than Elizabeth Cady Stanton?
>
> The very idea was scary. For a woman to speak to an audience of men was hard enough, but to speak to the men who governed the state of New York! The men who made the laws in her father's law books! This would be the highest fence that Elizabeth had ever tried to jump over. But she was thirty-eight years old and she had held herself back too long. Of course she would do it. She would take Amelia Willard and the three youngest children, put them up in an Albany hotel while she took on what she called the "great event" of her life. She enlisted the help of Susan, and for two months, she worked on her speech.

First I read the passage aloud. Then I chorally read it with a student, who had volunteered to be part of the demonstration. Next, my partner and I each read the passage three times and offered feedback and suggestions to each other. Finally, we discussed how reading the passage multiple times helped us to read more fluently and to understand the passage better. Then we invited questions from the rest of the class and I explained that we would all be doing Repeated Readings with a partner in the next step.

GUIDE: To guide students, I read aloud the first two paragraphs on page 37 of the book *You Want Women to Vote, Lizzie Stanton?* Then students and I chorally read the same paragraphs. Next the student partners took turns reading the paragraphs three times, giving feedback after each partner had finished reading. I circulated as the partners read, providing feedback and suggestions as necessary.

PRACTICE: To practice, students read the next two pages of the text. When possible, I paired a more able reader with a less able one. The students read the passage chorally, then took turns being the teacher and student and provided each other with compliments and suggestions. Once they had each read the passages several times, they discussed what they had read and how Repeated Readings had helped them to read more fluently.

REFLECT: To reflect, we talked about how reading the same passage several times helped make the passage easier to read and, therefore, helped us to read it more fluently. Stephen said, "I liked when my partner gave me good comments and suggestions to make my fluency better. It made me feel good about my reading and let me know that I was getting better. It also helped me to know what to focus on the next time I read the passage." We also talked about how this technique made it easier for us to understand the text.

(STAGE 2) Teacher-Guided Small-Group Instruction

TEXT: *Dear Benjamin Banneker* (Pinkney, 1994) (Texts varied according to the students' abilities.)

REVIEW: To review, I reminded students that Repeated Readings helps us to be more fluent readers and better comprehend what we are reading. I explained that we would be reading another book using Repeated Readings.

GUIDE: To guide students, I introduced the text *Dear Benjamin Banneker* and asked students to open their books to the Author's Note in the beginning of the story. First I read a short section aloud while students followed along. Next we chorally read this section. Then students read the passage aloud to a partner three times and offered positive feedback. As the pairs read, I made observations as I listened to each reader. Finally, we discussed what we had read.

PRACTICE: To practice, students worked with an assigned partner and continued reading *Dear Benjamin Banneker*. After they had all finished reading the book, we discussed the story. Then students revisited the story, focusing on three passages I had previously flagged with sticky-notes. When students reached a sticky-note, they engaged in Repeated Readings of a passage marked on that page. Students read those passages three times and provided positive feedback to their partner.

REFLECT: To reflect, we discussed how reading a passage multiple times helped us to read it more fluently. We also talked about how listening to someone else read helped us with our own reading. We also discussed the fact that we liked the positive feedback and helpful hints we got from our partners. Jack said, "It was also good because if I didn't know how to pronounce a word the first time, my partner helped me. Then, the next time I read the page, I remembered how to say the word, and that made me feel really good because then I knew I learned the word and I could read more fluently."

Student-Facilitated Comprehension Centers

DRAMA CENTER: Partners selected short "sports announcer" scripts I had left at the Drama Center and engaged in Repeated Readings. They used various sports props as they called a baseball game, a car race, or a tennis match. The students thoroughly enjoyed this center and eagerly practiced the scripts, which I had written based on recent sporting events.

THEME CENTER: The students chose different books and articles from the Biography/Autobiography Center and, with a partner, engaged in Repeated Readings.

Student-Facilitated Comprehension Routines

CROSS-AGE READING EXPERIENCES: Students read biographies or autobiographies with cross-age partners and engaged in Repeated Readings, with the older students sharing the role of teacher with younger partners.

LITERATURE CIRCLES: At the conclusion of the Literature Circles, students used passages I had marked in their current novel to engage in Repeated Readings.

(STAGE 3) Teacher-Facilitated Whole-Group Reflection and Goal Setting

SHARE: In small groups, students shared their Repeated Reading experiences from Stage Two. They discussed what they enjoyed about reading with their partner and how they found Repeated Readings to be helpful. After sharing in small groups, some students volunteered to share with the whole group.

REFLECT: We reflected on how Repeated Readings helped us to improve our fluency and our comprehension. Alexandria said that she liked how she got to feel like the teacher when she was giving her partner feedback and that she remembered the things she told her partner to do when it was her turn to read. All the students agreed that by the final time they read the passage, they felt really confident in their reading, and they could easily retell what the passage was about.

SET NEW GOALS: Students decided that they could engage in Repeated Readings when they read independently, and that each time they read the passage they could focus on their expression and rate. We decided that we were ready to try another strategy to improve our fluency.

Assessment Options

I primarily used observation to assess the students' fluency and engagement in Repeated Readings. When working with special education students, I was careful to pair them with a student with a higher reading ability for assistance and modeling. I noticed that with each reading, they were more comfortable with the reading and read more confidently. I assessed this by noting improvements made with each reading. Similarly, when working with ELLs during this lesson, I had students read along while listening to the book on tape to tap into both visual and auditory aspects of reading. I noticed that by hearing the words on tape first, students gained more confidence when reading with a partner. I assessed their performance by listening to them read throughout the different stages and noting their progress.

LESSON 4 Radio Reading
Theme: Fantasy

(STAGE 1) Teacher-Directed Whole-Group Instruction

TEXT: *Tuck Everlasting* (Babbitt, 1975)

EXPLAIN: I began by asking students what they thought fluency was. Marco said, "I have heard that word before. I think it means you read with expression." Others in the class added that they thought it meant you read with flow—without stopping after you read each word. I explained that we would continue to read the novel *Tuck Everlasting*, but we would begin today by focusing on fluency using a technique called Radio Reading. I said, "Radio Reading is similar to Readers Theater, but it includes sound effects to make the reading sound like an old-time radio show." Since we had already engaged in Readers Theater, I explained that we would be Radio Reading selected sections of texts to help improve our fluency. I said, "During Radio Reading we will have a script and read the parts of different characters using our voices to communicate our message, just as we did in Readers Theater. The difference is that in Radio Reading we will add sound effects."

Then I played a short tape of a brief Radio Reading I had previously recorded. It was based on a mystery and students immediately realized that the creaking doors, approaching footsteps, and howling animals were all examples of sound effects we would add to our scripts as we read. They were intrigued with the entire concept. For example, Eugenia said, "I like this idea. We'll use our voices to tell the story like we did in Readers Theater, and we'll use the sound effects to sort of back up our voices—to try to help us get our message across."

DEMONSTRATE: To demonstrate, I read aloud a very short selection from *Tuck Everlasting* and focused on the sound effects that might occur during that segment of the book. The section I read was one we had previously read and discussed. Before I began reading, I made sure students were following along on the copies I had provided. "Notice that the sound effects are included as directions in the dialogue. So, when I am reading the script, I am going to pay special attention to the dialogue and the sound effects. We can make some sound effects using our voices, but we will need to use props to make the others." Then I showed students some of the props I would be using, including coconut shells, a pitcher of water, and pine needles, and began Radio Reading the script I had prepared. I read with expression and when the text said, "We're home! This is it, Winnie Foster!" I made sound effects to represent the horse's hooves (coconut shells) and sliding needles on the ground. When the text said, "'Oh, look!' cried Winnie. 'Water!'" I focused on sound effects to represent the boys jumping in the pond and laughter.

GUIDE: To guide students, I introduced the next segment of the script based on *Tuck Everlasting*. (See below for an excerpt from the script.) The students took a few minutes to read through the script, first silently, then in small groups. I asked for volunteers to read each character's part as well as volunteers to make the sound effects, and we engaged in Radio Reading as a fluent model for the class. Then I provided props for each small group and they engaged in Radio Reading the script. They did this twice, changing roles for the second reading. The students thoroughly enjoyed this process. When we were discussing our participation in Radio Reading, Jaden said, "I thought when I was doing the sound effects it would be easy, but I needed to read along to know the right time to make the sounds and I had to listen to the readers to know whether to make the sounds louder or softer."

MAE:	It don't take 'em more'n a minute to pile into that pond. (*both boys heard laughing in the background*) You can go in too if you like.
WINNIE:	(*footsteps heard shifting backward*) Oh no, I couldn't.
TUCK:	(*big boots heard walking forward*) Where's the child? (*horse heard snorting in the background*)
MAE:	Here she is, right behind me.

TUCK:	There's just no words to tell you how happy I am to see you. It's the finest thing that's happened in . . . Does she know?
	(Mae heard laughing in the background)
MAE:	Of course she knows. That's why I brought her here.

PRACTICE: To practice, I introduced the next segment of the Radio Reading script. We briefly discussed it, and the students took a few minutes to practice reading it. Then the small groups chose parts to read and sound effects to make and engaged in Radio Reading twice—changing roles for the second reading. When we were discussing this segment of the script, Ellen said, "I liked it when I read a character's part *and* when I made the sounds. It's almost like the sounds are other voices we can add to the reading. I mean, when we make a sound we're still doing it with expression—just like we do with our voices."

REFLECT: The students all agreed that Radio Reading was a great technique for improving fluency. They also agreed that having opportunities to read and to make sound effects helped them to understand that everything that happens during Radio Reading contributes to the fluent reading of the script.

(STAGE 2) Teacher-Guided Small-Group Instruction

TEXT: *The Lion, the Witch, and the Wardrobe* (Lewis, 1994) (Texts varied according to the students' abilities.)

REVIEW: To review, we discussed the characteristics of fluent reading, including reading with expression, paying attention to punctuation, and reading at a good pace. We also discussed how Radio Reading helps us to improve our fluency. Then I reminded students that we would be adding sound effects to the scripts as we engaged in Radio Reading. Finally, I introduced the text on which our scripts were based, *The Lion, the Witch, and the Wardrobe.*

GUIDE: To guide students I shared the first segment of the script. (See following page.) I asked them to read it with a partner to become familiar with the passage and the sound effects. Following that, we briefly discussed the content of the script. Next, they selected character roles and responsibilities for sound effects and began reading the script. I listened as students read and jotted notes about their fluent reading and the integration of the sound effects.

LUCY (*feeling a little uneasy*): What's that noise?

EDMUND: It's only a bird, silly. (*bird heard chirping in the background*)

PETER: It's an owl. (*"hoo...hoo" heard in the background*) This is going to be a wonderful place for birds. I shall go to bed now. I say let's go explore tomorrow.

(*steady rain heard falling*)

EDMUND (*obviously annoyed*): Of course it would be raining!

SUSAN: Do stop grumbling, Ed. Ten to one it'll clear up in an hour or so. And in the meantime we're pretty well off. There's a wireless and lots of books.

PETER: Not for me. I'm going to explore in the house.

(*doors creaking and footsteps heard as the children wander about the house; footsteps heard walking away from Lucy*)

LUCY: Let me try the door of the wardrobe. (*door heard opening*) I am going to see what is behind these coats. (*hangers and coats heard shuffling around*)

PRACTICE: To practice, students finished reading the script. First they read it silently. Then they engaged in Radio Reading twice, changing roles and sound effects for the second reading.

REFLECT: We discussed the text and how fluency contributed to our understanding. The students all agreed that Radio Reading helped them focus on fluency while they were reading. Noel said, "When we switch parts we know we need to read differently." Robert said, "It's like that with sound effects, too. They're all different depending on when they happen in the story, so we have to listen to the voices and then make the sounds those voices would need." Finally, we discussed how we may use Radio Reading in the comprehension-based centers and routines.

Student-Facilitated Comprehension Centers

POETRY CENTER: The students worked with partners and selected poems from a group of story poems I had left at this center. First they read their poem silently. Next they partner-read the poem. Then they discussed the poem and added what they thought would be appropriate sound effects. They read the poems with the suggested sound effects twice more—changing roles for the second reading.

THEME CENTER: Students worked in small groups to do Radio Reading of theme-related passages I had provided at the center. They began by discussing a short introduction I had provided for each script, and then they followed the procedures they had engaged in earlier. First they read the script silently to become familiar with it. Next they engaged in Radio Reading twice, switching character roles and sound effects for the second reading. Finally, they completed their Comprehension Center Student Self-Assessments (page 204) and placed them in their Literacy Portfolios.

Student-Facilitated Comprehension Routines

LITERATURE CIRCLES: We adapted the Literature Circles to include Radio Reading scripts of the chapters students had read for their meeting. After the Literature Circles were completed, students chose roles and sound effects and engaged in Radio Reading as an extension activity. Finally, they completed their Literature Circle Student Self-Assessments (page 206) and put them in their Literacy Portfolios.

(STAGE 3) Teacher-Facilitated Whole-Group Reflection and Goal Setting

SHARE: The students used their self-assessments and Radio Reading scripts to share their work from Stage Two. The students met in their guided reading groups so each group could read a segment of their Radio Reading script for the class.

REFLECT: The students said that they really enjoyed engaging in Radio Reading. Their comments included that they learned a lot from matching the sound effects with the oral interpretation of the texts, that the sound effects added to the meaning of the text, and that it was fun. Hannah said, "I liked that I felt like I was a teacher when I got to decide how to read the passage and add the sound effects." Tomas said, "I really like Radio Reading. My favorite part was when we got to put our own sound effects in the poems at the Poetry Center, but I liked it all because having the sound effects made me want to read more. Now when I read, I think about what sound effects I could put in."

SET NEW GOALS: The students and I agreed that Radio Reading was a great way to improve our fluency, and students felt fairly comfortable using it. We decided that we would continue to use it, and students wanted to integrate it when they were turning sections of text into scripts.

Assessment Options

I mostly used observation to assess Radio Reading. I made comments about each student and his or her progress as a fluent reader. I also reviewed the self-assessments students used at the centers and in their Literature Circles. When working with special education students I made sure students had enough time to practice the scripts. To help with this, I reviewed the scripts with these students before I introduced them to the class. I also worked with them on the sound effects. They very much enjoyed Radio Reading—especially the sound effects. When working with ELLs, I provided the scripts on tape a few days before we used them in class so students could practice reading and integrating the sounds. I also limited the length of the scripts we used in class and assessed students on their effort and progress.

LESSON 5 The Fluent Reading Model
Theme: The Holocaust

STAGE 1 Teacher-Directed Whole-Group Instruction

TEXTS: "Holocaust" (Sonek, 2005)

The Yellow Star (Deedy, 2000)

Lily's Crossing (Giff, 1997)

EXPLAIN: To begin, I explained to the students that to become better readers it is important to listen to other people read, especially better, more experienced readers. "To become better readers, we need to read fluently," I said. "Someone who reads fluently reads with expression. When they read, their sentences flow, and so does the author's message. Fluent readers are good reading models." The students noted that knowing all the words in a passage also helped them to read more fluently. Rosemary said, "In social studies there are sometimes names of people and places that I don't know. When I read those passages it is harder to keep my reading flowing." I explained that when we need to stop to figure out how to say the words, it slows down our reading and makes it sound choppier. To show the difference between word-by-word reading and fluent reading, I read a poem titled "Holocaust" by Barbara Sonek. The first time I read the poem I read it word by word, with little or no expression, and I did not pay attention to any of the punctuation marks. Then I read the poem fluently. When I finished, I asked students to comment on the two readings. They quickly noted the differences. Veronica said, "I could understand the poem much better when you read it the second time. When you read it the first time, it didn't make sense." Lynette said, "The first time you read it, I could hear the words, but I couldn't figure out the ideas. The second time you read it, I could hear the ideas." I acknowledged the students' ideas and added that I did three things differently in my second reading. First, I read with expression. Second, I paid close attention to the punctuation marks—taking a breath if I saw a comma and stopping briefly if I saw a period. Third, I read at a good rate—not too quickly, but not too slowly.

I told students that they were now going to listen to me read *The Yellow Star* by Carmen Agra Deedy. I explained that this was the legend of King Christian X of Denmark, a very brave leader who defied the Nazis by rescuing Jewish people. We briefly discussed others we had read about who had helped the Jews during the Holocaust. Then I asked students to pay special attention to three things as I read: my expression, my use of punctuation clues, and the rate at which I read.

DEMONSTRATE: To demonstrate, I shared the book *The Yellow Star* with students. They followed along on copies I had provided for them. As I read I was sure to pay close attention to my expression, the use of punctuation, and the rate at which I read. For example, when "reading" the punctuation, I wanted my students to see the difference between a comma and a period, so I paused for a shorter time when a comma appeared. The second time I read the story I stopped at various points to discuss the author's use of short phrases and also how dialogue should be read. I asked, "How do you think we should read a passage that includes dialogue?" The students agreed that because different people speak in dialogue, the way we read it should reflect those people's feelings. Finally, I read the story again, changing my expression to accommodate different characters. Afterward, students made comments about my fluency. Ben said, "When you changed the tone of your voice, it was easier to understand how important the events were."

GUIDE: To guide students, I read the first few paragraphs of Chapter 13 in *Lily's Crossing*, a book we had been using for our whole-class theme read-aloud. Each of the students had a copy of the text, so it was easy for them to follow along as I read. The students worked with partners so they would be able to discuss important aspects of fluency. Again, I modeled how to read dialogue with expression, use the punctuation properly, and read at an appropriate rate. After reading the first page of the chapter, I asked the pairs of students to raise their hands when they heard a pause or change in my expression or rate. The students raised their hands frequently as I read different characters' parts in dialogue.

I continued reading the remainder of the chapter, pausing occasionally for the students to share their ideas. We discussed the chapter and predicted what might happen next. Then we discussed fluency. Some students said they liked when I read the story aloud because they were able to make sense of unfamiliar words by listening and using context clues. All agreed that my expression, attention to punctuation, and rate showed that I was a fluent reader.

PRACTICE: To practice, I asked students to reread Chapter 13 with me. Before we read the chapter aloud, we reviewed the three important factors in becoming a fluent reader: reading with expression, using punctuation correctly, and reading at an appropriate reading rate. After we finished reading the chapter, I asked students to read it that evening to their parents or siblings. They all agreed they would be pros by then, because they had sounded so good when we practiced.

REFLECT: We reflected on the factors involved in becoming fluent readers, and we discussed how fluency also helped us to comprehend better. The students all agreed that with each oral reading, the text made more and more sense and the big picture became clearer. Tyler said, "I think that sometimes I can't understand what I read because I get stuck at certain words and I lose my focus." Several students agreed with Tyler and shared their own frustrations in trying to read something when they didn't know all the words. Then Lucy said, "If practicing reading passages helps us become more fluent readers, I think reading a lot will help make us more fluent, too." Everyone agreed, and we discussed our overall goal, which was to become fluent silent readers.

(STAGE 2) Teacher-Guided Small-Group Instruction

TEXT: *Number the Stars* (Lowry, 1989)
(Texts varied according to the students' abilities.)

REVIEW: To review, I reminded students about fluent readers reading with expression, using punctuation clues correctly, and reading at an appropriate rate. I told students that we would be using the text *Number the Stars* to continue to improve our fluency. The students had been enjoying reading this text and were excited to read the next chapter.

GUIDE: To guide students, I introduced Chapter 14 of our text. Each of the students had a copy of the novel, so it made it easy for them to follow along as I read aloud to provide a fluent reading model. I began reading the text, stopping at various points to ask students to reread the text with me. After we finished reading Chapter 14 aloud, students led a group discussion about it. Because I had provided a fluent reading model and we had reread the chapter, I felt students truly had a better understanding of the text. The questions students had about the text seemed deeper and their comprehension of the chapter seemed greater than in previous chapters.

PRACTICE: To practice, I had partners take turns reading Chapter 14 aloud to practice fluent reading. I listened to each set of partners and made notes on students' performance, especially those I felt were experiencing difficulty.

REFLECT: The students' comprehension of this chapter was deeper and our discussions were noticeably richer. I noticed that some of the students who were reluctant to read in front of the class now volunteered. The students shared with me that they were more confident in their reading abilities and that they would continue to practice their fluency with various texts.

Student-Facilitated Comprehension Centers

LISTENING CENTER: The students listened to various short selections recorded on tape, using a copy of the text to read along. They did this twice. Then students read the text as a partner listened to them. The partners shared comments and suggestions about how fluently each of them read.

POETRY CENTER: Students wrote their own poems about the Holocaust and read them to partners to demonstrate their fluency. Then students recorded their poems on tape. Finally, if time permitted, students illustrated the poems and shared them with their partners.

THEME CENTER: The students worked with partners to read various poems related to the Holocaust. They practiced reading the poems aloud several times and then read them for a partner, who provided comments and suggestions.

(**STAGE 3**) Teacher-Facilitated Whole-Group Reflection and Goal Setting

SHARE: The students each read a selection of text that they had read several times. Most of the students chose poems that they found about the Holocaust to read to the class. All of the students in the class made positive comments on how the poem was read, and we also made comments on the amount of expression that was used.

REFLECT: We reflected on how fluency contributes to our reading. We all thought it was a good idea to have other people read to us, and I was happy to hear that more than half the students in my class were still read to on a weekly basis at home. The students said they were surprised how much better they understood the text after they reread it a few times. The students told me that they would continue to improve their fluency throughout the year by practicing. From a teacher's perspective, I noticed that when a fluent reading model was provided the students' comprehension increased. As Joey said, "It's easier for me to read a book if I know how it sounds when a really fluent reader reads it."

SET NEW GOALS: Our goal was to continue to work on our fluency by reading with expression, using punctuation clues, and adjusting reading rate. We decided that we would think about these things whenever we read. We decided to begin by practicing using these tools when we read informational texts.

Assessment Options

To assess the students I relied on observation and listening in all stages. I made notes about students throughout the lesson, especially those I thought were having difficulty. The students engaged in peer assessment at several points during the lesson. When working with special education students, I made sure they had access to many fluent reader models and enough time to practice reading along with selected short, taped passages at appropriate levels. When working with ELLs, I made "fluent reader text tapes" of the passages we were reading so students could practice reading along with them while at home. I also made notes on their fluency progress.

LESSON 6 Choral Reading
Theme: Poetry

STAGE 1 Teacher-Directed Whole-Group Instruction

TEXTS: "Stopping by Woods on a Snowy Evening" by Robert Frost, in *World's Best Loved Poetry* (2002)

Student-selected poems from *Winter Poems* (Rogasky, 1994)

EXPLAIN: I began by explaining to students that we would be reading a poem titled "Stopping by Woods on a Snowy Evening" by Robert Frost. We briefly discussed the title of the poem and made connections to various snowy evenings we had experienced. Next, I said, "We're going to chorally read the poem. Can anyone tell me what choral reading is?" Dimitri replied, "I think it is similar to what we do in chorus. There we all sing the same words together. In reading we all read the same thing together as a class." I told him that he was correct and that we would be reading the poem together. I said, "Choral reading helps us to become more fluent readers, because we can listen to the fluent reading of those around us as we read." I gave each student a copy of the poem and I explained that I would read the poem alone first to provide a fluent reading model, and then we would read the poem together.

I read the poem, and we briefly discussed it. Joshua said, "I could picture the snowy woods. I think it must have looked a lot like it looks here when the snow is falling and has already covered the ground." Sally said, "I pictured how the snow-covered ground looks when I'm waiting to hear if we'll have a snow day." James said, "I know what he meant when he said he had 'miles to go.' He must have needed to get somewhere where he had other things to do." I explained to students that we would now chorally read the poem stanza by stanza. I reminded them of my reading of the poem and that fluent readers change their expression and the rate at which they read to make what they are reading more interesting. Alexi said, "This reminds me of how the librarian read at story hour when I was younger. She used to change her expression a lot and we all enjoyed hearing her read. The books were easier to picture in my head when she read." The rest of the class made similar comments, and we agreed that reading was more interesting when the reader used various tones and expressions.

DEMONSTRATE: To demonstrate, I read the first stanza of the poem and students listened. The first time I read the stanza I used a monotone voice and I did not stop or pause at the appropriate punctuation. I asked students to give me feedback on how I read, and they told me that they didn't really understand what I read because it was too fast. I read the stanza a second time and used various tones in my voice and I also made sure I paid attention to the punctuation and the rate of my reading. Nick said, "I noticed where you paused when you read. I also noticed how the tone of your voice changed and I liked it better this way. I could understand it better." Next, the students and I read the stanza chorally. We emphasized our expression and rate and paused at the appropriate points in the text.

GUIDE: To guide students, I explained that we would be reading the next three stanzas of the poem chorally. To help them prepare for the choral reading, I suggested that they practice by whisper-reading the rest of the poem. When the students were ready, we read the poem chorally as a whole class. The students noticed that in the second and third stanzas there weren't as many pauses as in the first. My students also noted that in both of these stanzas the tone of voice should represent the puzzled thoughts the horse may have had. In the fourth stanza the students identified the number of commas in the text and noticed that the ending word of each line rhymed. Henry said, "The pattern of the words that rhyme changed from the first three sections to the fourth. I think the author did that on purpose to make it stand out." Others agreed. Again we discussed expression, punctuation, and reading rate. Then we read the entire poem chorally and decided that was our best reading. Rachel said, "I feel more comfortable reading aloud when we do it together. If I get stuck on a word, no one hears—except for me." Many of the other students shared similar thoughts.

PRACTICE: To practice, pairs of students selected various poems from the book *Winter Poems*. I asked the partners to first whisper-read the poem they chose and then practice reading the poem chorally with their partner. I reminded the students to vary the tone of their voices when necessary, pause when appropriate and adjust the reading rate. After approximately ten minutes, when I knew students were comfortable reading their poems, they shared them with the class.

REFLECT: The students enjoyed hearing the poems read chorally. We all agreed that when the poems were read with expression and attention to rate and punctuation they sounded much better. We also decided that the poems sounded better every time we read them. The students said that it was easier each time they read the poem because they would start to feel the rhythm and beat.

STAGE 2   Teacher-Guided Small-Group Instruction

TEXT: "America the Beautiful" by Katharine Lee Bates, in *World's Best-Loved Poetry* (2002) (Texts varied according to the students' abilities.)

REVIEW: To review, I reminded students that we would be practicing reading chorally in our small group. I explained that we would be reading a poem that they would be very familiar with. I told students that they would know this poem because the words were also lyrics to a song they knew. The poem, "America the Beautiful," was a good choice because we were getting ready to celebrate Memorial Day. The children thought it was great that the poem had been turned into a song.

GUIDE: To guide students, I read the first stanza and was very careful not to sing the words. I made sure that I read somewhat slowly so that students would see the poetic nature of the text. Next, we discussed the poem. Sam said, "It sounds different from when we sing the words. I'm more focused on the words when there is no music." Linda agreed and said, "I think the message sounds more serious when we read the words as a poem." Then we read the first stanza of the poem chorally.

PRACTICE: To practice, I asked students to whisper-read the poem. After they had practiced, we read the entire poem chorally as a small group. I noticed that a few of the students were having difficulty with two of the words—*impassioned* and *thoroughfare*—so we engaged in word study. We discussed what it means to have a *passion* for something. Nicholas said, "I have a passion for baseball. It means I really like it a lot." We examined the context to see if this meaning of *passion* worked in the poem, and we decided that it did because the people who came to America had a passion for freedom. Then we reviewed the meaning of *im-*, which we knew from our study of prefixes. In fact, it was an entry on our affix wall. The students already knew that the prefix *im-* sometimes means "in, within." Then we noticed *impassioned* ended in *-ed*. The students knew that any word with the affix *-ed* meant it happened in the past. So, we concluded that *impassioned* meant "filled with passion." Next, we discussed *thoroughfare*, noting it was a compound word. We examined the context in which it appeared and decided that the definition would probably be close to a road. One of the students looked up the word in a dictionary to confirm our definition and found that a thoroughfare is a public road. We discussed both of the words and then we read the poem again chorally. We had small group discussion at this point about how proud and patriotic the poem should sound when read aloud.

REFLECT: To reflect, we discussed the importance of reading fluently and how it helped our overall understanding of the poem. The students mentioned that they felt more confident about their reading when they had time to practice what they needed to read.

Student-Facilitated Comprehension Centers

LISTENING CENTER: Trios self-selected two poems, listened to them on tape, practiced whisper-reading them, and then recorded their choral reading. I left a note at the center reminding the trios to record their names before they began their choral reading.

THEME CENTER: The students selected and chorally read poems from various books with a partner or small group. The students chose poems they felt the most confident reading and presented them to the parents at our end-of-theme celebration.

WRITING CENTER: The students self-selected topics and individually wrote poems. Then they provided a fluent reading model for a partner, provided practice time for whisper-reading, and chorally read each other's poems.

(STAGE 3) Teacher-Facilitated Whole-Group Reflection and Goal Setting

SHARE: Students discussed the poems they most enjoyed reading with a partner or small group. Next, we listened to the recordings of trios sharing poems. The students enjoyed listening to themselves read the poems and thought they did a great job.

REFLECT: To reflect, we discussed how fluency helps us become better readers. The students agreed that when they chorally read they were more confident. Overall, the students said that they were able to better comprehend what they were reading if they practiced reading it fluently.

SET NEW GOALS: We decided as a class that we would continue to improve our fluency by reading chorally or whisper-reading a text first before reading it aloud. Since we had practiced choral reading with poetry, we decided to try it with some excerpts from stories and informational text.

Assessment Options

I used observation to monitor each student's progress as we engaged in choral reading. I made notes about students who I thought read very fluently and students who would benefit from more practice. I also used the trio choral reading tapes and their self-authored poems. When working with special education students I sat near them when the class and I were chorally reading, to ensure that they were reading along with us. I invited students to use their fingers to follow along and this seemed to really help. I also made notes about their progress. When working with the ELLs, I used illustrated poems to help them understand the author's message. These students also used poems on tape at home and read them with me the next day. I made notes on their progress and effort.

Final Thoughts on This Chapter

In this chapter we integrated research findings and current beliefs about best practices in teaching fluency. Each lesson featured a model—whether a teacher, a peer, a book on tape, or a cross-age tutor. The instructional strategies we used in these lessons are described in detail in Appendix B. In the next chapter, we examine the role of vocabulary in the reading process. We begin by exploring the theory that underpins current beliefs about vocabulary instruction. Then we present a variety of strategy-based lessons focused on teaching vocabulary in the intermediate grades.

What can we read to learn more about teaching fluency?

Rasinski, T. V. (2004). Creating fluent readers. *Educational Leadership*, 61(6), 46–51.

Rasinski, T. V. (2003). *The fluent reader*. New York: Scholastic.

Richards, M. (2000). Be a good detective: Solve the case of oral reading fluency. *The Reading Teacher*, 53(7), 534–539.

CHAPTER 4

Vocabulary

The most important information we know about teaching vocabulary can be simply summarized:

> Students must understand the meanings of the words they read in order to comprehend. (McLaughlin & Allen, 2002a; Richek, 2005)

> Knowledge of vocabulary is one of the best predictors of reading success. (Daneman, 1991)

We also now know that students need to do much more than write a word's definition to make the word part of their working vocabulary. They need to talk about words, take ownership of them, and use them in a variety of contexts. According to Asselin (2002), students learn between 2,500 and 3,000 new words every year. If we want our students to actively use these words, we need to motivate them to understand how words work. Graves and Watts-Taffe (2002) describe this as "word consciousness—the awareness of and interest in words and their meanings" (p. 144). That's the focus of this chapter: helping students to develop an interest in words.

Part One: Research Base

What is vocabulary?

Most of us think about our vocabularies as the words we use to communicate. We know that we learn words from our experiences as well as from our reading. In *The Literacy Dictionary*, Harris and Hodges (1995) support our thoughts and extend our thinking about vocabulary development, which they note is influenced by teaching practices, including using context clues and analyzing root words and affixes. They say, "Vocabulary is a list of words," whereas vocabulary development is "the growth of a person's stock of known words and meanings; [and] the teaching-learning principles and practices that lead to such growth, as comparing and classifying word meanings, using context, analyzing root words and affixes, etc." (p. 275).

What does the research tell us?

Themes that have emerged from research on vocabulary include the following:

- Vocabulary development and instruction play significant roles in students' reading comprehension.

- Reading widely enhances students' vocabulary.

- Repeated exposure to words helps students learn how to use them.

Both direct instruction and the use of context clues have been found to be effective in teaching vocabulary. Lessons that feature direct and guided instruction, as well as independent practice in a variety of settings, are featured in Part Two of this chapter. The lessons focus on the comprehension strategy Knowing How Words Work (see Appendix C). Research indicates that knowing and using vocabulary-related strategies contribute to students' reading comprehension (Blachowicz & Fisher, 2000; National Reading Panel, 2000).

The overarching conclusion of the research on vocabulary is that it affects students' comprehension. We cannot comprehend if we don't know what the words mean. Vocabulary instruction leads to gains in comprehension, but the methods must be appropriate to the age and ability of the reader. Students need to actively use the words—read them, hear them, write them, and speak them—in order for them to become part of their working vocabularies. Learning in rich contexts, having a wide variety of experiences, and using technology all facilitate students' acquisition of vocabulary.

Part Two: Lesson Overview

In this section we put research into practice by presenting six lessons that focus on various ways to teach vocabulary. As seen in the Lesson Overview, the lessons are theme-based and feature a variety of teaching ideas. The texts also vary. In Stage One, the teacher reads, so the text level may be easy, just right, or more challenging. In the guided reading groups, texts are at students' instructional levels, and at the centers and in the routines, independent level texts are used. Appendix C contains additional resources for teaching fluency. Appendix F features other texts and Web sites that can be used when teaching these themes.

THEME	TEACHING IDEA	STAGE ONE TEXT	STAGE TWO GUIDED READING TEXT
Mystery	Probable Passages	*The Westing Game*	*The Ghost of Lizard Light*
Survival	Context Clues	*Hatchet*	*Julie of the Wolves*
Biography	Semantic Question Map	*You Want Women to Vote, Lizzie Stanton?*	*Rosa Parks*
Fantasy	Semantic Map	*Tuck Everlasting*	*Harry Potter and the Sorcerer's Stone*
The Holocaust	Concepts of Definition Map	*Lily's Crossing*	*The Devil's Arithmetic*
Poetry	Vocabulary Bookmark Technique	"California Ghost Town," "Washington, D.C."	"Islands in Boston Harbor"

Vocabulary Lessons

LESSON 1 Probable Passages
Theme: Mystery

STAGE 1 Teacher-Directed Whole-Group Instruction

TEXT: *The Westing Game* (Raskin, 1978)

EXPLAIN: I began by telling students that we can use selected vocabulary to make predictions about text. "Understanding key words and concepts about a text can help us to better understand it," I said. For example, one kind of text we read is narrative or story text, and there is a vocabulary technique that we can use to make predictions about the story. It's called Probable

Passages." I showed them the Probable Passages blackline (see page 186) and told them that we would use certain words from the story to help us make predictions about the different story elements. I said, "In Probable Passages, we will use only four story elements: character, setting, problem, and solution. We're going to use words from a list to make predictions about these elements. Some of the words on the list may be familiar to us, others we may recognize but not know the meaning of, and some we may not know at all." Then I explained that we would be using these words in sentences to make our predictions about the story elements.

DEMONSTRATE: To demonstrate, I used preselected words from Chapter 8 of *The Westing Game* by Ellen Raskin. Since the chapter is long and has several story lines running through it, I chose to use only the first part of the chapter to model this teaching idea. I placed the following words and phrases on the chalkboard, using magnetized sentence strips: *clues, invalid, Chris, Westing Paper Products, murderer, Sunset Towers, Flora, corridors, Sydelle, Shakespeare, clue-chasing, emergency,*

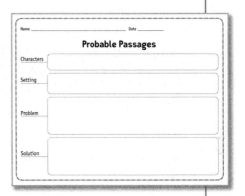

Turtle, heir, and *insensitive.* I read aloud all the words and explained to students that we would determine their meanings by making connections to other words and using our background knowledge. For words that students could not figure out, I provided sentences. For example, to explain the word *corridor* I said, "I walked down the *corridor* to get to the music room." With that description, students were able to figure out that *corridor* meant "hallway."

Then I said, "Since we have already started reading this book, I am going to use my knowledge of the characters and the events that have happened so far to help me make my predictions. I know that people's names are proper nouns and that they are capitalized. I know from previous reading that Chris, Flora, Sydelle, and Turtle are characters in the story, so on the Probable Passages chart I am going to write, 'The main characters are Chris, Flora, Sydelle, and Turtle.' Next, I want to look for words that have to do with the setting. Where it says 'Setting' on the chart, I am going to write, 'The setting is Sunset Towers and Westing Paper Products.' Now we are going to use the other words to make predictions about the rest of the story."

GUIDE: To guide students, I engaged them in a discussion about what the problem in this chapter might be, based on the clue words, and what they already knew from the prior chapters. As a group we agreed that the problem was probably that Sydelle and

Turtle needed to figure out the clues that would lead them to find out who the murderer was because if they did they would become heirs to Westing Paper Products. So, under "Problem" on the chart, I wrote, "The problem in this chapter is that Sydelle and Turtle have to discover who the murderer is so that can become the heirs to Westing Paper Products." Next we looked at the vocabulary words again to predict some possible events in the story. Together we came up with "The clue-chasing pair searched Sunset Towers for clues." Then students worked in pairs to predict two more events that may have happened based on the vocabulary words in the list. Each pair shared one idea with the class, and I recorded their responses on the chart. Examples of the students' ideas I included were "There was an emergency in one of the corridors" and "Some of the people were insensitive to Chris, who is an invalid."

PRACTICE: To practice, students completed their Probable Passages charts by using the clue words to predict a solution to the story. After we discussed their ideas, I wrote one of their predictions on our class blackline. Next, I read pages 46–51 of Chapter 8 aloud. After reading, we revisited our class Probable Passages blackline and confirmed or modified our predictions. For example, we confirmed that some of the main characters in this chapter were Turtle, Sydelle, Flora, and Chris. We modified the setting because although we were correct that it took place at Sunset Towers, none of the action took place at Westing Paper Products. We confirmed that they were searching Sunset Towers for clues and modified that the "someone" who was insensitive to Chris was Sydelle. We also specified the nature of the emergency: there was no electricity, there was a murderer out there somewhere, and the partners were searching for each other in the dark corridors. Then we discussed the chapter.

REFLECT: As a class, we reflected on how using Probable Passages helped us to make predictions about the story and allowed us to discover the meanings of some unknown words. The students talked about how they could tell what part of speech certain words were and therefore knew if they should be used to describe the setting or an event. Jack said, "I knew *emergency* was a noun and the events would be nouns, so I thought that the emergency might be one of the events." Wendy said, "I like Probable Passages because when I first looked at all the words on the list, I didn't know what some of them meant. After making the predictions for Probable Passages and making some changes after reading, I know all the words and what they mean."

STAGE 2 Teacher-Guided Small-Group Instruction

TEXT: *The Ghost of Lizard Light* (Woodruff, 1999) (Texts varied according to the students' abilities.)

REVIEW: To review, I asked students to recall the three cueing systems we can use to help us determine the meaning of an unknown word. Together we listed and described the graphophonic (sound/letter) cueing system, the syntactic (part of speech) cueing system, and the semantic (meaning) cueing system. Next we reviewed, using Probable Passages to help us understand new vocabulary, and then used that new vocabulary to make predictions about the story. I explained that we would be using Probable Passages before we read the first chapter of *The Ghost of Lizard Light* by Elvira Woodruff.

GUIDE: To guide students, I showed them a list of words that I had preselected from the first chapter. We read over the words together, and I had students work together to define them using their background knowledge. For words they did not know, I used the words in sentences and focused on using the cueing systems we had spoken about to help them define them. Next, we worked together as a group to come up with sentences for the Characters and Setting sections of the Probable Passages chart. For the characters, we predicted, "We think the characters are Ned, Jack, and Denton." For the setting we predicted, "We think the setting is a lighthouse."

Then students worked with partners to complete the problem. I circulated and provided prompts and reminders from our whole-group lesson as needed. The students shared the predictions that they had made so far.

PRACTICE: To practice, students completed the solution portion of Probable Passages. The students then shared the rest of their predictions and whisper-read the first chapter while I listened for fluency. After they finished reading the chapter, we revisited the Probable Passages chart to see if our original predictions were confirmed or if we needed to modify or refine them. We used our completed Probable Passages chart to orally retell the chapter.

REFLECT: To reflect, we discussed how we can use Probable Passages to help us better understand the meanings of unfamiliar words and how understanding that vocabulary can help us to make predictions about elements of the story.

Student-Facilitated Comprehension Centers

THEME CENTER: Students worked with partners to complete Probable Passages about various mystery books and articles I had left at the center. (I had left a list of words to be used in Probable Passages in each text.) They used the strategies we had discussed to define the given words. Then they wrote their sentences to predict the story elements. After completing Probable Passages, they discussed their predictions, modifying and refining as necessary. Then they partner-read the text and verified or modified their predictions. Finally, if time permitted, they used their completed charts to create oral summaries.

POETRY CENTER: Students wrote poems using formats such as acrostics, Bio-Pyramids, cinquains, and diamantes. Possible topics included words generally associated with mysteries like *mystery*, *case*, *detective*, *clues*, *suspect*, and *solution*. They were given the opportunity to share their poems during Stage Three.

Student-Facilitated Comprehension Routines

LITERATURE CIRCLES: Students completed Probable Passages for the chapters they were going to read. When they came to Literature Circle, they discussed what they had predicted and what had actually happened in the chapter they read. The students also completed their Literature Circle roles.

CROSS-AGE READING EXPERIENCES: Students read with cross-age partners after previewing the story using clue words I had provided. They completed Probable Passages together and read to verify or modify their ideas.

(STAGE 3) Teacher-Facilitated Whole-Group Reflection and Goal Setting

SHARE: In small groups, students shared their Probable Passages from Stage Two. They discussed the new words that they learned and shared the predictions they had made for the books they had read. They also shared how close their predictions were to the actual story.

REFLECT: The students reflected on how using Probable Passages helped them to better determine the meanings of unknown words and make predictions about what they were going to read. Joey commented that "learning the new vocabulary and using it before we read was really good. I was excited when I read it in the story because I knew what it meant and how I thought it might be part of the story. Before doing Probable Passages, I wouldn't have known some of the words."

SET NEW GOALS: We decided that we would continue to use Probable Passages to help us learn new vocabulary and make predictions about story elements. We decided that we would use our revised Probable Passages to create summaries of the chapter. We felt pretty good about using Probable Passages, so we decided to learn another vocabulary technique, the Semantic Question Map (see page 103).

Assessment Options

I used observation, students' completed Probable Passages, and student self-reflections as assessments. When working with special education students, I was careful to limit the number of words they were required to use, and provided larger blacklines with more room for them to write. I also color-coded the sections of the blackline using sticky dots. In addition, I provided picture cues as well as verbal cues to help them determine the meaning of the new vocabulary. When working with ELL students, I limited the amount of text they were required to read in a given setting, limited the number of new words they were required to use, and allowed extra time for more specific and individualized instruction. I assessed their performance both orally and in written format.

LESSON 2 Context Clues
Theme: Survival

STAGE 1 Teacher-Directed Whole-Group Instruction

TEXT: *Hatchet* (Paulsen, 1987)

EXPLAIN: I began by asking students to think of what they should do if they are reading and don't know the meaning of a word. Shelly said, "You can look it up in the dictionary." Roberto said, "It's annoying to have to stop and take out the dictionary every time you don't know a word. We can keep reading to see if we can figure it out on our own." I said, "These are good suggestions. There are times when it is necessary to use a dictionary, but it is a good idea to first try to figure out what the word means by using something we call Context Clues. Today we are going to use this technique to help us learn more about how words work. When we use Context Clues, we use a variety of cueing systems to help us figure out unknown words and make sense of the text we are reading. There are many types of Context Clues that will help us to understand words whose meanings we don't know, but today we are going to discuss only four: the grammar clue, the logic clue, the example/illustration clue, and the cause-and-effect clue."

Context Clues

GRAMMAR CLUE: How is the unknown word used in the sentence? What part of speech is it?

LOGIC CLUE: What words are related to the topic that would make sense here?

EXAMPLE/ILLUSTRATION CLUE: Is there an example in the text or a sketch or photo that give a clue to the word's meaning?

CAUSE AND EFFECT CLUE: What might have caused the event? What effect could the event have?

I placed a list containing the four types of Context Clues and their meanings on the overhead and distributed copies to students. Then I thought aloud about the different types of clues that were listed. I said, "The first is the grammar clue. To use this Context Clue, we need to think about how the unknown word is used in the sentence and what part of speech it is. If we can determine what part of speech the word is, that narrows the scope of possible meanings. We don't think about all words as possibilities, just nouns or verbs or whatever part of speech the word under investigation is. For example, if the word we were looking at was *abundance*, we could look at how it is used in the sentence to determine its part of speech. If the sentence was 'We served an *abundance* of food at the family picnic,' we could tell that *abundance* is a noun because it is preceded by *an* and it is the direct object.

"Logic is the next Context Clue. This means we use logic to narrow our list of possible meanings to words related to the topic we are reading about. For example, if the text we are reading is about school, it may be logical or fitting to narrow our search to school-related words.

"The next type of Context Clue is example/illustration. Often the text provides an example (words in text) or picture (sketch, photo, painting) that will help us figure out the meaning of the unknown word. For example, when we read Jon Scieszka's book *Baloney, Henry P.*, we didn't know that a *zimulis* was a pencil until we saw Lane Smith's illustration.

"The fourth Context Clue is cause and effect. This can be used when there is a cause and a resulting action. For example, if it were raining (cause), you may use an umbrella (effect) when walking outside. When we use Context Clues, we often use more than one clue at a time, but we rarely—if ever—use all four of the clues to determine the meaning of one word."

DEMONSTRATE: I demonstrated how to use Context Clues by using a read-aloud of *Hatchet* by Gary Paulsen, a think-aloud, and the overhead projector. I still had the list of the four types of Context Clues on the overhead as I began to read aloud from Chapter 7 of *Hatchet*. As I read the first page, I thought aloud when I came to the word *abdomen*, which I thought may be unfamiliar to some students. I said, "The word *abdomen* is unfamiliar, so I am going to look at my list of Context Clues and see if any of them can help me. I am going to begin by using the grammar clue. Based on the sentence in which *abdomen* appears, 'His whole abdomen was torn with great rolling jolts of pain . . . ,' I can tell that the word *abdomen* is a noun because it is the subject of the sentence. So now I know the unknown word is a noun.

"Next, I will use the logic clue. If I go back to the previous sentence, it says that he had a pain in his stomach, and then it says that his abdomen was torn with 'jolts of pain.' So, logically, if the text is talking about the stomach, which is a part of the human body, I am going to conclude that the abdomen is a part of the body. I think I am on the right track because a part of the body would be a noun. So now I know I am looking for a noun that is part of the human body. I noticed when I read the previous sentence, it said he had a pain in his stomach, and then it said his abdomen was torn with pain. Now I'm going to use the example/illustration clue; even though there is no illustration, there is the example that speaks first of the stomach's pain and then the abdomen's pain. Based on the three Context Clues I have used, I am going to guess that abdomen means 'stomach.' I'm going to confirm with the dictionary, just to verify that my conclusions are correct." When I checked the dictionary, it defined *abdomen* as "stomach." Then I continued reading, stopping twice more to demonstrate using Context Clues. The words I focused on were *peck* and *streaming*.

GUIDE: I guided students to respond in pairs as I read aloud the next segment of the text. I had preselected words that we would focus on. The first word was *vicious* and the second was *receded*. I read up to the sentences that contained those words and asked the pairs which Context Clues we could use to help them determine each word's meaning. I circulated as they discussed the first word, *vicious*. Meghan volunteered the idea that she and Johann had discussed. She said, "It worked out well when you started with the grammar clue, so that's what we tried first. There is a dog in our neighborhood that people think is vicious. *Vicious* describes the dog, and describing words are adjectives, so we think *vicious* is an adjective." Johann added, "Then we used the logic clue. The sentence said, 'Then he saw the sun streaming in the open doorway of the shelter and heard the close, *vicious* whine of the mosquitoes and knew' [page 69]. The sentence after said, 'He brushed his face, completely covered with bumps and bites.' We know that mosquitoes bite and that their bites are really itchy. I get really mad when I have them because sometimes they hurt. We knew that *vicious* described the mean dog in our neighborhood and that mosquito bites can be itchy and painful. So we used the logic clue to help us figure out that *vicious* means 'mean or nasty.'"

PRACTICE: To practice, I asked students to raise their hands when I read a word they wanted to investigate with a partner using Context Clues. Then I continued to read the chapter aloud. The first word students suggested was *stave*. The sentence ended with the words ". . . just enough to stave off the hunger a bit" (page 70). This time Jaime was first to respond. He said, "I used the grammar clue first. In this sentence, I think *stave* is a verb because it comes after the word *to*, and usually verbs follow *to*, like *to speak* or *to write*." Connie added, "If we use the logic clue, we know from the sentences before that Brian is really hungry, and he is talking about eating some of the cherries that he had gotten sick on. If he eats something, it will stop him from being hungry, so I think that *stave* must mean to stop or put off." James and Shelby had a similar conversation about the word *gorge*. James said, "First we started with the grammar clue. The sentence was 'Soon, as before, his stomach was full, but now he had some sense and he did not gorge or cram more down' [page 100]. We could tell it was a verb because it is an action—he did not *gorge*." Shelby said, "Next we tried the logic clue. We knew that before Brian had eaten too many of the cherries and had gotten sick. This sentence says that he was full and had the sense not to *gorge*. That made us think that *gorge* must mean to stuff himself with more food. Finally we used the example clue because the sentence said '*gorge* or cram more down.' I know that my mom has told me not to cram too many cookies into my stomach or I will get sick, so we figured that *gorge* must mean the same thing—to stuff yourself."

REFLECT: To reflect, we talked about how using the different types of Context Clues helped us to determine the meaning of a word. Joey said, "The first couple times I needed to figure out the meaning of a word, I looked at the list to see which Context Clue I should use, but after using the list a few times, I started to remember the clues without looking at the list." Jacquelyn said, "I like using Context Clues. It's like figuring out a mystery, and the mystery is what the word means." Timothy said, "I like how we start with the grammar and logic Context Clues. That helps us to narrow the possibilities."

(STAGE 2) Teacher-Guided Small-Group Instruction

TEXT: *Julie of the Wolves* (George, 1972) (Texts varied according to the students' abilities.)

REVIEW: To review, I reminded students how important it is for us to understand how words work and how to use Context Clues. We briefly reviewed the four clues we discussed. The students had their copies of the Context Clue list with them and I also still had the list on the overhead projector. Then I reminded students that we seemed to do well using Context Clues, when we started with the grammar and logic clues. I explained that we would be using Context Clues to help us decode unfamiliar words in the book *Julie of the Wolves* by Jean Craighead George.

GUIDE: To guide students, I introduced the text. After a brief discussion, we turned to the first chapter. I guided students' reading and asked that when they came to an unfamiliar word they stop, discuss it with another group member, and work together to use Context Clues to determine the word's meaning. I provided a blackline on which they could record their thinking (see page 185). I monitored this process so I could follow their reasoning and make sure the meanings they determined were correct.

PRACTICE: To practice, students continued reading Chapter 1 of *Julie of the Wolves*. Each time they came across an unfamiliar word, they stopped to determine which Context Clues they could use to help them decipher its meaning. Then they shared their reasoning.

REFLECT: To reflect, we discussed how using Context Clues helped us to determine the meanings of unfamiliar words and how we could use them with different kinds of text.

Student-Facilitated Comprehension Centers

THEME CENTER: I provided numerous theme-related texts at various levels at this center. Students worked in pairs to read theme-related books and articles, using Context Clues to determine unfamiliar words and the blacklines to record their reasoning.

Student-Facilitated Comprehension Routines

CROSS-AGE READING EXPERIENCES: Students read with cross-age partners and used Context Clues to help them determine unfamiliar words.

LITERATURE CIRCLES: In addition to their assigned roles, all students played the role of Word Finder (see page 13). They used Context Clues while reading and shared their ideas about various unknown words during the circle.

(STAGE 3) Teacher-Facilitated Whole-Group Reflection and Goal Setting

SHARE: In small groups, students shared their work from Stage Two. They discussed words that they were unsure of and which Context Clues they used to determine their meanings. After sharing in small groups, some students volunteered to share with the whole group.

REFLECT: The students reflected on how using Context Clues helped them to better determine the meanings of unknown words and, therefore, better understand what they had read. Kelly said, "I never knew there were so many clues to help me figure out a word that I didn't know. My partner and I would use a couple at a time, just to make sure we were right."

SET NEW GOALS: We decided that we would continue to use Context Clues to help us determine the meanings of words we didn't know. We agreed that this would be a good strategy to use when reading other types of text, especially informational text.

Assessment Options

I used observation and student self-reflections as assessments. When working with special education students, I was careful to make sure their texts were at appropriate levels. To help them focus, I used colored dots to mark different parts of the Context Clue Organizer blackline. When students were in paired settings, I made sure each of these students was partnered with a more knowledgeable student. I also had the book on tape available for them to listen to and read along with. Whenever possible, I engaged these students in conversations about their learning and offered multiple modes of response. When working with ELL students, I made sure their texts were at appropriate levels and allowed extra time for more specific and individualized instruction. Books on tape were also utilized when needed. I assessed their performance both orally and in written format.

LESSON 3 Semantic Question Map
Theme: Biography

STAGE 1 Teacher-Directed Whole-Group Instruction

TEXT: *You Want Women to Vote, Lizzie Stanton?* (Fritz, 1995)

EXPLAIN: I began by explaining to students that we would be continuing to develop our understanding of how words works by using a graphic organizer to examine a key idea related to our story. "Today we are going to learn how to use a Semantic Question Map. Semantic Question Maps help guide our thinking by asking us specific questions about a focus word or phrase. Using Semantic Question Maps will help us understand the important aspects of the focus word." I explained that we would first answer the questions using what we already knew and later, after reading, add information we learned from the text.

DEMONSTRATE: To demonstrate how to use a Semantic Question Map, I used a read-aloud, a think-aloud, and an enlarged copy of a Semantic Question Map blackline (see page 188) that I had already prepared. Since I had previously read aloud Chapter 1 of our text, I began by reading aloud the title and reviewing that this book was about Elizabeth Cady Stanton, who was a pioneer in women's rights. We had also begun a unit in social studies on equal rights, so I knew that the students had

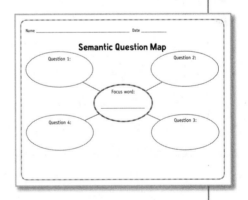

some background knowledge on the topic. Next, I shared a copy of the enlarged Semantic Question Map, which contained a center oval for the focus word and four question ovals. Our focus phrase was Women's Rights, which I had already written in the center oval. Each of four questions branched out from the center oval. The questions were "Who were the key people involved in women's rights?," "What were they fighting for?," "What events took place to support women's rights?," and "What major dates are associated with women's rights?" I said, "Let's notice that 'Women's Rights' is written inside the center oval because that is the focus phrase on this map. Now I need to think about what I already know about women's rights." I pointed out that in the Semantic Maps that we had previously used, we had all offered ideas and then decided which categories emerged. Semantic Question Maps are different in that the questions are provided and are the categories.

I read the first question aloud: "Who were the key people involved in women's rights?" I said, "Since the book is about Elizabeth Cady Stanton, and I know from the title that she wants women to vote, I think she must be a key person, so I will write her name underneath this question. I can also add information under the second question, 'What were they fighting for?,' because I know that women's right to vote was one thing they were fighting for." After I added that information under the second question, I thought aloud about what I knew about the remaining questions. The third question was "What events took place to support women's rights?" I wrote "conventions" as one response. The fourth question was "What major dates are associated with women's rights?" I wrote "middle to late 1800s."

After recording these initial responses on our Semantic Question Map, I said, "Now I am going to read information about women's rights and revisit the Semantic Question Map to verify or revise the ideas I've written. I will also add any new information I learn from the text." Then I read aloud Chapter 2 of *You Want Women to Vote, Lizzie Stanton?* When I finished reading I said, "Now I will go back to the Semantic Question Map and verify that what I have written is confirmed by the text. The text continued to talk about Elizabeth, so I know that my information under the first question is correct. Elizabeth and her husband did go to a convention, but it wasn't about women's rights. However, I am going to leave *conventions* on our list and see if I can verify that information as I read on. I also can't confirm the dates yet, but since the last date this chapter spoke about was 1840, and they haven't really begun to fight for women's rights yet, I think my guess of middle to late 1800s may be correct. Again, we will have to read on to find out for sure." Next, I looked at the questions again to see if there was any new information I could add to the map. We added "Lucretia Mott" under "Who were the key people involved in the fight for women's rights?" and "June 1840" under "What major dates are associated with women's rights?" because that was when Elizabeth and Lucretia, two of the key figures, first met.

GUIDE: I guided pairs of students to think about the categories in our Semantic Question Map as I read aloud the next chapter of *You Want Women to Vote, Lizzie Stanton?* The text provided more information to add to our map, and students volunteered suggestions such as "Jane Hunt," "to be able to choose their type of work," "Women's Rights Convention," and "1848" for questions one through four, respectively. I recorded the students' responses on our map under the appropriate question.

PRACTICE: Students practiced by adding more details to our Semantic Question Map as I read aloud Chapter 4 of the text. Then we used our completed Semantic Question Map to write a summary of what we knew so far about women's rights. Our completed Semantic Question Map appears in Figure 4-1.

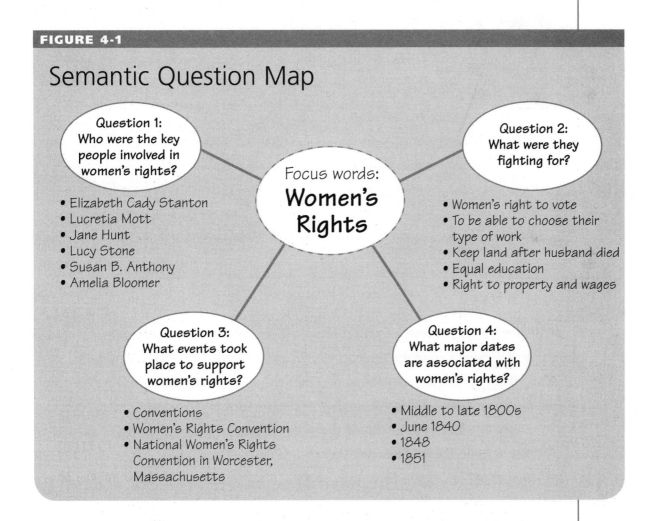

FIGURE 4-1

Semantic Question Map

Question 1:
Who were the key people involved in women's rights?

- Elizabeth Cady Stanton
- Lucretia Mott
- Jane Hunt
- Lucy Stone
- Susan B. Anthony
- Amelia Bloomer

Focus words:
Women's Rights

Question 2:
What were they fighting for?

- Women's right to vote
- To be able to choose their type of work
- Keep land after husband died
- Equal education
- Right to property and wages

Question 3:
What events took place to support women's rights?

- Conventions
- Women's Rights Convention
- National Women's Rights Convention in Worcester, Massachusetts

Question 4:
What major dates are associated with women's rights?

- Middle to late 1800s
- June 1840
- 1848
- 1851

REFLECT: As a class we reflected on what we had learned about women's rights and how the Semantic Question Map had helped us to organize the information. We decided that we would leave our Semantic Question Map on display and that as we continued to read the book *You Want Women to Vote, Lizzie Stanton?* we would add more information to the categories. We talked about how the Semantic Question Map helped us to organize and remember the information we had added to it. Finally, we discussed how we would use Semantic Question Maps in other settings.

(STAGE 2) Teacher-Guided Small-Group Instruction

TEXT: *Rosa Parks* (Weidt, 2002) (Texts varied according to the students' abilities.)

REVIEW: I began by reviewing the comprehension strategies good readers use and focused on Knowing How Words Work (see Appendix C) and Semantic Question Maps. I introduced *Rosa Parks* by Maryann N. Weidt and explained that this book contained information on Rosa Parks, a woman who was a key figure in the civil rights movement. I shared the cover and title and read aloud the introduction. We had a brief discussion, and the students contributed other information from their prior knowledge of Rosa Parks. Then we began working on our Semantic Question Map, which focused on the civil rights movement, and I provided copies for students. This time there were only three questions: "Who was involved in the civil rights movement?," "What was the civil rights movement fighting for?," and "What were the major events in the fight for civil rights?"

GUIDE: After the students had recorded what they already knew on their individual maps, I guided them in reading the first chapter of the text, providing assistance as needed. They paused when they had finished reading, and we discussed the information and made additions to our Semantic Question Map. Under the question "What was the civil rights movement fighting for?" they added "an end to separate restaurants and water fountains" and "same schools for all children." They also confirmed the ideas they had written before reading.

PRACTICE: To practice, I had students continue to read the text. When they had finished the second chapter, they added "an end to segregation on buses" and "equal rights for all citizens" under "What was the civil rights movement fighting for?" and added "the NAACP" under "Who was involved in the civil rights movement?"

REFLECT: To reflect, we discussed how we can use the Semantic Question Map to help us better organize the information we learn about a specific topic. We decided that as we continued to read *Rosa Parks*, we would add information to our Semantic Question Map. Our Semantic Question Map about the civil rights movement from our guided small-group lesson appears in Figure 4-2.

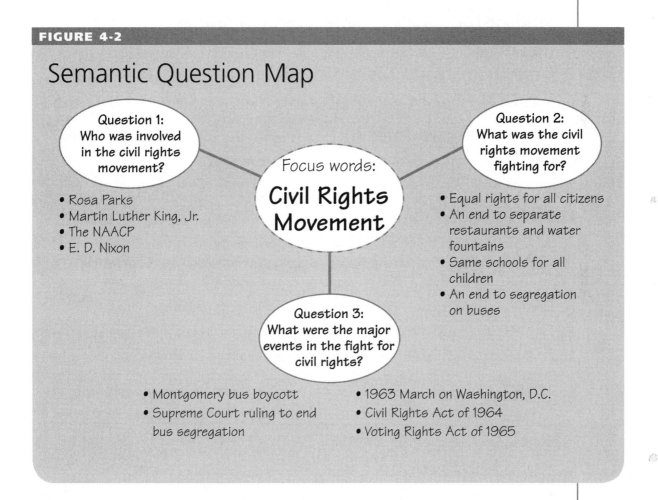

FIGURE 4-2

Semantic Question Map

Question 1:
Who was involved in the civil rights movement?

- Rosa Parks
- Martin Luther King, Jr.
- The NAACP
- E. D. Nixon

Focus words:
Civil Rights Movement

Question 2:
What was the civil rights movement fighting for?

- Equal rights for all citizens
- An end to separate restaurants and water fountains
- Same schools for all children
- An end to segregation on buses

Question 3:
What were the major events in the fight for civil rights?

- Montgomery bus boycott
- Supreme Court ruling to end bus segregation
- 1963 March on Washington, D.C.
- Civil Rights Act of 1964
- Voting Rights Act of 1965

Student-Facilitated Comprehension Centers

POETRY CENTER: Students used Semantic Question Maps they had previously completed to write and illustrate acrostic, diamante, or cinquain poems.

THEME CENTER: Students self-selected and read biographies from the Theme Center. I had prepared Semantic Question Map blacklines, and they worked either individually or with a partner to complete the maps.

WRITING CENTER: Students used Semantic Question Maps they or the class had previously completed to write paragraphs about the focus words or phrases.

Student-Facilitated Comprehension Routines

LITERATURE CIRCLES: We adapted the Literature Circle so students could use the Semantic Question Map to take notes as they read the biography the group had selected. After reading the text and completing the maps, students used them to facilitate discussion.

CROSS-AGE READING EXPERIENCES: Students read with cross-age partners. They began filling out the Semantic Question Map before they began reading. As they read, they added information as necessary. Then they used the completed map to create an oral summary.

(STAGE 3) Teacher-Facilitated Whole-Group Reflection and Goal Setting

SHARE: In small groups, students shared their Semantic Question Maps from Stage Two. They also shared the poems and summaries they had created. After sharing in small groups, some students then volunteered to share with the whole group.

REFLECT: We reflected on how using Semantic Question Maps helped to guide our reading and how well we could use them. Jaime said, "The Semantic Question Map really helped me focus on what I was reading. I knew that I needed to find information to answer the questions, so I was really paying attention to what I was reading." Kelly said, "I liked knowing what I was supposed to be looking for before I started reading." The students seemed to be proud of their ability to use Semantic Question Maps. They especially liked how the completed maps could be used as a basis for discussion and writing.

SET NEW GOALS: We decided that we would continue to use Semantic Question Maps to help us organize information, but we wanted to learn another idea that would help us understand how words work. We decided we would learn about Concept of Definition Maps next (see page 178).

Assessment Options

I used observation, students' completed Semantic Question Maps, student writing, and student self-reflections to assess. When working with special education students, I was careful to limit the number of questions they were required to focus on. I also used colored dots to draw students' attention to different sections of the maps. I provided individual assistance as necessary to complete the task. I assessed them on these smaller components and their ability to complete them. When working with ELL students, I provided extra time for more specific and individualized instruction. I also made books on tape available. I assessed their performance both orally and in written format.

LESSON 4 Semantic Map
Theme: Fantasy

STAGE 1 Teacher-Directed Whole-Group Instruction

TEXT: *Tuck Everlasting* (Babbitt, 1975)

EXPLAIN: To begin, I explained to students that Knowing How Words Work helps us to make sense of what we read. "Knowing How Words Work is a reading comprehension strategy that helps us to understand words through strategic vocabulary development, including the use of our cueing systems." I explained that we would be focusing on the Semantic Map, a technique designed to help us understand what we already know about a word. I said that when we use a Semantic Map our focus is a word in or related to the text. I told students, "After we choose the focus word, we will share what comes to mind when we hear that word. For example, if our focus word were *weather*, some of our responses may be *rain*, *snow*, and *sleet*, and other responses may be *boots*, *raincoat*, and *umbrella*." I explained that after everyone had a chance to respond, we would place everyone's ideas into categories. So in our example, *rain*, *snow*, and *sleet* might be placed in the category "Types of Weather," while *boots*, *raincoat*, and *umbrella* might be placed in the category "Weather Gear."

I asked students to turn to a partner and see if they could think of other categories that might appear on a Semantic Map about weather. After a few minutes the pairs shared their ideas with the class, and we brainstormed some words that might be placed in that category. For example, Jose and Anne suggested "Severe Weather" and other students suggested we could put words like *hurricane*, *tsunami*, and *tornado* in that category. I said, "After putting the responses into categories, we would have a good overview of the focus word and could use the information to create a summary." I added, "Brainstorming what we already know about words will help us make connections, and when we have connections to words it is easier for us to know what the word means."

DEMONSTRATE: To demonstrate, I used a think-aloud, a read-aloud, and a laminated poster of the graphic organizer (see page 187 for blackline). I showed students a laminated, poster-size Semantic Map that I created on a poster machine. I used a think-aloud to demonstrate how to brainstorm related words and organize them into categories. I said, "In the center oval, I am going to write a focus phrase from our novel, *Tuck Everlasting*, and then I am going to brainstorm every word I can think of that relates to that phrase." I wrote the words *everlasting life* in the

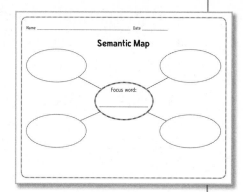

center oval of the map and brainstormed a few ideas that came to mind when I thought of this phrase. I used a think-aloud and said, "When I hear the words *everlasting life* I think of never getting old, being able to see everything in the world, and being healthy forever."

After brainstorming several ideas and writing them on the board, I said, "Now that I have some ideas, I need to think about a category I can place these words in. For example, I have *never-ending travel*, *never getting old*, and *being healthy forever*, so I need to think of a category that might work for these phrases. I think these sound like reasons we would want everlasting life." The class agreed, and I wrote "Reasons to Want Everlasting Life" inside the upper left oval and listed the related ideas, which included *never getting old*, *never-ending travel*, and *being healthy forever*, below it I crossed out each idea on the board as I wrote it on our Semantic Map.

GUIDE: To guide students I said, "Now it's your turn to brainstorm some ideas to add to our Semantic Map, so work with a partner to think of an idea you want to add to our list. I will record your ideas right next to the ideas I brainstormed, and then we will develop categories and complete our map. Remember, the question you and your partner need to answer is, What comes to mind when you hear the phrase *everlasting life*?" The pairs brainstormed and shared their ideas, which I recorded on the board.

To get them thinking, I said, "I wonder what other categories we could use to organize ideas on our Semantic Map." I looked at the list of phrases I had recorded on the board and read: *outliving friends*, *living dangerously*, *dealing with jealousy*, and *living through more wars* aloud to students. Then we thought about a category these might fit into. Mayan and Mandy suggested "Reasons Not to Want Everlasting Life." We all agreed that was a good choice because it was the opposite of the category I had created. I wrote "Reasons Not to Want Everlasting Life" in the upper right-hand oval and listed the related phrases underneath. As I wrote the ideas on the blackline, I crossed them off the board. Next, I read the words and phrases *secrecy*, *science experiments*, and *being found out* aloud, and we discussed possible categories. We decided that the category could be "Reasons for Hiding." I wrote the third category in the lower left-hand oval and wrote the related words and phrases below it.

PRACTICE: To practice, the partners determined a label for the last oval. The words that were left on the board were names: Mae, Winnie Foster, Tuck, and Jesse. We discussed students' ideas and finally agreed that the last oval should be titled "People Affected." I wrote this in the last oval on our poster and listed the characters' names below it. After the Semantic Map was completed, we had a class discussion about what we knew about everlasting life. For example, Nikita said, "I know I have watched movies and TV shows where people look for the fountain of youth so they can have everlasting life." Then we used all the information on the Semantic Map to create an oral summary of the concept of everlasting life. When we finished, I read Chapter 2 of *Tuck Everlasting* aloud to the class. After I read the chapter, students and I discussed evidence of everlasting life within the text. Jim said, "I think it is interesting that we said on the Semantic Map that people would have to hide so no one would catch on that you weren't aging, and in this chapter Mae is doing that." Marta said, "On our map we listed reasons to want everlasting life, but we don't see any of those in this chapter. I wonder if we will see those ideas later in the novel." The students made quite a few connections between the text and our map. Figure 4-3 shows our completed Semantic Map.

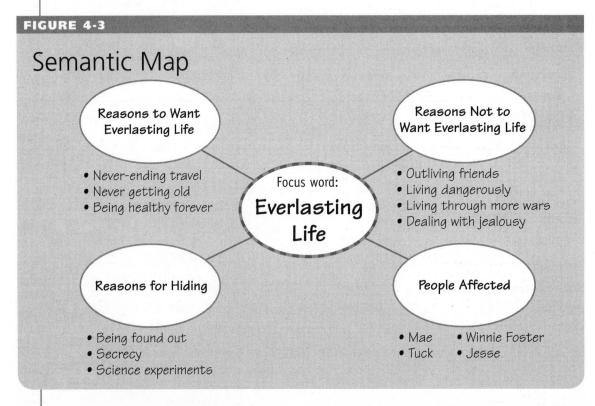

FIGURE 4-3

Semantic Map

Reasons to Want Everlasting Life
- Never-ending travel
- Never getting old
- Being healthy forever

Focus word: **Everlasting Life**

Reasons Not to Want Everlasting Life
- Outliving friends
- Living dangerously
- Living through more wars
- Dealing with jealousy

Reasons for Hiding
- Being found out
- Secrecy
- Science experiments

People Affected
- Mae
- Tuck
- Winnie Foster
- Jesse

REFLECT: As a class we talked about how Semantic Maps help us to understand how words work and how they help us understand what we read. The students commented on how they could see Semantic Maps working for science and social studies terms. Tyler said, "I think that it was fun to map the words and I think we can use maps with all kinds of text. I also like how we work together when we learn new ideas like the Semantic Map."

STAGE 2) Teacher-Guided Small-Group Instruction

TEXT: *Harry Potter and the Sorcerer's Stone* (Rowling, 1997) (Texts varied according to the students' abilities.)

REVIEW: I reviewed with students the importance of knowing how words work and making connections to words and ideas by using Semantic Maps. I also reminded students that by connecting our background information to the focus word we are better able to comprehend what we read. Then I introduced *Harry Potter and the Sorcerer's Stone* and explained to the students that we would be creating a Semantic Map using a focus word in the book. The students were very excited to be able to read a Harry Potter book. I asked if they could think of a focus word that we could use for our Semantic Map. Some of the words suggested were *wizardry*, *witchcraft*, *school*, *friends*, and *magic*. We decided that *wizardry* would be a good selection because we would be able to incorporate many of the other ideas with it.

GUIDE: To guide students, I invited Mario to write the focus word *wizardry* in the center oval of our poster-size Semantic Map. Because we were working in a small group and would have a limited number of responses if we began by brainstorming, we used a Semantic Map on which I had already recorded four categories: "Supplies," "Schooling," "Types of Classes," and "What Wizards Do." Students brainstormed words for each category, a fun task since they were familiar with the Harry Potter books and movies.

PRACTICE: To practice, partners used our Semantic Map to create and share oral summaries about wizardry. Next, the students read aloud a paragraph from Chapter 8. I listened to students whisper-read this paragraph. Lisa said, "In this paragraph it mentions telescopes, which could have been listed on the Semantic Map under 'Supplies.' This paragraph also shows that students take Herbology, which we could have listed under 'Types of Classes.'" So we added that information to our Semantic Map and decided we would continue to add information, as necessary, as we continued to read the book.

I suggested that we change the color marker we used for adding information, so we would know which information we had brainstormed and which had come from the text. Our Semantic Map, as completed at this point, is featured in Figure 4-4.

REFLECT: The students shared their thoughts about the Semantic Map with a partner. Then we engaged in an oral retelling of the events in this section of the novel. Finally, we discussed the importance of Knowing How Words Work and how this strategy helps us make connections and understand what we read.

FIGURE 4-4

Semantic Map

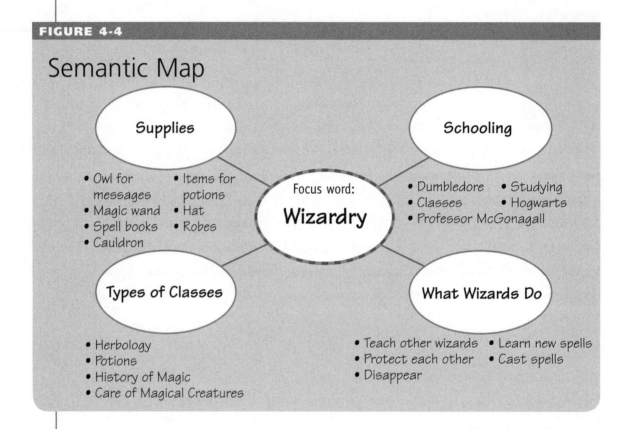

Supplies
- Owl for messages
- Magic wand
- Spell books
- Cauldron
- Items for potions
- Hat
- Robes

Schooling
- Dumbledore
- Classes
- Professor McGonagall
- Studying
- Hogwarts

Focus word:
Wizardry

Types of Classes
- Herbology
- Potions
- History of Magic
- Care of Magical Creatures

What Wizards Do
- Teach other wizards
- Protect each other
- Disappear
- Learn new spells
- Cast spells

Student-Facilitated Comprehension Centers

THEME CENTER: I placed a variety of fantasy books and Semantic Map blacklines at the Theme Center. I made sure to include books of various reading levels to accommodate all students. The Semantic Map blacklines, on which I had already written focus words, were tucked into each book. Students worked with a partner to complete a Semantic Map before reading. After reading, students discussed their completed Semantic Maps and shared oral summaries based on their maps.

WRITING CENTER: Students worked with a partner or individually to write short summaries based on at least three different Semantic Maps, which had been previously completed by the class or individual students. If time permitted, students also illustrated their summaries. (See page 189 for Semantic Map Summary blackline.)

Student-Facilitated Comprehension Routines

LITERATURE CIRCLES: Each group received a copy of a Semantic Map with the focus word and categories already filled in. The students completed and discussed their maps before reading their text. When the circle was finished, students created oral summaries based on their map. They also agreed to continue to add information to their Semantic Map as they read the rest of the text.

(**STAGE 3**) Teacher-Facilitated Whole-Group Reflection and Goal Setting

SHARE: Students shared their thoughts and completed Semantic Maps from Stage Two in small groups. The students were eager to share their completed maps, and group members orally summarized a few of them.

REFLECT: We discussed how we would be able to use Semantic Maps with other texts and how the graphic organizer and categories make it easier to remember the information. Niki said, "I like that we map a word from the text. It helps me understand what the word means and then I read better." The students all agreed. Jackie said that he liked the brainstorming because he had to "check with his brain" to see what he already knew about the word.

SET NEW GOALS: The class decided that everyone was very confident using the Semantic Map with narrative text, but they wanted to learn how to use it with informational text. So, using Semantic Maps with informational text became our new class goal.

Assessment Options

Throughout each stage of the lesson I observed students as they made contributions to the Semantic Maps. I also reviewed their Semantic Maps and listened to or read their Semantic Map Summaries to ensure that they understood how to use them. I made notes on the progress of each student and held individual "on my feet" conferences with them. When working with special education students, I scaffolded their learning by partnering them with more capable students at the start of the lesson. I also made sure they were given extra time when needed and paired them with other students throughout Stage Two. ELLs worked with partners throughout the lesson. I noticed that the Semantic Map graphic organizer was effective for all students.

LESSON 5 Concept of Definition Map
Theme: The Holocaust

(STAGE 1) Teacher-Directed Whole-Group Instruction

TEXT: *Lily's Crossing* (Giff, 1997)

EXPLAIN: To get started, I explained Knowing How Words Work and focused on the Concept of Definition Map. "Knowing How Words Work is a key reading comprehension strategy," I said. I explained that we use Concept of Definition Maps to help us understand how words work. I added that Concept of Definition Maps help us to make connections between what we already know and words we are trying to learn about. I explained that we would write a focus word in the center of the map, complete as much of the map as we could before we read the text, and make changes or modifications after we read. Finally, I explained to students that we would use our completed Concept of Definition Maps to create summaries. I said, "Knowing how to use a Concept of Definition Map will help us expand our understanding of words and make connections between the focus word, what we already know, and what we learn from the text."

DEMONSTRATE: I demonstrated by using a think-aloud, a poster-size Concept of Definition Map (see page 184 for blackline), and a read-aloud of Chapter 1 of *Lily's Crossing*. I began by showing students a laminated poster-size copy of the Concept of Definition Map. Next, I read aloud the various categories that we would need to complete. I wrote our focus word, *war*, in the center of the map and said, "To complete this Concept of Definition Map, we will need to provide all the information requested on the graphic organizer. Let's start with the box that says 'What is it?' Okay. We need to think of what war is. I know that war happens when two or more countries have tried everything else to get along but they feel a need to fight for what they believe in." So in the top box I wrote, "When two countries fight for what they believe in."

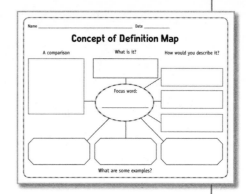

Next, I looked to the right of my focus word and read aloud the next category, "How would you describe it?" I told students that we could use single words as well as phrases to describe war. I thought aloud and said, "I know that war is very scary for everyone involved, so I am going to write *scary* in the first box." I asked students to turn to a partner and think about how they would describe war. After a few minutes I invited them to share. Alyssa and Jore said, "We think war is confusing." Mark and Diana said, "We think that war is very loud because of the guns and tanks." I wrote *confusing* and *loud* in the remaining two boxes in the "How would you describe it?" section.

GUIDE: Next, I asked students to direct their attention to the category at the bottom of the map, "What are some examples?" I asked students to brainstorm with a partner some examples of war and they came up with World War I, World War II, Desert Storm, Iraq, the Civil War, and the American Revolution. As students shared their thoughts, we discussed them and I wrote class-selected ideas on the map. The final section asked for a comparison. I said, "I know a comparison is something that is similar, so I need to think of something that is similar to war. Let's close our eyes and picture what war looks like." I closed my eyes and said, "I see bombs going off, planes machine-gunning cities, and missiles being launched. What do you see?" Students offered several responses, and we decided we would write *conflict* in the box labeled "A comparison," because war is similar to conflict. Then we discussed our completed map. Our completed Concept of Definition Map is featured in Figure 4-5.

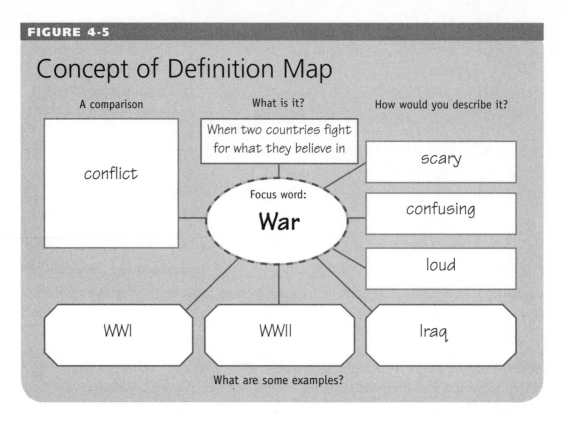

FIGURE 4-5

Concept of Definition Map

A comparison

What is it?

How would you describe it?

conflict

When two countries fight
for what they believe in

Focus word:

War

scary

confusing

loud

WWI

WWII

Iraq

What are some examples?

PRACTICE: To give students practice, I wrote "Concept of Definition Map Summary" on the board and encouraged students to join me in creating a Concept of Definition Map Summary. We used our completed map and I wrote, "War is similar to conflict. War happens when two countries fight for what they believe in. War is very scary, loud, and confusing. The American Revolution, the Civil War, and World War II are three examples of wars." I explained to the students that often when we write summaries, we need to extract or pull important information out of the text. But when we have a completed Concept of Definition Map, all of the important information is already on the map, so all we need to do is create the summary from the information provided.

Next I introduced the novel *Lily's Crossing* to the students by sharing the cover and reading the title. I said, "I wonder why the author chose the title *Lily's Crossing*." Some of the students thought that Lily was going to cross into a different stage in her life. Other students suggested that the world was changing around her because of a war and she was crossing into a new way of thinking. I said, "I wonder if the author will be clear about why the title is *Lily's Crossing* or if we will have to infer what it means." The students said they hoped they would find out what the meaning of the title was as we started reading. Then I read the first chapter of the novel aloud as students followed along. When I finished reading, I again asked students what they thought the title meant. The students replied that they thought that the title meant that Lily was crossing into a new stage in her life, a stage where war was everywhere and it had changed the lives of many. They decided that the war had a strong impact on the relationships Lily had in the book.

REFLECT: We reflected on how using the Concept of Definition Map helped us to understand what we read. We also talked about how the map made it easy to remember information because each section contained ideas about a particular aspect of the focus word. David also noted how easy it was to summarize when using a completed map. He said, "Using the finished map makes summarizing really easy. We can also tell what kinds of information to put into summaries by looking at the categories—what is it, how to describe it, what are some examples." The students all agreed with him. I was pleased that David had raised this point, because oftentimes determining which information is important enough to be included in a summary can be challenging for students. Finally, we discussed how we could use Concept of Definition Maps with other texts in other settings.

(STAGE 2) Teacher-Guided Small-Group Instruction

TEXT: *The Devil's Arithmetic* (Yolen, 1988) (Texts varied according to students' abilities.)

REVIEW: I reminded students about the strategies good readers use and focused on Knowing How Words Work using Concept of Definition Maps. I also reminded them that Knowing How Words Work helps us to make connections to words and ideas and to better understand what we read.

GUIDE: I gave each student in the small group a copy of a Concept of Definition Map blackline with the focus phrase *concentration camps* written in the center. The students had just started studying the Holocaust in social studies, so this was a phrase I knew wasn't totally new to them. We discussed what we knew already about concentration camps, and I encouraged students to write a response for the first category, "What is it?" Amy and a few other students wrote "a place where Jews were relocated during the Holocaust," and TJ and a few other students wrote "a place where Jews had to live and had no freedom." I encouraged students to write their ideas in the "What is it?" section of the map.

I continued to guide students as they completed the next section, "How would you describe it?" The responses included *cruel*, *frightening*, and *unfair*. The students recorded their answers on their maps. Next, I directed the students' attention to the bottom of the map, "What are some examples?" The students filled in one of the boxes with the word *Auschwitz* and mentioned that this was the only example they could think of. I said,

"That's fine. Sometimes we can complete the entire map before reading; other times we need information from the text to help us complete it. I know that in our text we will read about other examples of concentration camps, so we will complete the other two examples after we have read the text."

I introduced *The Devil's Arithmetic* by showing the cover and the title, reading pages 3–5, and engaging in a brief discussion with students. The students instantly noticed the picture on the bottom of the cover. They thought it looked like people in a concentration camp, so we talked about that. Then they whisper-read the first two chapters of the novel, and when everyone in the small group was finished, we discussed the story. The students completed the remaining examples needed at the bottom of their map with *Bergen Belsen* and *Dachau*, concentration camps they had read about in the text. They also filled in the last category, "A comparison." The students decided after they read a section of the text that they could compare concentration camps to a jail. Some of the students also compared the camps to the Japanese internment. Lee said, "I think concentration camps and the Japanese internment can be compared to each other because in both circumstances people were relocated from their homes and taken to live in places very far away." The students added the information to our Concept of Definition Map and we briefly discussed our completed map.

Finally I asked, "What will we write in our Concept of Definition Map Summary?" The students used the format we had used in Stage One. They wrote their summary on a sheet of poster paper. It read, "Concentration camps were places where Jews were relocated during the Holocaust. Concentration camps were cruel, frightening, and unfair. Auschwitz, Bergen Belsen, and Dachau were three examples of camps. Concentration camps were like jails."

PRACTICE: The students practiced by reading the next few chapters of the text with a partner. After they finished, we discussed the information we had on our Concept of Definition Maps. I asked students if any information on the map was confirmed as they read. Mario said, "Grandpa Will has the flashback at the beginning of Chapter 2 where he shows how frightening and cruel the concentration camps were. Those were two of the words we used to describe our focus word." Maria said, "In Chapter 6 they mention that Grandpa had no pictures of his family because you couldn't bring anything to the death camps. That shows how cruel, frightening, and unfair the concentration camps were."

REFLECT: To reflect, we discussed how Concept of Definition Maps help us to more fully understand different ideas and how Concept of Definition Map Summaries provide us with essential information. Then we discussed how we might use the maps in other settings.

Student-Facilitated Comprehension Centers

POETRY CENTER: At this center students used completed Concept of Definition Maps to write poetry about the Holocaust. Their completed poems were hung in our Theme Corner and shared with the class in Stage Three.

THEME CENTER: I placed a number of theme-related books at various reading levels at this center. Students selected books and completed the Concept of Definition Maps I had placed in each text. I had already provided the focus word/phrase for each map, and individual students worked to complete the maps before reading and added information as necessary after reading.

Student-Facilitated Comprehension Routines

LITERATURE CIRCLES: I provided students with Concept of Definition Map blacklines for whatever segments of the novel students had agreed to read for a particular meeting. I had already written a focus word/phrase on the blacklines. The students worked on completing the maps as they read and added information after reading as necessary. The group discussed the Concept of Definition Maps and created Concept of Definition Map Summaries as extension activities after the Literature Circle discussions were completed.

(**STAGE 3**) Teacher-Facilitated Whole-Group Reflection and Goal Setting

SHARE: Students shared their Concept of Definition Maps and Summaries from Stage Two in small groups. The entire class visited our Theme Corner so students could share the poems they had written.

REFLECT: We reflected on how Knowing How Words Work and Concept of Definition Maps helped us to understand what we read. We talked about how we might use Concept of Definition Maps and summaries with informational text and how this would help us remember the facts about a subject we were studying.

SET NEW GOALS: The students felt comfortable using Concept of Definition Maps and summaries when they were reading narrative texts, so we decided our new goal would be to learn how to use them when reading informational text.

Assessment Options

I carefully observed students in all stages of this lesson. I also used their completed Concept of Definition Maps and summaries to assess their understanding. When working with special education students, I placed particular emphasis on the graphic organization of the Concept of Definition Map. Students said that having the completed maps really helped them to summarize. When working with ELLs, I made sure I provided extra time and guidance as needed. For example, I encouraged students to sketch summaries of the information on the completed Concept of Definition Maps and provided picture clues whenever possible. In addition, I made the texts used in Stage Two available as books and books on tape, so any student who needed could read along with the tapes. I also ensured that books at appropriate levels were available at the centers and in the routines.

LESSON 6 Vocabulary Bookmark Technique
Theme: Poetry

STAGE 1 Teacher-Directed Whole-Group Instruction

TEXTS: "California Ghost Town" by Fran Haraway and "Washington, D.C." by Rebecca Kai Dotlich in *My America* (Hopkins, 2000)

EXPLAIN: I began by explaining to students that we would be using a new technique—the Vocabulary Bookmark Technique—to learn more about how words work. I said, "When we use the Vocabulary Bookmark Technique, we will select the words we want to study. When reading story text or informational text, we will write the word, what we think it means, why we think it means that, and the page and paragraph numbers on which it appears on a Vocabulary Bookmark." (See page 190 for the Vocabulary Bookmark blackline.) I added that since we were studying poetry, we would adapt the bookmark and include the stanza and line number instead of page and paragraph. I said that when we had finished our bookmarks we would discuss our words and confirm our definitions with the dictionary. "This will help us to understand the meaning of the words, how they are used in the text, and how we can use the words in our everyday world." Michelle said, "I think it will be fun to look for words we want to study. I like that we get to pick words we think are important." The rest of the class shared similar comments about how important they thought it was to pick out their own words.

DEMONSTRATE: To demonstrate, I used a think-aloud and an oversize version of the Vocabulary Bookmark blackline. To begin, I introduced the poem "California Ghost Town" by Fran Haraway. We briefly discussed what the title could mean. I gave each student a copy of the poem to follow along, and then I read it aloud so we could all enjoy listening to it. Then we briefly discussed the poem. During my second reading, I paused at the word *warped* in the first line. The line read, "Buildings blackened, boards warped, pushed askew." On a poster-size, laminated copy of the bookmark I wrote the word *warped* and thought aloud as I wrote what I thought the word meant. I wrote, "I think *warped* means to bend or twist something out of its original shape. I think this must mean that the boards on some of the buildings are not in the same shape or condition that they were in a long time ago." I also made sure that I wrote *stanza 1, line 1* at the bottom of the bookmark.

After this, students and I read the first line together. We discussed the word and its relation to the text. Nikita said, "By using the word *warped*, the author helps us to picture what the town might look like. I think that the boards of the buildings look worn and twisted and the town looks run-down." We decided that we should check the meaning of *warped* in the dictionary. It said *warped* meant "twisted out of shape," which was very close to the meaning of the word that I had written on the Vocabulary Bookmark. I explained that we should always confirm our word's meaning in a dictionary.

GUIDE: To guide students, I continued to read the rest of the poem aloud and invited students to choose words they thought the class should discuss. Some of their word choices were *askew*, *remains*, and *indifference*. Pairs of students wrote the word they chose on a bookmark and also what they thought the word meant, followed by the stanza and line number on which it appeared. I walked around the room as students chose their word and discussed what they thought the word meant. As a group, we discussed the words.

The only definition that was not initially confirmed by the dictionary was *indifference*. Alexia and John said, "The line of the poem that contains the word *indifference* is 'By winds and winter's harsh indifference.' We think *indifference* means 'totally different.'" When we checked the dictionary, we discovered that the meaning was "showing neither interest or dislike." We discussed the dictionary definition and examined how that meaning would work in the text. Alexia and John agreed that the dictionary definition made more sense in

Vocabulary Bookmark

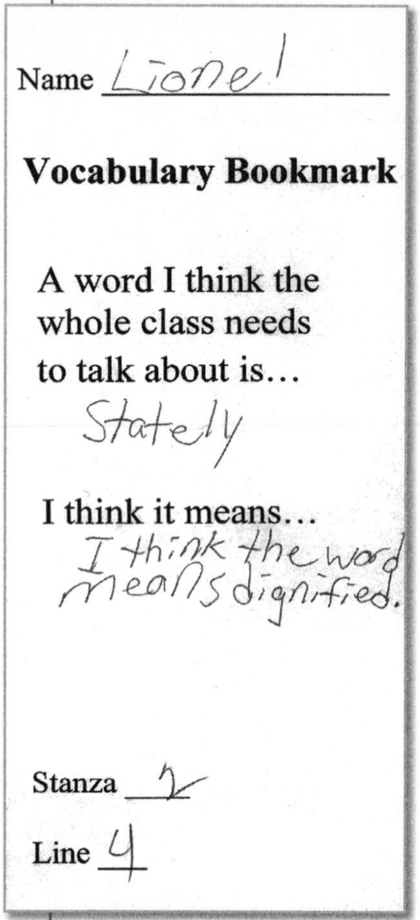

Name *Lionel*

Vocabulary Bookmark

A word I think the whole class needs to talk about is…

Stately

I think it means…

I think the word means dignified.

Stanza *2*

Line *4*

FIGURE 4-6

the poem. Then we discussed the importance of using context clues when we were trying to determine a word's meaning and how knowing what words meant helped us with our comprehension.

PRACTICE: To give students practice, I introduced "Washington, D.C." by Rebecca Kai Dotlich, and we briefly discussed what we thought the poem may be about. I gave each student a copy of the poem, then I read the poem aloud, so we could all listen and enjoy it. After a brief discussion of the poem's contents, I read aloud the first two stanzas of the poem, and students wrote on their Vocabulary Bookmarks a word they thought the whole class should discuss. I reminded students to think carefully about the word's possible meaning and to include the stanza and line number on their bookmark. The students discussed the words' possible meanings and where they were located. For example, Lionel chose *stately*. He noted that it was located in stanza 2, line 4, and thought that *stately* meant "dignified." When we verified the meaning of *stately* in the dictionary, we realized that it was very similar to what Lionel had suggested. Then we used *stately* in a variety of sentences. Figure 4-6 shows Lionel's bookmark.

REFLECT: The students truly enjoyed this activity. They clearly felt empowered when they self-selected the vocabulary words. We decided that it is good to select words we want to learn and to predict possible meanings. They agreed that the Vocabulary Bookmark Technique was a great way to learn new words and they knew they would be able to use it with other types of texts. Maria said, "I think Vocabulary Bookmarks would be great to use with social studies. There are always so many new words to learn that it would be fun to choose ones we wanted to learn!"

Teacher-Guided Small-Group Instruction

TEXT: "Islands in Boston Harbor" by David McCord, in *My America* (Hopkins, 2000) (Texts varied according to the students' abilities.)

REVIEW: To review, I reminded students about the Vocabulary Bookmark Technique and how using context clues can help us figure out what a word means. I also reminded them of the strategies good readers use. We remembered that we would need to include the vocabulary word, what we thought it meant and why, and the paragraph or stanza and line number on our Vocabulary Bookmarks.

GUIDE: To guide students, I introduced the poem "Islands in Boston Harbor" by David McCord. I gave each student a copy of the poem and the Vocabulary Bookmark blackline. I invited students to read the poem silently to become familiar with it. Then we read the poem aloud for enjoyment and briefly discussed it. During the third reading, we focused on the first four stanzas and the words students selected for their Vocabulary Bookmarks. For example, Marco chose the word *boast*, which appeared in line 1. Marco said, "I think the word *boast* is similar to the word *talk*." Many of the students began to discuss what they thought the word meant. After our discussion students agreed that it meant to talk, but in a proud way. When we checked the dictionary, it said "to praise oneself or one's possessions," so we knew it verified the students' thinking. Marco said, "I understand it now. I could say, 'I boasted about the number of baskets I made during the game.'"

PRACTICE: To practice, students read the rest of "Islands in Boston Harbor" with a partner. They chose words they wanted our group to discuss and wrote them and their possible meanings on their bookmarks. Some of the words they chose were *spectacular*, *cormorants*, and *granite*. As students worked to determine the meaning of the words, I observed. Next, we discussed the words' possible meanings and verified them in the dictionary. Finally, we talked about how we could use the words when speaking or writing. Nick's completed bookmark appears in Figure 4-7.

Name _Nick_

Vocabulary Bookmark

A word I think the whole class needs to talk about is...

granite

I think it means...

I think the word granite means a type of stone

Stanza _8_

Line _5_

FIGURE 4-7

REFLECT: We reflected on how much the Vocabulary Bookmark Technique helped us to understand new words. Justine said, "We could use Vocabulary Bookmarks all the time —when we read stories and in social studies, math, and science!"

Student-Facilitated Comprehension Centers

POETRY CENTER: I placed poetry books at a variety of levels at this center. Each student chose two poems, read them, and completed two Vocabulary Bookmarks. The students consulted a dictionary to make sure their definitions were correct.

(STAGE 3)   Teacher-Facilitated Whole-Group Reflection and Goal Setting

SHARE: Students shared their Vocabulary Bookmarks from Stage Two in small groups.

REFLECT: Students again discussed how much they liked using the Vocabulary Bookmark Technique because everyone got to choose words they thought were important. Many students also said that they gained a lot of information during the class discussion of the words.

SET NEW GOALS: We decided that we would continue to broaden our knowledge of vocabulary by using the Vocabulary Bookmark Technique with narrative and informational text.

Assessment Options

During this lesson, I used observation and the students' completed Vocabulary Bookmarks to assess. I also reviewed students' self-assessments. When working with special education students, I simplified the Vocabulary Bookmark blackline and worked with students individually as needed. When working with ELLs, I assessed them orally, in writing, and through sketching. I offered additional time and worked with students in pairs as needed. I was also careful to monitor students' understanding as the lesson progressed.

Final Thoughts on This Chapter

One of the challenges of teaching and learning vocabulary is keeping the students interested. In this chapter, we integrated self-selection and sketching in students' vocabulary study to help engage them in learning and encourage ownership of the words they were studying. Appendix C features detailed descriptions of the strategies used, as well as copies of the blackline masters. In the next chapter, we examine the role of the other Guided Comprehension strategies in the reading process. We begin by examining current theoretical beliefs about reading comprehension and then explore classroom applications through a variety of lessons.

What can we read to learn more about teaching vocabulary?

Blachowitz, C. L., & Fisher, P. (2000). Vocabulary instruction. In M. L. Kamil, P. Mosenthal, P. D. Pearson, & R. Barr (Eds.), *Handbook of reading research* (Vol. 3, pp. 503–523). Mahwah, NJ: Lawrence Erlbaum Associates.

International Reading Association. (2002). *IRA Literacy Study Groups vocabulary module*. Newark, DE: International Reading Association.

McLaughlin, M., & Allen, M. B. (2002a). *Guided comprehension: A teaching model for grades 3–8*. Newark, DE: International Reading Association.

CHAPTER 5

Comprehension

As reading teachers, our ultimate goal is to help our students construct meaning—to comprehend what they read. This is a personal process, and we know that the more background knowledge our students have about a given topic, the more deeply they will comprehend. Reading widely and having a variety of background experiences enhance background knowledge and facilitate our personal construction of meaning.

To help our students comprehend various types of text, we need to teach them how to be active, strategic readers. This is supported by the recent, renewed focus on teaching comprehension strategies (Pearson, 2001) that has shaped reading instruction in the intermediate grades. Our goal is to teach these strategies so students can develop a repertoire and use them as needed.

Essentially, every aspect of the reading process contributes to comprehension. In Chapter 2, we discussed how word study helps us to discover various grammatical, spelling, and structural clues that aid us in analyzing words. In Chapter 3, we discussed how fluency contributes to comprehension by eliminating word-by-word reading. And in Chapter 4, we focused on vocabulary, noting that we cannot comprehend if we do not know words' meanings. In this chapter, which builds on the preceding ones, we focus on reading comprehension strategies.

Part One: Research Base

What is comprehension?

> Comprehension is the construction of meaning of a written or spoken
> communication through a reciprocal, holistic interchange of ideas between
> the interpreter and the message in a particular communicative context. Note that
> the presumption here is that meaning resides in the intentional problem-solving,
> thinking processes of the interpreter during such an interchange, that the content
> of meaning is influenced by that person's prior knowledge and experience, and
> that the message so constructed by the receiver may or may not be congruent
> with the message sent. (Harris & Hodges, 1995, p. 39)

In other words, when we read, we need to activate any background knowledge we have
related to the topic. For example, if we were reading one of the Harry Potter books, any
knowledge we had about author J. K. Rowling, the popularity of the Harry Potter series,
essentials of the story line, sorcerers, and so on would interact with our reading of the text
to help us construct personal meaning.

What does the research tell us?

Reading is a social-constructivist process. Constructivists believe that comprehension takes
place when students connect what they know and have experienced with the text they are
reading. The more experience learners have with a topic, the easier it is for them to make
these connections (Anderson, 1994; Anderson & Pearson, 1984). Cambourne (2002)
notes that constructivism is based on three core assumptions:

- What is learned cannot be separated from the context in which it is learned.
- The reader's purposes or goals are central to what is being learned.
- Knowledge and meaning are socially constructed through the processes of
  negotiation, evaluation, and transformation.

Research (Askew & Fountas, 1998; Duke & Pearson, 2002; Pressley, 2000) tells us that
good readers

- are active and use comprehension strategies to help them derive meaning from text.
- have goals and constantly monitor the relation between the goals they have set and
  the text they are reading.
- spontaneously generate questions.
- construct and revise meaning as they read.
- have an awareness of the author's style and purpose.
- read widely.

Part Two: Lesson Overview

In this section we put research into practice by presenting six lessons that focus on ways to teach reading comprehension. As seen in the Lesson Overview, the lessons are theme-based and feature a variety of teaching ideas. The texts also vary. In Stage One, the teacher reads, so the text level may be easy, just right, or more challenging. In the guided reading groups, texts are at students' instructional levels, and at the centers and in the routines, independent level texts are used. Appendix D contains additional resources for teaching comprehension strategies. Appendix F features additional texts and Web sites that can be used when teaching these themes.

THEME	TEACHING IDEA	STAGE ONE TEXT	STAGE TWO GUIDED READING TEXT
Mystery	Self-Questioning, "I Wonder" Statements	*The Westing Game*	*From the Mixed-Up Files of Mrs. Basil E. Frankweiler*
Survival	Bookmark Technique, Monitoring	*Hatchet*	*Island of the Blue Dolphins*
Biography	Summarizing, Bio-Pyramid	*You Want Women to Vote, Lizzie Stanton?*	*What's the Big Idea, Ben Franklin?*
Fantasy	Making Connections, Connection Stems	*Tuck Everlasting*	*Harry Potter and the Prisoner of Azkaban*
The Holocaust	Previewing, Story Impressions	*Lily's Crossing*	*The Butterfly*
Poetry	Visualization, Draw and Label Visualizations	"The Raven"	"My Shadow"

Comprehension Lessons

LESSON 1 Self-Questioning
Theme: Mystery

STAGE 1 Teacher-Directed Whole-Group Instruction

TEXT: *The Westing Game* (Raskin, 1978)

EXPLAIN: I began by asking students why we ask questions. Responses included "Because we want to find out more about something than we already know" and "To see if someone else knows the answer to something we don't know." We discussed their responses, and I explained that asking questions also helps us gain a greater understanding about things and allows us to seek more information about what has happened or might happen. I said, "Today we will be using a reading comprehension strategy called Self-Questioning, which will help us to monitor what we read. To help us, we are going to use 'I Wonder' Statements. Using 'I Wonder' Statements will help us to become more active readers and generate questions and make speculations about what we are reading." I explained that we would be using the I Wonder Bookmark and writing questions that popped into our minds as we were reading. "For example," I said, "you might question why a character chose to say or do something in the story."

Next, I showed students the I Wonder Bookmark (see page 199), which I had displayed on the overhead projector. I thought aloud about the information that was required on the bookmark and noted that I needed not only to provide an "I Wonder" Statement but also to explain why I was wondering that. Then I explained that using "I Wonder" Statements helps us to generate questions that guide our thinking while we're reading. I continued, "If we wonder about what is going on in the story as we read, we are really questioning what the author is telling us. By asking questions we become more active readers. We are better able to make predictions and develop a greater understanding of events and characters. It also helps us to set our purpose for reading."

Name_____

I Wonder Bookmark

Page_____

I wonder _____

_____

_____

because _____

_____

_____

Page_____

I wonder _____

_____

because _____

_____

_____

DEMONSTRATE: I demonstrated how to create "I Wonder" Statements by using a read-aloud, a think-aloud, and an overhead projector. I displayed a copy of the I Wonder Bookmark on the overhead projector. I began by showing the cover of the book *The Westing Game* to the students, and I read aloud the title. Then I said, "My first wonder comes from the title, so where the bookmark says 'page' I am going to write 'cover.'" I did so and continued, "Now I am going to complete my first 'I Wonder' Statement." I thought aloud and said, "'I wonder what type of game this is and who will be playing it.' This is my first wonder, so I am going to write it on the bookmark where it says, 'I Wonder.'" Next I pointed out that I need to have a reason for my wonder. I said, "Where it says 'because,' I will explain why I wondered this. I will write, 'I have never heard of a Westing game and I know that you need people to play a game.'" Then I opened the book to Chapter 1 and began reading. As I read aloud, I continued to write my wonders on bookmarks, emphasizing the phrase *I wonder* and the word *because*. Then I said, "Creating 'I Wonder' Statements helps us to make predictions and question what the author has written. Wondering as we read helps us become more active, strategic readers."

GUIDE: I guided students to work in pairs to create "I Wonder" Statements. I continued to read aloud, pausing to allow partners to write their wonders on bookmarks. Once the students had finished their first "I Wonder" Statements, I invited them to share with the class. Keir and Chris said, "On page 2, we wondered why it said that Barney Northrup didn't exist, because he was giving the tours." Jennifer and Dylan said, "Our 'I Wonder' Statement is from page 4. We wondered how Barney knew how much the Wexler's house cost, and what else he knew about them, because no one had ever told him." All the pairs provided good examples, and I complimented them on remembering to explain why they wondered what they did.

PRACTICE: To practice, students worked on their own and used the bookmarks to record and explain their wonders as I read aloud the rest of the chapter. Then we shared our "I Wonder" Statements. Erik said, "On page 6, I wonder why he rented the apartment to a burglar and a bomber, because that would be dangerous!" Alina said, "I wonder why Barney kept saying there was only one apartment left each time he showed the apartment to someone, because he really had apartments for everyone."

REFLECT: The students and I reflected on how our wonders helped us to question what we read. Charlie said, "While I was reading, I was really paying attention to asking why certain things were happening. I felt more involved in the story because I kept questioning what was happening." Carly added, "It was like I was an extra character looking in and questioning everything that was happening. I think this will help me solve the mystery faster, because I am already wondering about all the clues." I reminded students that it was important not only to wonder about what they were reading but also to make sure they had a *reason* for their wonders. Cody said, "We know! Whenever we say *I wonder*, we need to explain why and say *because*."

STAGE 2 Teacher-Guided Small-Group Instruction

TEXT: *From the Mixed-Up Files of Mrs. Basil E. Frankweiler* (Konigsburg, 1967) (Texts varied according to the students' abilities.)

REVIEW: I began by reviewing the strategies all good readers use, and focused on how we can use "I Wonder" Statements to help us question.

GUIDE: I introduced the text, *From the Mixed-Up Files of Mrs. Basil E. Frankweiler*, by sharing the cover and title and reading the first page of Chapter 1. The students and I briefly discussed and wondered about what I had shared. They realized immediately that we were about to read another mystery and recorded their wonders and reasons on their I Wonder Bookmarks. For example, Ami wondered why Claudia was running away, because someone wouldn't run away without a good reason. Maddy wondered what the old-fashioned kind of running away was, because she didn't know there was an old way to do it. We discussed our wonders and then I guided students to begin reading. I monitored and provided help as needed as students continued to read the next few pages. After the third page, we stopped again to discuss our wonders and reasoning.

PRACTICE: The students continued to read the rest of Chapter 1 and individually recorded their "I Wonder" Statements on their bookmarks as they read. At the end of the chapter we discussed all of our wonders and reasons. We discovered that many of us had wondered similar things but for different reasons. This created further discussion about what was happening in the story and why.

REFLECT: We reflected on how "I Wonder" Statements help us to engage with the text and become actively involved in what we are reading. Melissa said, "Wonders made me think a lot more about what I was reading and helped me to guess what would happen next."

Student-Facilitated Comprehension Centers

MYSTERY CENTER: I had left a number of texts at the Mystery Center. Students read in pairs, but completed their own I Wonder Bookmarks as they read. The students stopped periodically to complete the bookmarks and discuss their wonders. Students placed their completed bookmarks in their literacy folders.

ART CENTER: After completing "I Wonder" Statements for books they read in the Mystery Center, the students chose different art media to create visual representations for those "I Wonder" Statements. We displayed the completed works in our class gallery.

LISTENING CENTER: Students chose a partner and listened to a mystery book on tape. Before reading, the partners decided where they would stop to create and discuss their wonders. Partners generally chose to stop after a few paragraphs or after each page to discuss their "I Wonder" Statements.

Student-Facilitated Comprehension Routines

LITERATURE CIRCLES: We adapted the Literature Circles to include the students using the I Wonder Bookmarks as they were reading. Each student shared their wonders with the group and further discussed any similarities or differences they had in their wonders.

CROSS-AGE READING EXPERIENCES: Students read with cross-age partners and completed bookmarks and discussed "I Wonder" Statements as they read.

(STAGE 3) Teacher-Facilitated Whole-Group Reflection and Goal Setting

SHARE: Students shared the "I Wonder" Statements they had created during Stage Two in small groups. Next, students toured our class gallery to view and share the drawings and other artistic representations of the "I Wonder" Statements.

REFLECT: We reflected on the way "I Wonder" Statements helped us to monitor what we were reading by causing us to question what was happening with the characters and events. They also helped us to become more actively involved in what we were reading.

SET NEW GOALS: We decided that we were confident in using "I Wonder" Statements to help us self-question as we read narrative text. Then we decided we would learn how to use this technique to help us question as we read informational text.

Assessment Options

I used observation, the students' completed "I Wonder" Statements, their artistic representations, and student self-reflections as assessments. I also completed running records with selected students during guided reading. When working with special education students, I was careful to limit the number of "I Wonder" Statements required. I also accommodated students' needs by allotting more time to complete the task, as necessary. I sometimes noticed these students needed assistance to remain on task and avoid becoming frustrated. I offered more teacher support and gradually scaffolded instruction to accommodate these needs. I assessed the special education students based on smaller components and their ability to complete them. When working with ELL students, I limited the number of "I Wonder" Statements required and allowed extra time for more specific and individualized instruction. I also used the Draw and Label Visualizations blackline (see page 200), to provide ELL students with opportunities to communicate their ideas through sketching. I assessed their performance orally, in written format, and through students' sketching, dramatizing, and singing.

LESSON 2 Bookmark Technique
Theme: Survival

STAGE 1 Teacher-Directed Whole-Group Instruction

TEXT: *Hatchet* (Paulsen, 1987)

EXPLAIN: I began by asking students what *monitoring* means. Tom said, "Well, I know that a hall monitor watches what is going on and makes sure no one does anything wrong, so I think that monitoring is to watch something." I responded, "What does the hall monitor do if someone does something wrong?" Caitlin answered, "They have to do something to fix it." I asked students how monitoring could be connected to reading. Mayo replied, "When you are reading, you have to pay attention to what you are reading and make sure that it makes sense. If what you're reading doesn't make sense, you have to do something to fix it." I said, "Yes! Monitoring our reading is important because it helps us to make sure what we are reading makes sense. When we monitor our reading, we constantly ask, 'Does this make sense?' and if it doesn't, we think about ways we can help make sense of our reading."

Next, I explained that one way we can monitor our reading is to use the Bookmark Technique (McLaughlin & Allen, 2002a). I showed students the Bookmark Technique blacklines (See pages 201–202), which I had enlarged and hung on the chalkboard. I explained that we would be using the bookmarks to record our thoughts about various parts of the book as we read. Then I explained the four different bookmarks that we would be using: "We will use Bookmark One to record what we think is the most interesting part of the story. We will use Bookmark Two to record the most confusing part of the story. On Bookmark Three we will write a word we think the whole class should discuss, and on Bookmark Four we will write about an illustration, chart, map, or graph that helps us understand what we read." Then I reminded the students that the Bookmark Technique helps us monitor our reading and that

by writing our ideas on the bookmarks, we can easily go back to the text and share our ideas with a partner or the whole class.

DEMONSTRATE: I demonstrated how to use the Bookmark Technique by using a read-aloud of the book *Hatchet* by Gary Paulsen, a think-aloud, and the enlarged Bookmark Technique blacklines I had hung on the chalkboard. I had already read aloud chapters 1 and 2, so I began my reading with Chapter 3. After reading the chapter, I said to the class, "Now I need to complete Bookmark One, the most interesting part of the chapter. I think the most interesting part was when the author described how Brian was able to crash-land the plane into the lake, so I am going to write that on Bookmark One. Underneath that I am going to sketch a picture of the plane over the lake and write 'pages 28–30' for the page numbers. Since this part of the story happens throughout several paragraphs, I am going to write 'all' where it says *paragraph*." I explained to students that it is important to write down the page and paragraph numbers so that we can easily find our information when we discuss our bookmarks with others.

GUIDE: I suggested the students work with partners. Then I guided the pairs to complete Bookmark Two, which asks for something that confused them. As the students discussed this issue, I circulated, providing feedback and assistance as needed. Then the students wrote on their Bookmarks, and we discussed their responses. Ideas they shared included:

> We were confused when Brian was sent on the plane with just the pilot. We wondered why there was no one else on the plane and why his mother would let him do that. Our mothers wouldn't let us do that.

> We thought that Brian flying the plane was the most interesting and the most confusing part. We can't figure out how he knew what to do.

PRACTICE: To practice, the students continued to work with partners to complete Bookmarks Three and Four, which asked for a word they thought the whole class needed to discuss and an illustration, chart, map or graph that helped them understand what they read. I reminded the students that the words they chose could be either words they didn't know or words that they thought would be interesting to discuss. Each pair wrote a word, what they thought it meant, and the page number and paragraph in which it could be found. Next, volunteers shared their word choices. Michael and Jonah said, "We picked the word *abated* on page 33, paragraph 7, because we didn't know what it meant at first. But after reading more, we guessed that it meant *stopped*." We discussed what we thought *abated* meant and checked the dictionary to verify our thoughts. We noted others who had that response and talked about why they had chosen it, and then Michael and Jonah suggested that we add *abated* to our word wall so we would all remember to use it in our writing and discussions. Then we discussed other students' words choices and added them to our word wall. Students' bookmark word choices included *altitude*, *rudder*, *secret*, *wrenching*, and *muck*.

For Bookmark Four, I explained that since the book did not have any illustrations, students could sketch their own based on something they had visualized while listening to the story. Examples included views of lakes from the air and crashing planes. Finally, students volunteered to share their sketches with the class. Amelia and Joanne's bookmarks are featured in Figure 5-1.

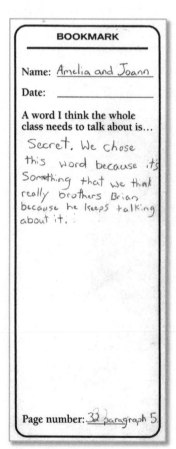

FIGURE 5-1

REFLECT: We reflected on how using the Bookmark Technique helps us to monitor or think about what we are reading. Sammi said, "The bookmarks helped me pay attention better to what I'm reading, because I knew I was looking for certain things." Nicolas said, "If I didn't understand something that I read, I could write it down and then talk about it with the class to help me understand it better. I also got to draw, which was fun!"

TEXT: *Island of the Blue Dolphins* (O'Dell, 1960) (Texts varied according to the students' abilities.)

REVIEW: I began by reviewing strategies good readers use and focused on how we can use the Bookmark Technique to help us monitor our reading.

GUIDE: I introduced the text, *Island of the Blue Dolphins*, by sharing the cover and title and reading aloud the first three pages. Next, I guided students to finish reading aloud Chapter 1. After they read the chapter, they completed Bookmarks One and Two. I reminded them to make sure they recorded the page numbers and paragraphs, so we could refer back to their ideas later.

PRACTICE: To practice, the students completed Bookmarks Three and Four. When they finished, they shared their bookmarks with the rest of the group, referring back to the specific pages and paragraphs where they had found their ideas, explaining why they had made their choices, and sharing the illustrations they had sketched. Juan's completed bookmarks are featured in Figure 5-2.

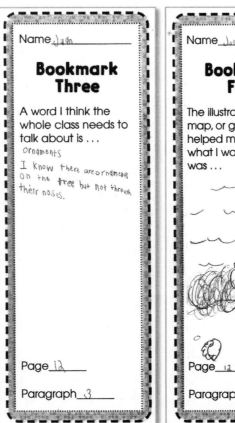

FIGURE 5-2

REFLECT: We reflected on how the Bookmark Technique helps us to think about what we are reading and monitor our comprehension of the text. Finally, we talked about how we could use bookmarks when reading informational text.

Student-Facilitated Comprehension Centers

ART CENTER: Students self-selected and read books and informational articles from the Theme Center. Then they used different media to create artistic representations of their bookmarks. We displayed their completed works of art in our class gallery.

THEME CENTER: Students chose partners and then each pair selected a book or informational article from either their book baskets or the texts I had left at the Theme Center. After reading, they completed the Bookmark Technique and shared and discussed their bookmarks with their partner.

Student-Facilitated Comprehension Routines

LITERATURE CIRCLES: We adapted the Literature Circle format to allow students to use the Bookmark Technique while reading the group text. The bookmarks were then shared and discussed when the group met in their circle. For example, the Discussion Director encouraged students to share their completed copies of Bookmarks One and Two to prompt discussion. The Word Finder used Bookmark Three to share his word and then encouraged other group members to share and discuss the words on their bookmarks.

Finally, the Artful Artist, or Illustrator, used Bookmark Four to encourage group members to share their illustrations. (See page 13 for a description of the Literature Circle roles.)

STAGE 3 Teacher-Facilitated Whole-Group Reflection and Goal Setting

SHARE: Students shared the bookmarks they had created during Stage Two in small groups. Then we toured the class gallery so that we could see the artistic representations of their bookmarks.

REFLECT: We reflected on how using the Bookmark Technique helps us to monitor our reading by causing us to focus on different aspects of what we were reading. Curtis said, "I liked using bookmarks because they gave me reasons for reading. I knew that there were four different things I was looking for." Sarai said, "I was really paying attention to what I was reading because I wanted to find the best ideas for each bookmark. I kept asking myself, 'Is this the most interesting word?' or 'Does this make sense?' I think using the bookmarks will help me when I am reading other things."

SET NEW GOALS: We decided that we felt comfortable using the Bookmark Technique with narrative text and would try using it with informational text.

Assessment Options

I used observation, students' completed bookmarks, their artistic interpretations, and student self-reflections as assessments during the lessons. I also completed running records with a few students during guided reading. When working with special education students I was careful to limit the number of bookmarks required, depending on the individual student's needs. I noticed that breaking down the task into smaller chunks helped to reduce frustration at completing the task. Pairing the students with another student of a higher ability who could serve as a model was also beneficial in helping special education students actively participate in the activity. In addition, I used books on tape and offered students the option of responding orally. I assessed these students on smaller components and what they were able to complete. When working with ELLs during this lesson, I began by limiting the number of bookmarks required and allowing time for more specific and individualized instruction. I also encouraged students to complete the bookmarks by sketching and labeling what they were thinking. I assessed their performance on what they completed both orally and in written format. I also incorporated the use of books on tape.

LESSON 3 Summarizing
Theme: Biography

STAGE 1 Teacher-Directed Whole-Group Instruction

TEXT: *You Want Women to Vote, Lizzie Stanton?* (Fritz, 1995)

EXPLAIN: I began by asking students what it means to summarize. Responses included "to tell events that happened" and "to retell something using only the most important parts." I added that summarizing is important because it helps us to recount or retell the events of a story or the important points in informational text. I said, "Summarizing is a strategy that helps us synthesize important ideas." I explained that today we would be creating a summary of the story we had finished reading and discussed earlier in the day, *You Want Women to Vote, Lizzie Stanton?*, using a Bio-Pyramid. I explained that creating a Bio-Pyramid is one strategy we can use to summarize a person's life.

After showing students the Bio-Pyramid blackline (see page 203), which I displayed on the overhead projector, I thought aloud about what information each line of the Bio-Pyramid required. I said, "The Bio-Pyramid begins with a person's name and then provides more information about the person in each succeeding line. For example, line two asks us to provide two words that describe the person, and line three asks us to write three words that tell about the person's childhood. Then I explained that a Bio-Pyramid is a way to organize the information we have learned about a person's life in a very specific way. I also noted that after we organize our information, we can use the Bio-Pyramid to help us do an oral or written summary.

DEMONSTRATE: I demonstrated how to complete a Bio-Pyramid by reading aloud Jean Fritz's book *You Want Women to Vote, Lizzie Stanton?* When I finished reading, I used a think-aloud and an overhead projector. I placed a copy of the Bio-Pyramid blackline on the projector for students to see and began modeling how to complete it. I thought aloud and said, "The first thing I need to do is write a person's name in the space on line one. I will write *Elizabeth* because the book is about her." Next, I said, "In line two, I need to write two words to describe Elizabeth Cady Stanton. In the first blank of the second line, I will write the word *determined* because in the book we found out that she worked her entire life speaking and getting petitions signed for the cause of women's suffrage. In the second blank, I will write *hardworking* because in the book it tells us that not only did she write and give speeches and attend conventions, she also raised seven children." Then I pointed to lines one and two and said, "So far, we know this Bio-Pyramid is about Elizabeth Cady Stanton and that she was determined and hardworking."

GUIDE: I guided students to work with partners to complete the following three lines of the Bio-Pyramid—three words describing the person's childhood, four words indicating a problem the person had to overcome, and five words stating one of her accomplishments. First I asked the partners to think of a three-word phrase to describe Elizabeth's childhood. I emphasized that this did not have to be a complete sentence and that they could leave out words like *a, an, the,* and *of* in order to make their idea fit the number of spaces provided in each line. I circulated among the pairs as they discussed their ideas, prompting and providing assistance as necessary. After a few minutes, I asked volunteers to share their ideas for line three. After listening to several responses, we decided that *father wanted sons* best described Elizabeth's childhood because she worked very hard to study Greek and learn to ride horses so that she could be "brave and strong" like a boy. Then the partners worked to complete line four—four words indicating a problem the person had to overcome. Again I circulated among the pairs and they shared several different responses. We decided that *not being treated equally* was the best way to summarize a problem Elizabeth had to overcome. Finally, the pairs created a response to line five—five words stating one of her accomplishments. Since we had been taking notes on important events from the book as I read it aloud, I encouraged students to look over their notes if necessary to determine what they felt were her most important accomplishments. After we discussed several possible responses, we decided to write the words *first to demand women's suffrage,* an idea offered by Annika and Jenna.

PRACTICE: To practice, students worked on their own to complete the final lines of the Bio-Pyramid—six words stating a second accomplishment, seven words stating a third accomplishment, and eight words stating how humankind benefited from the accomplishments. The students completed the remaining three lines and shared their ideas with a partner. Several students also shared with the whole class. We discussed which phrases to add to our group Bio-Pyramid. For line six, we selected *spoke to New York State Legislature.* For line seven, we chose *in 1866, ran for seat in Congress.* For line eight, the final line, we wrote *because of her, women eventually got to vote.* Then we used the completed Bio-Pyramid to orally summarize the life of Elizabeth Cady Stanton. Our completed Bio-Pyramid is featured in Figure 5-3.

REFLECT: The students and I reflected on how the Bio-Pyramid helped us to summarize Elizabeth Cady Stanton's life. Jerry said, "I liked using the Bio-Pyramid because it helped me to focus on one thing at a time. Usually when I have to do a summary my thoughts get all mixed up. This was organized." Manuel said, "I like that every line of the Bio-Pyramid is labeled, so we know what information we should add." Sophie said, "It's fun to try to put our ideas into just the right number of words." Then we discussed how we can use the Bio-Pyramid in other settings, such as Guided Comprehension Centers and Literature Circles.

Elizabeth
person's name

determined hardworking
two words describing the person

father wanted sons
three words describing the person's childhood

not being treated equally
four words indicating a problem the person had to overcome

first to demand women's suffrage
five words stating one of his/her accomplishments

spoke to New York State Legislature
six words stating a second accomplishment

in 1866 ran for seat in Congress
seven words stating a third accomplishment

because of her women eventually got to vote
eight words stating how humankind benefited from his/her accomplishments

FIGURE 5-3

STAGE 2 Teacher-Guided Small-Group Instruction

TEXT: *What's the Big Idea, Ben Franklin?* (Fritz, 1976)

(Texts varied according to the students' abilities.)

REVIEW: I began by reviewing with the students strategies all good readers use and focused on summarizing using Bio-Pyramids.

GUIDE: I guided students to revisit a text they had recently finished partner-reading, *What's the Big Idea, Ben Franklin?* I encouraged them to recall the highlights of the book and then guided them to work with a partner to complete the first three lines of their Bio-Pyramid. I observed as students began their work. When they finished this section, each pair summarized what they had written about Ben Franklin's life in lines one, two, and three. Ben and Matt said, "Benjamin Franklin was a creative and diplomatic man. As a child he had to work."

PRACTICE: To practice, students completed the remaining lines of their Bio-Pyramids independently. I circulated, observing what they were writing and providing feedback and assistance as needed. Then students shared their completed Bio-Pyramids and used them to orally summarize Ben Franklin's life. The Bio-Pyramid that Matt began with Ben and finished on his own is featured in Figure 5-4.

Ben Franklin
person's name

creative diplomat
two words describing the person

spent childhood working
three words describing the person's childhood

didn't like being apprentice
four words indicating a problem the person had to overcome

used kite to discover electricity
five words stating one of his/her accomplishments

was signer of Declaration of Independence
six words stating a second accomplishment

he published Poor Richard's Almanac in 1733
seven words stating a third accomplishment

he organized mail system, fire company, and hospital
eight words stating how humankind benefited from his/her accomplishments

FIGURE 5-4

REFLECT: We reflected on how Bio-Pyramids help us to remember specific information about people and how we can use that information to summarize people's lives.

Student-Facilitated Comprehension Centers

THEME CENTER: I left a variety of biographies and autobiographies at this center. Students selected titles and created Bio-Pyramids. When they completed their work, they met with a classmate, shared their Bio-Pyramids, and created oral or written summaries based on their work.

ART CENTER: After completing Bio-Pyramids, students used different media to create artistic representations of that person's life. We displayed the completed works in our class gallery.

Student-Facilitated Comprehension Routines

LITERATURE CIRCLES: Students jotted notes while reading their group-selected biography. When they finished reading the text, they completed a group Bio-Pyramid. Students discussed the Bio-Pyramid and then used it to create a summary of the person's life.

STAGE 3 Teacher-Facilitated Whole-Group Reflection and Goal Setting

SHARE: Students shared the Bio-Pyramids they had created during Stage Two in small groups. Then we toured the class gallery so students could review their Bio-Pyramid artistic representations.

REFLECT: We reflected on how Bio-Pyramids help us to remember and organize information to summarize a person's life. The students liked that they could have lines that were different from other students' but still have a Bio-Pyramid that accurately presented information about a person's life.

SET NEW GOALS: We decided that we were confident using the Bio-Pyramid to help summarize a person's life and decided we would like to learn another way to summarize.

Assessment Options

I used observation, the students' completed Bio-Pyramids, their artistic interpretations, and student self-reflections as assessments during this lesson. I also completed running records with a few students during guided reading. When working with special education students, I was careful to pay particular attention to individual students' needs. For example, I noticed some of the students needed special assistance to remain on task without becoming frustrated, so I paired them with a student of a higher ability. I also used colored dot stickers to help draw their attention to the different lines of the Bio-Pyramid. When working with ELL students, I allowed extra time for more specific and individualized instruction. I also adapted the Bio-Pyramid format and encouraged the ELL students to use it to sketch and label their responses. In both cases I assessed their strategy use through multiple informal measures, including observation, discussion, and sketched and written responses.

LESSON 4　Making Connections
Theme: Fantasy

STAGE 1　Teacher-Directed Whole-Group Instruction

TEXT: *Tuck Everlasting* (Babbitt, 1975)

EXPLAIN: I began by explaining the concept of Making Connections, noting that there are three different connections we can make—text-self, text-text, and text-world. I said, "We make text-self connections when we connect what we are reading to our own lives. For example, if I were reading a book about dogs, I would make a connection to dogs I know. If you were reading a book about dogs, what text-self connection could you make? Turn to your neighbor and share your text-self connection." All the students made text-self connections. Examples included "I would make a connection to my dog" and "I would make a connection to a dog I see every day in the park."

Then I said, "We make text-text connections when make a connection between what we are reading and other books we have read. For example, if we were reading a book about dogs, I would make a text-text connection between the book we were reading and *Murphy Meets the Treadmill*—a book about a yellow Lab who exercises on a treadmill. If we were reading a book about dogs, what book could you make a connection to? Turn to your neighbor and share your text-text connection." I monitored their responses and heard book titles including *Because of Winn Dixie, Old Yeller,* and *Call of the Wild.*

"The third kind of connection," I said, "is text-world. So, if we were reading a book about dogs and we wanted to make a text-world connection, we would need to think of the roles dogs play in our world. I might make a connection from the book to things we know about dogs in our world, for example, 'Dogs make good pets.' If we were reading *Murphy Meets the Treadmill* about the exercising dog, we could make a connection from the book to 'Exercise is good for animals and people.'"

Then I explained that Connection Stems (McLaughlin & Allen, 2002b) are phrases we can use at the beginning of sentences to help us make our connections. I shared the following Connection Stems with students:

> That reminds me of . . .
>
> I remember when . . .
>
> I have a connection . . .
>
> An experience I have had like that . . .
>
> I felt like that character when . . .
>
> If I were that character, I would . . .

I noted that, if I were making a text-self connection about the book on dogs, I could use a Connection Stem and say, "That reminds me of a dog I know . . ." or "I remember when my dog did something like that . . ."

DEMONSTRATE: I demonstrated by using a read-aloud, a think-aloud, and a poster of the Connection Stems (see Figure 5-5). I read the first three pages of Chapter 10 in *Tuck Everlasting* aloud. Then I used a think-aloud to point out my connections to the beginning of this chapter. I said, "The first Connection Stem says, 'That reminds me of . . .' At this point I could make a text-self connection because these pages talk about a mouse being in the house and I once had a mouse in my home. I didn't welcome the mouse like they did in the story, but my connection will help remind me of some of the details in the story. I will write, 'That reminds me of the time I had a mouse in my home.'" The students laughed as I wrote my connection on the poster. As I continued to read, Mary said, "This part of the story reminds me of my aunt's house. The description is almost exactly what her house looks like. It looks like a mess." I said, "That's a fine text-self connection, and you used the Connection Stem 'This reminds me of. . .'" As I continued to read through the chapter I stopped periodically to discuss my connections. I said, "The next stem says

'I remember when. . .' I have a text-text connection at this point." On the poster I wrote, "I remember when Harry Potter had to hide from different people within Hogwarts." The students had various connections that they also wanted to share.

GUIDE: After reading Chapter 11 of *Tuck Everlasting* to the students, I directed their attention back to the Connection Stem poster. I said, "The next stem says, 'I have a connection. . .' Remember to try to think of text-self, text-text, and text-world connections." I completed the Connection Stem by saying, "I have a connection to the beginning of the chapter. Winnie is eating with the family and she is unsure of how to eat with them without being rude, and then she realized there were no rules for how they ate. This reminds me of when I went to a really fancy restaurant when I was very young and I watched everyone else to see what fork they were using and how they ate." I explained to students that this was an example of a text-self connection because I was able to make a connection with something that had happened in my own life.

We Can Make Connections!

There are 3 kinds of connections:

1. Text—Self
2. Text—Text
3. Text—World

These stems can help us make connections:

1. That reminds me of…
2. I remember when…
3. I have a connection…
4. I felt like that character when…
5. I read about a similar character in…
6. I read about this topic before in…
7. An experience I've had like that…

FIGURE 5-5

Again I showed students the connections I had to the text so far and encouraged them to turn to a neighbor and share one of their own connections to the text. The students shared their connections with their partner, and a few shared with the class. The students and I had a discussion about each of the connections and whether they were text-self, text-text, or text-world. Most of the connections were text-self, so I encouraged students to think of other books they could connect to and how the information in the book related to the world in which we live. After this, students shared more connections with their partners. Avi said, "I have a connection to the family wanting to take Winnie out on the boat. My family has a boat on the lake and we love to go out on it." Avi and the class decided that his connection was text-self because it was a personal connection to an experience in his life.

PRACTICE: I continued to read the novel aloud to the students. As I read Chapter 12, the students thought of different connections they had to the story and shared them. Mark said, "For one of my connections I wrote, 'I felt like the character when Winnie found out that the family had everlasting life and she was upset and confused. I remember when my family tried to tell me my grandfather was really sick and I didn't understand and was confused." The class continued to do this for the rest of the novel, and as they became more comfortable with making connections they were able to tell the type of connection it was.

REFLECT: We reflected on how important making connections was and how it helped us to understand what we read. The students decided that the more connections they made to the different events in the novel, the better they understood the story. The students talked about sharing their connections and how much they liked hearing the class's connections as well. Finally, we discussed how we could use Connection Stems with other types of text.

(STAGE 2) Teacher-Guided Small-Group Instruction

TEXT: *Harry Potter and the Prisoner of Azkaban* (Rowling, 1999) (Texts varied according to the students' abilities.)

REVIEW: I reminded students about the strategies good readers use and focused on Connection Stems. We reviewed the different types of connections: text-self, text-text, and text-world. We also talked about how making connections helps us understand what we read.

GUIDE: I introduced *Harry Potter and the Prisoner of Azkaban* by sharing the cover and reading the first three pages. The students had already read the first two books in the Harry Potter series, so they were very quick to make text-text connections with the characters and setting. Haylie said, "I remember that in both of the Harry Potter books I read, it started with Harry at the Dursleys' house." The class shared different connections about the events in the first few pages. I continued to read the chapter aloud and asked the students to take note of any connections they had to the text. At the end of the chapter students shared their thoughts and connections.

PRACTICE: The students read Chapter 2 and made various connections as they read. The students also noted what type of connections they were. I encouraged students to make at least three connections as they read. We stopped periodically so they could share their connections with a partner.

REFLECT: We reflected on how Connection Stems helped us to understand what we read and how we would use Connection Stems with other texts in other settings.

Student-Facilitated Comprehension Centers

ART CENTER: Students read theme-related books and engaged in Draw and Label Visualizations (see page 200), sketching and sharing their connections with a partner.

THEME CENTER: I placed various theme-related texts at various levels at this center along with copies of the Connection Stems. The students whisper-read the text with a partner, stopping periodically to make and share their connections.

WRITING CENTER: Students used their Connection Stems to write a paragraph about the connections they had to *Harry Potter and the Prisoner of Azkaban* or to *Tuck Everlasting*.

Student-Facilitated Comprehension Routines

LITERATURE CIRCLES: The Connector (see page 13) used Connection Stems to share ideas with the circle members. The members made connections as they read in preparation for Literature Circle.

STAGE 3 Teacher-Facilitated Whole-Group Reflection and Goal Setting

SHARE: The students shared their completed Connection Stems from Stage Two in small groups. They seemed to really enjoy sharing their connections and connection types.

REFLECT: We reflected on how Connection Stems helped us to make connections from the texts we were reading to other texts, the world, and ourselves. We also reflected on the way these connections helped us to understand what we read. Students discussed that hearing classmates' connections also helped them to understand what they were reading.

SET NEW GOALS: The students decided to extend their goal and learn how to make connections while reading informational text.

Assessment Options

I observed students as they made their connections in Stages One and Two. I also assessed students on their completed Connection Stems. The completed Connection Stems showed me the students' abilities to use this technique, and I made notes on their progress. I also completed running records with selected students during guided reading. When working with special education students, I encouraged them to engage in Draw and Label Connections so they could sketch their connections and write a sentence to label them. I also paired them with a strong reader in partner settings. When working with ELLs, I provided assistance as needed and monitored their responses to ensure that they understood the distinctions among the three different kinds of connections.

LESSON 5 Previewing
Theme: The Holocaust

STAGE 1 Teacher-Directed Whole-Group Instruction

TEXT: *Lily's Crossing* (Giff, 1997)

EXPLAIN: I explained to the students that when we preview a text we can activate prior knowledge, make predictions, and set a purpose for reading. Then I said, "One way that we can preview text is to write Story Impressions. When we create Story Impressions, we use a series of seven to ten clues taken from the story to write our impression of the story. The clues are about different story elements: characters, setting, problem, and solution. We write Story Impressions in small groups before we read the original story. They help us to make connections with the story elements and provide a framework for our writing." Then I explained that the clues had to be used in the order in which they were presented, because that's the order in which they appeared in the original story. Finally, I said, "We usually write Story Impressions about books, but today we're going to write ours about the next chapter in our read-aloud novel, *Lily's Crossing.*

DEMONSTRATE: I demonstrated by using an overhead projector, a think-aloud, and a Story Impression blackline (see page 198). I began by showing students a list of words I had taken from Chapter 6 of *Lily's Crossing*. The words were:

Lily ⟶ radio ⟶ soldiers ⟶ living room ⟶ waves ⟶ seagull ⟶ train

I reminded students that these words came from various story elements—characters, setting, problem, and solution. I also reminded them that the sequence of the clues in the Story Impression was very important. I showed students the arrows between the words and noted that this was the order in which the clues appeared in the original chapter. I read the first word, *Lily*, and said, "I already know Lily is our main character, so I will start by writing 'One day Lily. . .'" The students used information from earlier chapters to start a discussion about what Lily might be doing in this chapter. I continued to use a think-aloud to finish the first sentence of my Story Impression. I wrote, "One day Lily was thinking about the war and how it would change her life." The students agreed that this was a good start. I looked at the next two clues and added, "Then she heard on Gram's radio that the soldiers were invading other parts of Europe." I showed students that I added details to the words to make my prediction but still used the clues in the order in which they were presented.

GUIDE: To guide students, I asked them to look at the next clue—*living room*—and I told them to think about how the story might continue. I reminded them that they needed to think of the story elements while they were creating their Impressions. The students shared their thoughts in their small groups, and when they were finished we decided on "Lily ran into the living room to ask Gram if the soldiers would invade the United States, but Gram was sleeping."

PRACTICE: To practice, students took on the role of "detectives" and used the remaining clues to create the rest of the Story Impression. For example, for their next section, Mario, Sabrina, Jim, and Maria wrote, "Lily decided to walk to the beach. She sat on the sand watching the waves and a seagull flying overhead. She wondered if she should tell Gram what she had heard on the radio." Then students wrote about the final clue—*train*.

Here is the Story Impression we began as a class and that Mario, Sabrina, Jim, and Maria completed:

> One day Lily was thinking about the war and how it would change her life. Then she heard on Gram's radio that the soldiers were invading other parts of Europe. Lily ran into the living room to ask Gram if the soldiers would invade the United States, but Gram was sleeping. Lily decided to walk to the beach. She sat on the sand watching the waves and a seagull flying overhead. She wondered if she should tell Gram what she had heard on the radio. As it grew dark, Lily decided to go home. On her way she stopped at the train tracks and wondered if soldiers would take the train to her town.

When all the small groups had finished writing their Story Impressions, each group shared what it had written. We applauded after each group's presentation. The Story Impressions were all different, even though they had used the same clues in the same order. Each impression was also interesting. After students finished sharing, I explained that I would be reading Chapter 6 aloud, and when I finished we would compare and contrast what happened in our Story Impressions with what actually happened in the chapter.

As I read, I stopped at several points and we had a class discussion to talk about the similarities and differences between our Story Impressions and the novel. For example, the chapter could be summarized as follows:

> Lily, the main character, uses a key to gain entry into her best friend's house. Her best friend, Margaret, and her family moved to Detroit because jobs were tough to find during the war. Margaret left the key so Lily could have a peaceful place to write stories. Lily's father has just told her that he is leaving Rockaway, New York, and going overseas to help rebuild after the war is over. Lily is saddened by the thought of her father leaving her with Gram, but she tries to make it look as if it doesn't bother her. She tries to stay in the attic of Margaret's house to write, but she decides to try to see if her father's train back to the city has left yet. She runs to the viaduct hoping that her father will see her and wave good-bye.

The actual story was very different from most of the impressions the students had written prompting them to look at where and how the "clue words" were used. After I finished reading the chapter, we concluded our discussion, orally retold what had happened in Chapter 6, and predicted what might happen next.

REFLECT: The students were very excited about Story Impressions and they all agreed that this technique really helped them to make predictions, learn vocabulary, and focus on what they were about to read. We discussed the importance of previewing a text, and students said they were eager to write Story Impressions again. We also talked about what it would be like to write Story Impressions before reading our next novel.

STAGE 2 Teacher-Guided Small-Group Instruction

TEXT: *The Butterfly* (Polacco, 2000) (Texts varied according to the students' abilities.)

REVIEW: I reviewed the different strategies good readers use and focused on previewing using Story Impressions. I reminded students that we would be using clues taken from the original text to create a prediction, or impression, of the text we were about to read.

GUIDE: I showed students the cover of *The Butterfly,* written by Patricia Polacco. We had a discussion about the illustration on the cover and what the title of the book might mean. Tulio said, "I think that the girl on the front cover looks sad. I also see the Nazi symbol in the lower left-hand corner so I think she is sad because the Nazis took over her town." Rachel said, "I think that the little girl is going to find a butterfly near her house and that it will make her happy during a sad time."

Next, I reminded students that the clues I was about to share were taken from *The Butterfly*, and they needed to be used in the order in which they were presented, because that's the way they appear in the original story. Then I shared the clues with students, reminded them that the clues were related to the story elements, and reminded them again that the words needed to be used in the order in which they were listed. The clues in the box at right were on the list.

I asked students to look at the words and start to think about their Story Impression. I reminded students that Story Impressions are written in small groups, so our group would be writing our impression together. The students looked at the first two words, and we decided to write, "In her bedroom, Monique sat and wondered about what she would do the next day." I guided students to use the next two words to

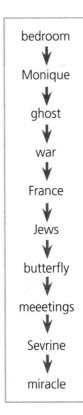

bedroom
↓
Monique
↓
ghost
↓
war
↓
France
↓
Jews
↓
butterfly
↓
meeetings
↓
Sevrine
↓
miracle

create the problem of the story. We wrote, "As she wondered, Monique thought she saw a ghost. He was dressed in a uniform, and Monique thought he may have been a soldier in some war."

PRACTICE: To practice, students used the remaining clues to complete the Story Impression. Then Jim read it aloud. Here is the Story Impression that Tulio, Hannah, Lisa, and Jim wrote:

> In her bedroom, Monique sat and wondered about what she would do the next day. As she wondered, Monique thought she saw a ghost. He was dressed in a uniform, and Monique thought he may have been a soldier in some war. The ghost said that he had been to France and that the war should be coming to an end. Monique asked if the Jews were going to be freed and he said he thought they were. He mentioned that he had seen a butterfly and that was a good sign. He saw many people flying to different meetings about ending the war. It was at Sevrine, France, that the miracle happened and the war finally ended.

Next, we whisper-read the text, stopping after every three pages to make new predictions or to change the ones we had already made. The students continued to do this until they had finished reading the text. Then we discussed how our Story Impression was similar to and different from the story Patricia Polacco had written.

REFLECT: We talked about writing Story Impressions. The students enjoyed working with a small group to write a prediction using the clues. Many of the students asked when we would be using this technique again. They also mentioned that they enjoyed seeing how their predictions compared to and contrasted with the original story. We talked about how some groups' predictions were similar to the original story and some groups had very different ideas about how the story would turn out. Harold said, "I like Story Impressions. The clues help us to know what to write about next. Then we can see how our story is like and unlike the original story."

Student-Facilitated Comprehension Centers

THEME CENTER: I placed a variety of theme-related books at various levels at this center, along with Story Impression blacklines. I had a list of clues already printed on the blacklines, which I tucked into each volume. First, students worked in small groups to create Story Impressions. Then they partner-read the text, using the Read–Pause–Predict pattern (see pages 66–70). After reading the story, students compared their Story Impression with the original story. The students shared their completed Story Impressions in Stage Three.

POETRY CENTER: The students used lists of poem clues to write Poem Impressions. I placed a variety of story poems and clue lists at this center. The students worked with a partner and used the clue lists to write Poem Impressions. Then they read the story poems and compared and contrasted what they had written with what they had read. When they finished reading the text, they wrote a summary in poetic form. The students shared their completed poems in Stage Three.

Student-Facilitated Comprehension Routines

LITERATURE CIRCLES: Each Literature Circle group was given a list of clues for the next chapter they would be reading. The students worked together to create their Story Impression and wrote their prediction on poster paper. Next, students partner-read the text and had a group discussion about the predictions and the actual events in the story.

STAGE 3 Teacher-Facilitated Whole-Group Reflection and Goal Setting

SHARE: Students shared their Story Impressions from Stage Two. Each group also shared ideas about using Story Impressions with chapters, stories, and poems.

REFLECT: First we reflected on the benefits of using Story Impressions to preview text. The students noted that it was fun to use clues about the story elements to predict what may happen in the story. Students enjoyed writing as a group. They also said that it was very helpful to compare and contrast their prediction with the original story, because it helped them to see different perspectives. They also thought their stories were often better than the original stories!

SET NEW GOALS: The students felt confident using the Story Impression, so we decided to learn another technique for previewing text.

Assessment Options

I observed students throughout all the stages in this lesson. I noted their verbal contributions as well as their completed Story Impressions. During guided reading, I completed running records with selected students. When working with special education students I made sure that they were partnered with a stronger reader within the Story Impression small groups. I also used color-coded dots to draw their attention to different parts of the Story Impression blackline. The students seemed to enjoy writing the Story Impressions—perhaps because they were brief and the clues provided direction. When I was working with ELLs, I placed them in small groups with a few stronger readers. I also provided individual assistance as necessary.

LESSON 6 Visualization
Theme: Poetry

STAGE 1 Teacher-Directed Whole-Group Instruction

TEXTS: "The Raven" by Edgar Allan Poe, in *A Child's Introduction to Poetry* (Driscoll, 2003)

EXPLAIN: To start, I explained to the students that visualizing is a very important strategy good readers use to comprehend. I explained that visualizing means creating pictures in our minds based on verbal and written cues. Next, I introduced Draw and Label Visualizations to students and shared the blackline on the overhead (see page 200). I explained the blackline by showing where we would be sketching the pictures we created in our minds and where we would write a detailed sentence describing our sketch. We discussed the skills necessary to sketch what we were picturing in our minds and decided that we didn't need to have perfect drawings to express our thoughts. I showed the students examples of basic shapes and lines that we could all use to create our sketches.

DEMONSTRATE: I demonstrated Draw and Label Visualizations by using a read-aloud of Edgar Allan Poe's "The Raven," a think-aloud, and a poster-size laminated copy of the Draw and Label Visualizations blackline. I introduced the poem by providing some brief background information about Edgar Allan Poe. For example, I said, "Edgar Allan Poe lived in the 1800s, and he is best known for his poems and short stories. He is often credited with inventing the detective story." I was surprised that several of the students knew about Poe. Then I shared the title of the poem. (I didn't share the illustrations with students before the read-aloud because I did not want to influence their mental images.) Next, I read a section of the poem aloud and thought aloud about the mental image I was creating as I read. Referring to the first stanza of the poem, I said, "In the beginning of the poem I formed a mental image of the room the man was in, and I know this will probably be the main setting of the story poem. I also think that since the poem is titled 'The Raven,' a bird will appear at some point in the poem." As I read more of the poem, I continued to share my mental images with students. These included the lonely state of the narrator, the frustration he seemed to be facing, and his irritation toward the raven.

After I read the first stanza of the poem, I began to sketch my initial mental images on the poster-size Draw and Label Visualizations blackline. I sketched a large, empty room with a man seated by an open window. At this time, I also asked students if they thought I should add anything to my sketch, and they all agreed that I needed to somehow show that it was nighttime. I agreed and drew a moon in the open window. I reminded students that our ideas were more important than our drawing abilities and that it was fine to use simple lines and shapes to sketch. Then I wrote this sentence as the label for my sketch: "The narrator in this poem appears to be lonely and extremely frustrated about the world in which he lives." I drew the students' attention to my label, and we discussed the importance of using a complete sentence, proper spelling, and capitalization when labeling. Then I read the second stanza of the poem and engaged in another Draw and Label Visualization. I said, "As I read this stanza of the poem, I pictured a dark, quiet room with a man sitting in it wondering where his beloved Lenore had gone."

GUIDE: I read aloud the next two stanzas of the poem and guided students to create their own mental images and sketch what they were thinking as I read. The students sketched using pencils and copies of the Draw and Label Visualizations blackline that I had provided. Mary asked, "Is it okay if I do two sketches if I am visualizing two different things?" I told her to do both sketches if she was visualizing two things and to include both visualizations in her sentence. The students each sketched what they were thinking as I read and then used a think-aloud to share their thoughts with a partner. When they were finished, I sketched on the poster-size Draw and Label Visualizations blackline the mental images I had as I read the third and fourth stanzas. Next, the students and I shared our sketches and our labels. Most of the sketches included pictures of the raven and various parts of a lonely room. Even though some of the students included different details, they all depicted the bird as a very menacing creature. Joanna said that the bird's constantly repeating the word "Nevermore" was similar to a time when her younger brother had kept repeating everything everyone in the family said. Then we discussed how our personal experiences affect the way we see things.

PRACTICE: The students practiced by continuing to create Draw and Label Visualizations and sharing them with their partners as I continued to read the rest of the poem aloud. When I finished reading the poem, the students finished up their sketches and labels and we shared our images with the class. Many of the students had similar sketches and enjoyed sharing the similarities. I also finished my sketches and labels and shared them with the class. We discussed the amount of frustration in the narrator's voice and the feeling of darkness in the poem. The students prompted a discussion about the communication between the narrator and the bird. Lucinda noticed that the language in the poem was different from the language we use today, and we talked about the time period in which the poem was written and the educational background of Edgar Allan Poe, including that he had spent five years in school in England. We decided that the amount of detail Poe used in his poetry made it easier for us to picture the events in our minds, which also it made it easier to do our sketches. Examples of student work are featured in Figure 5-5.

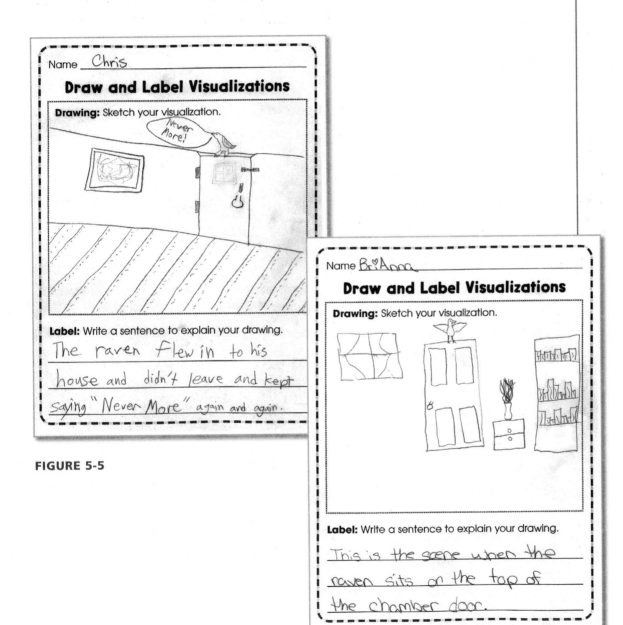

FIGURE 5-5

REFLECT: We reflected on how using Draw and Label Visualizations helped us to imagine the story and understand what we were reading. We also discussed how helpful Draw and Label Visualizations would be as we read various texts throughout the year.

STAGE 2 Teacher-Guided Small-Group Instruction

TEXT: "My Shadow" (from *World's Best-Loved Poetry*, 2002) (Texts varied according to students' abilities.)

REVIEW: I quickly reviewed the reading comprehension strategies good readers use and focused on visualizing and Draw and Label Visualizations. Then I introduced the new poem, "My Shadow," by Robert Louis Stevenson. We briefly discussed the title. Hannah said, "The title reminds me of a really sunny day last year when I jumped around and tried to lose my shadow." All of the students smiled when they heard this. It seems at some point they had all tried to lose their shadow. Miguel said, "You cannot lose a shadow it always goes with you," and everyone smiled in agreement. Next, I asked students to create mental images and sketch and label what they were visualizing as I read the title and first stanza. I also sketched and labeled my mental image. When we finished, the students shared their Draw and Label Visualizations, and then I shared my sketch of a boy with a shadow peeking out behind him and my label: "The shadow follows the young, carefree boy everywhere he goes."

GUIDE: I gave students a few minutes to read the rest of the poem silently, then I guided them to partner-read the next stanza of the poem, create mental images, and sketch and label their visualizations. I offered assistance as needed. I noticed that many of the students were excited to share their sketches and labels with their partners.

PRACTICE: The students continued this pattern with the next two stanzas of the poem. At the end of each stanza, the students stopped to individually sketch their mental images. Then students shared their sketches and labels with their partners. I monitored their discussion and provided assistance when necessary. Examples of Jerre's and Susan's Draw and Label Visualizations are featured in Figure 5-6.

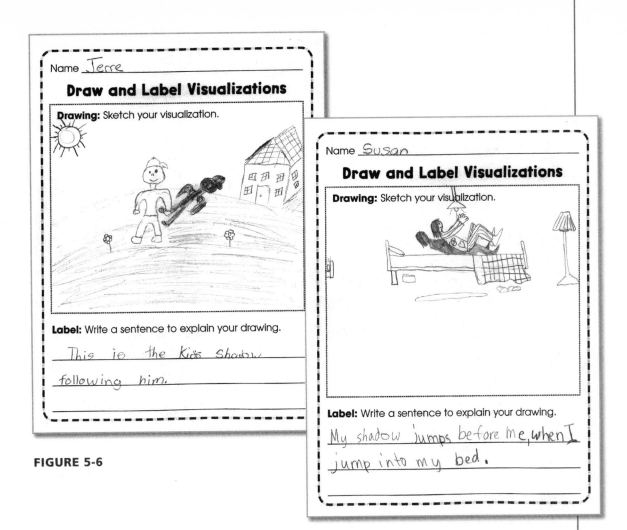

FIGURE 5-6

REFLECT: The students engaged in one more reading of the poem. They whisper-read as I walked around the room listening to a few students and making notes about their fluency. When everyone was finished reading, we did an oral retelling of the poem. After this, we discussed how everyone had their own personal visualizations even though we all had read the same poem. We discussed how using Draw and Label Visualizations helped us to understand what we were reading, and we all agreed it would help us remember the content better because we would have mental images about the text in our minds. All the students agreed that when they were completing this activity they were thinking of a day when they saw their own shadow (see Figure 5-6).

Student-Facilitated Comprehension Centers

LISTENING CENTER: Students worked with a partner and chose two poems to listen to on tape. The tapes chimed at three different points so the students could pause and complete Draw and Label Visualizations.

THEME CENTER: I left a wide variety of poetry books of various levels at this center. Students selected two poems and engaged in Draw and Label Visualizations. When they finished, partners shared their completed visualizations.

WRITING CENTER: Students wrote poems, indicating at least two points where readers should stop to complete their Draw and Label Visualizations. Peers used the student-authored poems as the basis of their visualizations.

Student-Facilitated Comprehension Routines

POETRY CIRCLES: The students read a variety of poems by a group-selected author and completed Draw and Label Visualizations as they read. The students used their completed visualizations as discussion prompts in their poetry circles.

CROSS-AGE READING EXPERIENCES: Students worked with cross-age partners to read poems and create Draw and Label Visualizations. The students stopped at designated points to create mental images and sketch and label their visualizations. (I had previously inserted sticky-notes in the poems to indicate where to stop.) Then the students shared and discussed their creations with their cross-age buddies.

(STAGE 3)   Teacher-Facilitated Whole-Group Reflection and Goal Setting

SHARE: The students shared their Draw and Label Visualizations in small groups. Then we had a whole-group discussion about our work.

REFLECT: We reflected on how much we enjoyed using Draw and Label Visualizations and that we liked to be able to create mental images and sketch and label them, especially since it helped us understand what we were reading.

SET NEW GOALS: The students were very confident in their ability to engage in Draw and Label Visualizations with poetry, and their work bore this out. We decided that we would try this technique with informational text.

Assessment Options

I observed students as they worked in whole-group, small-group, partner, and individual settings. I made various notes about students' abilities throughout the stages of this lesson. The students and I held brief conferences about their self-assessments from the centers and routines. I also reviewed and commented on each Draw and Label Visualization the students completed, and completed running records with selected students during guided reading. When working with special education students, I reminded students to create pictures in their minds while reading. I suggested they close their eyes and picture what we were reading about. I was also careful to extend the amount of time needed to complete the Draw and Label Visualizations, when needed. When working with ELLs, I paired students with peers of stronger abilities in partner settings. The students seemed quite confident in their drawing and clearly communicated their ideas. I assessed the students based on their effort and their progress throughout the lesson.

Final Thoughts on This Chapter

The topics of the previous chapters—word study, fluency, and vocabulary—all contribute to students' comprehension, but this chapter focused on specific reading comprehension strategies. The goal was for students to learn a repertoire of strategies to call upon as needed when reading independently. In the next chapter we summarize our goals and examine some of the challenges we face as we teach word study, fluency, vocabulary, and comprehension in the intermediate grades.

What can we read to learn more about teaching comprehension?

Farstrup, A., & Samuels, S. (Eds.). (2002). *What research has to say about reading instruction* (3rd ed.). Newark, DE: International Reading Association.

Kamil, M. L., Mosenthal, P. B., Pearson, P. D., & Barr, R. (Eds.). (2000). *Handbook of reading research* (Vol. 3). Mahwah, NJ: Lawrence Erlbaum Associates.

McLaughlin, M., & Allen, M. B. (2002a). *Guided Comprehension: A teaching model for grades 3–8.* Newark, DE: International Reading Association.

Continuing the Journey

As reading professionals, we know that teaching is a lifelong learning experience and we fully embrace it. We constantly question what we know and how we can use our knowledge to benefit our students. We are always looking for new ways to motivate them, and we are constantly searching for up-to-the-minute information that will help them to learn to the best of their abilities. Teaching word study, fluency, vocabulary, and comprehension will help us do that.

As we have noted at various points throughout this book, none of these elements of literacy is new to us. What is new is the current emphasis on teaching them, and from our perspective, that is a good thing. As reading teachers, we have all known the joy of seeing a student who once struggled comprehend well for the first time. We have heard students' fluency continue to develop in the intermediate grades because they were nurtured by fluent reading models. We understand that vocabulary is an essential component of comprehension, and we know that the latest research tells us that intermediate-grade students are very capable of learning and using comprehension strategies.

We are living in an age of possibility. We know that teaching these elements of reading will help our students. Yet challenges remain. Finding time for and access to meaningful professional development isn't always easy. Funding for classroom support (reading specialists, literacy coaches, aides) and innovative materials and the space in which to use them is also not always easy to come by. In addition, reducing the number of assessments we give to fewer, more meaningful measures that will provide information about our students and inform our teaching is something we should strive for.

And yes, as we try to keep pace with these challenges, we may occasionally need to be reminded that we, as teachers, are the single most important influence on our students' learning (International Reading Association, 2000; National Commission on Teaching and America's Future, 1997; Ruddell, 2004). We think that information cannot be emphasized enough.

In our introduction, we thanked you for joining us in our quest to help our students reach their greatest potential. We thank you now for continuing to honor that commitment.

Appendix A

Ideas for Teaching Word Study

Cinquain

A cinquain is a form poem that contains five lines, each requiring the use of a different part of speech. In these poems writers are required to use nouns, adjectives, participles, phrases, and synonyms. The focus of a cinquain is the noun that appears on line one and its synonym, which appears on line five. In addition to providing direction for students' writing, cinquains help students to demonstrate their understanding of vocabulary, synonyms, and parts of speech and how they function.

(See Chapter 2, Lesson 2, pages 33 and 34 for completed cinquains.)

Diamante

A diamante is a form poem shaped like a diamond that contains seven lines, each requiring the use of a different part of speech. In these poems writers are required to use nouns, adjectives, participles, phrases, and antonyms. The focus of a diamante is the noun that appears on line one and its antonym, which appears on line seven. The first three lines of the diamante describe the noun on line one; the final three lines describe the antonym on line seven. The focus of the poem changes on line four. In addition to providing direction for students' writing, diamantes help students to demonstrate their understanding of vocabulary, antonyms, and parts of speech and how they function.

(See Chapter 2, Lesson 5, pages 47 and 48 for completed diamantes.)

Homonyms

According to *The Literacy Dictionary*, a homonym is "a word with different origin and meaning but the same oral or written form as one or more other words, as *bear* (an animal) vs. *bear* (to support) vs. *bare* (exposed). Note: In this sense, homonyms includes homophones and homographs" (Harris & Hodges, 1995, p. 109). When working with homonyms, students learn the words' meanings, spellings, and pronunciations, as well as how to use them in context. The following are examples of homonyms: ate/eight; aunt/ant; scent/cent/sent; one/won; peace/piece; and to/too/two.

(See Chapter 2, Lesson 3, pages 36–40, for sample lesson. See extended list of homonyms on page 171.)

Prefixes

A prefix is a type of affix that involves adding a syllable or letter(s) to the beginning of a word to change its meaning or part of speech. Working with prefixes helps students to understand structural analysis. The following are examples of prefixes: ad- (to, toward); ante- (before); anti- (against); extra- (beyond); micro- (small).

(See Chapter 2, Lesson 6, pages 52 and 53, for student work involving prefixes. See extended list of prefixes on page 172.)

Root Mapping

This technique provides an overview of a Latin or Greek root and words that are derived from it. A root is selected to be the focus of the map. Then words containing that root are added at the ends of branches that connect to the root. As the map is completed, it has the potential to continue growing, because as each new word is added, other words may branch from it. The following are examples of roots: bio (life); chromo (color); psycho (mind); thermo (heat); zoo (animal).

(See Chapter 2, Lesson 1, page 28, for a sample Root Map. See extended list of roots on page 174.)

Suffixes

A suffix is a type of affix that involves adding a syllable or letter(s) to the end of a word to change its meaning or part of speech. Specifically, according to *The Literacy Dictionary*, a suffix is "an affix attached to the end of a base, root, or stem that changes the meaning or grammatical function of the word" (Harris & Hodges, 1995, p. 246).

Working with suffixes helps students to understand structural analysis. The following are examples of suffixes: -able (can be done); -ic (relating to); -ist (one who practices); -ology (study of).

(See Chapter 2, Lesson 4, pages 42 and 44, for student work involving suffixes. See extended list of suffixes on page 173.)

Name _____ Date _____

Cinquain

_____

one word – noun

_____ _____

two adjectives describing line one

_____ _____ _____

three *-ing* words telling actions of line one

_____ _____ _____ _____

four-word phrase describing a feeling related to line one

_____

one word – synonym or reference to line one

Diamante

_____

one word – noun

_____ _____

two adjectives describing line one

_____ _____ _____

three *-ing* words telling actions of line one

_____ _____ _____ _____

four nouns – two relating to line one, two relating to line seven

_____ _____ _____

three *-ing* words telling actions of line seven

_____ _____

two adjectives describing line seven

_____

one word – antonym of line one

© McLaughlin, Homeyer, & Sassaman. (2006) *Research-Based Reading Lessons: Grades 4–6.* New York: Scholastic. Page 170

Homonym List

accept/except	ad/add	affect/effect
ant/aunt	ate/eight	bear/bare
brake/break	bread/bred	by/bye/buy
carrot/carat	cent/scent/sent	cereal/serial
chews/choose	choral/coral	discreet/discrete
eye/I	flea/flee	flower/flour
fourth/forth	hare/hair	herd/heard
hire/higher	hoarse/horse	hole/whole
its/it's	knead/need	knew/new
knight/night	know/no	knows/nose
maize/maze	meet/meat/mete	one/won
pair/pear	piece/peace	plain/plane
principle/principal	rain/rein/reign	right/write/rite
ring/wring	role/roll	sea/see
sew/so	soared/sword	stair/stare
there/their/they're	threw/through	to/too/two
vain/vein	wail/whale	wait/weight
weather/whether	whose/who's	your/you're

Prefix List

PREFIX	MEANING	EXAMPLE
ab-,abs-, a-	from, away	abstain
anti-	against	antifreeze
auto-	self	autobiography
bi-	two	bimonthly
con-	with	concert
contra-	against	contraband
di-	two	diameter
dis-	opposite	disrespect
ex-	out, from	excavate
extra-	beyond	extracurricular
in-, il-, im-, ir-	not; in, within	immature
inter-	between	interstate
intra-	within	intramurals
mis-	bad	misbehave
mono-	single	monotone
non-	not, opposite from	nonviolent
omni-	all	omnipotent
post-	after	postpone
pre-	before	predetermine
re-	again	reappear
semi-	half	semicircle
sub-	under	submarine
un-	not	unwilling

Suffix List

SUFFIX	MEANING	EXAMPLE
-able, -ible	can be done	comfortable
-al, -ial	relating to	personal
-ation, -ition, -ion, -tion	act, process of	animation
-dom	quality/state	freedom
-ed	past tense for verbs	voted
-en	made of	wooden
-er	one who	dancer
-ful	full of	hopeful
-ic	relating to	characteristic
-ile	quality/state	juvenile
-ist	one who practices	zoologist
-ity, -ty	state of	infinity
-ive, -itive, -ative	adjective form of a noun	quantitative
-less	without	homeless
-ly	characteristic of	happily
-ment	action or process	excitement
-ness	condition of	sadness
-ology	study	biology
-ous, -eous, -ious	quality, state	joyous
-s, -es	more than one	desks
-tion	quality/state	preservation
-y	characterized by	jumpy

Word Roots List

ROOT	MEANING	EXAMPLE
anthropo	man	anthropology
astro	star	astronaut
bio	life	biology
cardio	heart	cardiologist
cede	go	precede
demos	people	democracy
derma	skin	dermatologist
dyna	power	dynamic
geo	earth	geology
hydro	water	hydroplane
hypno	sleep	hypnosis
magni	great, big	magnify
man(u)	hand	manuscript
mono	one	monoplane
ortho	straight	orthodontist
psycho	mind	psychology
script	write	manuscript
terra	earth	terrace
thermo	heat	thermometer
zoo	animal	zoology

Appendix B

Ideas for Teaching Fluency

Choral Reading

In Choral Reading, the teacher and the students read together. When engaging in choral reading, the individual reader feels less pressure than she may feel reading aloud alone, so there is more of a tendency to focus on the fluent manner in which the poem or text segment is being read. Participating in Choral Reading also provides everyone with good fluency models.

(See Chapter 3, Lesson 6, pages 85–89.)

The Fluent Reading Model

Providing fluent reading models for students helps them become fluent readers. Teachers, parents, cross-age volunteers, and books on tape can all be good fluency models for students.

(See Chapter 3, Lesson 5, pages 80–84.)

Pattern Partner Reading

Pattern Partner Reading provides a structure for focused, strategic, interactive partner reading of narrative and informational text. This technique involves two students reading together with each taking a turn reading aloud. Before they begin reading, the students choose (or the teacher suggests) a pattern to use while reading. The patterns are strategy-based and include ideas such as Read–Pause–Question, Read–Pause–Sketch, Read–Pause–Retell or -Summarize, Read–Pause–Make Connections, and Read–Pause–Say Something. When the students engage in Pattern Partner Reading, a partner reads a segment of the text, they both pause, and then they apply the strategy. For example, in the Read–Pause–Retell or -Summarize pattern, partner one would read, both students would pause, and partner two would retell or summarize what had been read. Then reading would continue and the roles would be reversed. Pattern Partner Reading helps to keep both readers focused on the text.

(See Chapter 3, Lesson 2, pages 66–70.)

Radio Reading

Radio Reading is similar to Readers Theater, because in both activities students read scripts, using their voices to communicate the scripts' meanings. What makes Radio Reading distinctive is that sound effects are added. The goal is to use the sound effects to create the impression of an old-time radio show in which both voices and sound effects are used to help communicate the script's meaning.

(See Chapter 3, Lesson 4 , pages 76–78 for examples of scripts.)

Readers Theater

Readers Theater does not involve producing a class play; instead it is like a read-through of a script. A narrator often introduces the work, sets the scene, and provides transitional information during the performance. The readers use their voices to create the scene and bring the characters to life. Books that have a lot of dialogue can be used for Readers Theater. A number of Web sites also provide scripts for this technique.

(See Chapter 3, Lesson 1, pages 59, 61, and 63–64 for sample scripts.)

Repeated Readings

Repeated readings of text help students read it more fluently. The process "consists of reading a short, meaningful passage several times until a satisfactory level of fluency is reached. Then the procedure is practiced with a new passage" (Samuels, 1979, p. 376). This improves comprehension, because as the reading becomes more fluent, less emphasis is placed on decoding and more on comprehension.

(See Chapter 3, Lesson 3, page 71–75, for an adaptation of Samuels's Repeated Readings.)

Appendix C

Vocabulary-Building Strategies, Teaching Ideas, and Blacklines

STRATEGY	TEACHING IDEA	PAGE	BLACKLINE
Knowing How Words Work	Concept of Definition Map	178	184
	Context Clues	179	185
	Probable Passages	180	186
	Semantic Map	181	187
	Semantic Question Map	182	188
	Semantic Map Summary	181, 182	189
	Vocabulary Bookmark Technique	183	190

(TEACHING IDEA) Concept of Definition Map

Comprehension Strategies: Knowing How Words Work,
Summarizing (See blackline, page 184.)

TEXT: Expository

USE: Before and after reading, to build connections between background knowledge and new words; to summarize

PROCEDURE:

1. Explain Knowing How Words Work and what a Concept of Definition Map tells us about words.

2. Think aloud while demonstrating how to complete a Concept of Definition Map.

3. Select, or have students select, a word to be defined, and write the word in the "Focus word" oval.

4. Ask students to determine what broad category best describes the word in the "What is it?" section. Examples: Pizza is a food; a city is a place.

5. Ask students to provide a viable synonym for the section labeled "A comparison."

6. Ask students to provide some words that describe the focus word in the "How would you describe it?" section.

7. Ask students to provide some specific examples of the word in the "What are some examples?" section. These can be specific items or descriptions of examples.

8. If the map is complete, use it to create an oral or written summary. If the map is not complete, read a selection that will provide the missing information and complete the map after reading. Use the completed map to create an oral or written summary.

EXAMPLE LESSON: Chapter 4, Lesson 5, pages 116–122

SOURCE: Schwartz, R., & Raphael, T. (1985). Concept of definition: A key to improving students' vocabulary. *The Reading Teacher, 39*(2), 198–205.

(TEACHING IDEA) Context Clues

Comprehension Strategies: Knowing How Words Work

(See blackline, page 185.)

TEXT: Narrative, expository

USE: During reading to help determine the meaning of unknown words

PROCEDURE:

1. Explain to students the eight types of context clues and give examples of each:

   Definition: provides a definition that often connects the unknown word to a known word

   Example-Illustration: provides an example or drawing to describe the word

   Contrast: provides a comparison (similarity) or contrast (difference) to the word

   Logic: provides a connection (such as a simile) to the word

   Root Words and Affixes: provides meaningful roots and affixes that the reader uses to determine meaning

   Grammar: provides syntactical cues that allow for reader interpretation

   Cause and Effect: cause-and-effect example allows the reader to hypothesize meaning

   Mood and Tone: description of mood related to the word allows readers to hypothesize meaning

2. Use a read-aloud and think-aloud to demonstrate using one or more of the above clues to determine the meaning of a difficult and/or unfamiliar word in the text. (The think-aloud demonstrates the most effective clue based on the context of the sentence.) Readers use several of the clues to figure out unknown words.

3. If the context does not provide enough information, demonstrate other strategies for figuring out the meaning of the word.

4. Ask students to find difficult words in the texts they are reading and articulate the clues they can use to figure out the meanings. Guide if necessary.

EXAMPLE LESSON: Chapter 4, Lesson 2, pages 98–103

SOURCE: Vacca, R. T., & Vacca, J. L. (2002). *Content area reading: Literacy and learning across the curriculum* (7th ed.). New York: Longman.

(TEACHING IDEA) Probable Passages

Comprehension Strategies: Previewing, Making Connections

(See blackline, page 186.)

TEXT: Narrative

USE: Before reading to introduce vocabulary and make predictions related to the narrative elements: characters, setting, problem, and solution

PROCEDURE:

1. Select key vocabulary from the story to introduce to the students. Choose vocabulary that represents various elements of the story.

2. Have students use vocabulary to create Probable Passages they may find in the story. (Providing a story frame or story map may facilitate this process.)

3. Encourage students to share their Probable Passages with the class.

4. Read the story to confirm or modify original predictions.

EXAMPLE LESSON: Chapter 4, Lesson 1, pages 92–97

SOURCE: Adapted from Wood, K. (1984). Probable passages: A writing strategy. *The Reading Teacher*, 37, 496–499.

(TEACHING IDEA) Semantic Map

Comprehension Strategies: Knowing How Words Work, Previewing, Summarizing (See blacklines, pages 187 and 189.)

TEXT: Narrative, expository

USE: Before and after reading to gain an overview of a topic, make predictions about text, introduce vocabulary, and summarize information

PROCEDURE:

1. Choose a focus word related to the text and write it in the center oval of the Semantic Map graphic on the board or overhead projector.

2. Explain Knowing How Words Work and Semantic Maps.

3. Introduce the focus word and discuss.

4. Think aloud while demonstrating how to complete the map.

5. Begin by brainstorming a few words that come to mind when you think about the focus word. Then invite students to contribute words they associate with the focus word.

6. Record (or have students record) responses on the board.

7. After brainstorming, examine the list of related words to see what categories emerge.

8. Record a category in each of the four remaining ovals and list related words beneath each category.

9. After reading, revisit the map to revise, add, or delete information as necessary.

10. Use the completed Semantic Map to create an oral or written summary.

EXAMPLE LESSON: Chapter 4, Lesson 4, pages 110–116

SOURCE: Johnson, D. D., & Pearson, P. D. (1984). *Teaching reading vocabulary* (2nd ed.). New York: Holt, Rinehart and Winston.

(TEACHING IDEA) Semantic Question Map

Comprehension Strategies: Knowing How Words Work, Previewing, Summarizing (See blacklines, pages 188 and 189.)

TEXT: Narrative, expository

USE: Before and after reading, to gain an overview of a topic and make predictions about text

PROCEDURE:

1. Choose a focus word from the text, develop four related questions, and write them on the Semantic Question Map blackline.

2. Explain Knowing How Words Work and Semantic Question Maps.

3. Introduce the focus word and discuss.

4. Think aloud while demonstrating how to complete the map.

5. Invite students to respond to each question.

6. Record (or have students record) responses directly below each question.

7. Discuss the information on the map.

8. Read (or have students read) a text that will contribute information to the map.

9. Revisit the map to revise, add, or delete information as necessary.

10. Use the completed Semantic Question Map to create an oral or written summary.

EXAMPLE LESSON: Chapter 4, Lesson 3, pages 103–109

SOURCE: Adapted from Johnson, D. D., & Pearson, P. D. (1984). *Teaching reading vocabulary* (2nd ed.). New York: Holt, Rinehart and Winston.

(**TEACHING IDEA**) ## Vocabulary Bookmark Technique

Comprehension Strategies: Monitoring, Knowing How Words Work

(See blackline, page 190.)

TEXT: Narrative, expository

USE: During reading, to monitor comprehension, learn vocabulary, and understand how words work

PROCEDURE:

1. Explain Vocabulary Bookmark Technique. Explain that during reading, students will each choose a vocabulary word that they think the whole class should talk about. They will record (write or sketch) the word and what they think it means on the Vocabulary Bookmark blackline. They will also write the page number and the number of the paragraph where their word choice is located.

2. Think aloud while demonstrating how to use the Vocabulary Bookmark Technique.

3. Invite students to complete Vocabulary Bookmarks.

4. Use completed bookmarks as the basis of discussion. Have students explain what their words mean and how to use them. Revisit the text to locate words and check their meanings in context. Use dictionaries to verify the words' meanings, if necessary.

5. Add selected words to the class word wall, and encourage students to use the words in their speaking and writing vocabularies.

EXAMPLE LESSON: Chapter 4, Lessons 6, pages 122–127

SOURCE: McLaughlin, M. (2003). *Guided comprehension in the primary grades.* Newark, DE: International Reading Association.

© McLaughlin, Homeyer, & Sassaman. (2006). *Research-Based Reading Lessons: Grades 4–6.* New York: Scholastic. Page 184

Name _____ Date _____

Concept of Definition Map

A comparison

What is it?

How would you describe it?

Focus word: _____

What are some examples?

Name _____ Date _____

Context Clue Organizer

	Unknown Word	Page	Context Clues— What I Think It Means	What It Means
1.				
2.				
3.				
4.				
5.				
6.				

Name _____ Date _____

Probable Passages

Characters

Setting

Problem

Solution

Name _____

Date _____

Semantic Map

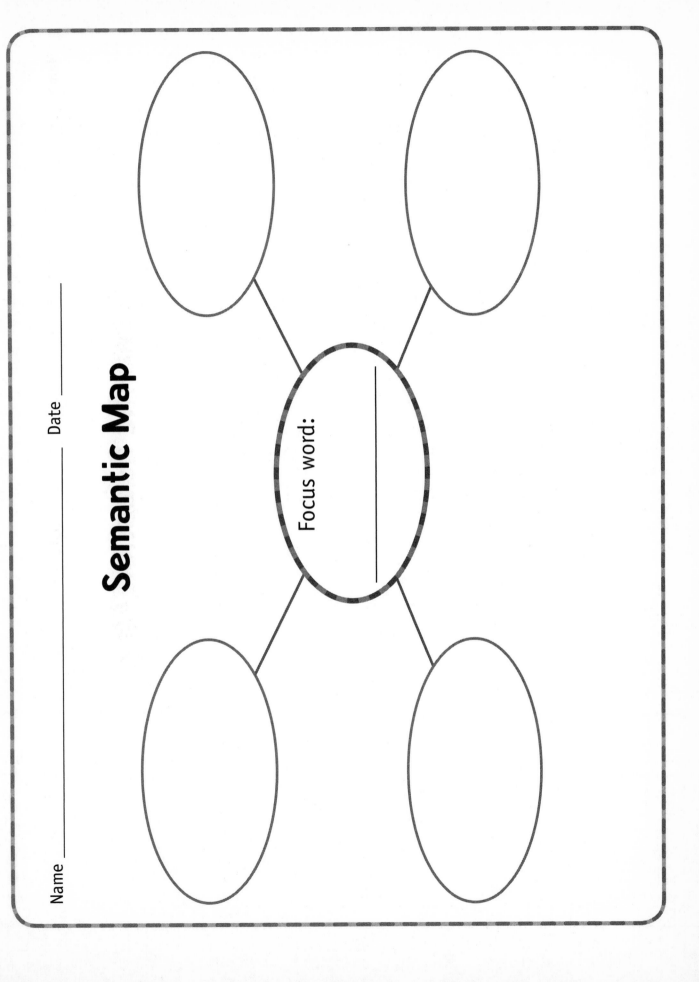

Focus word: _____

Name _____ Date _____

Semantic Question Map

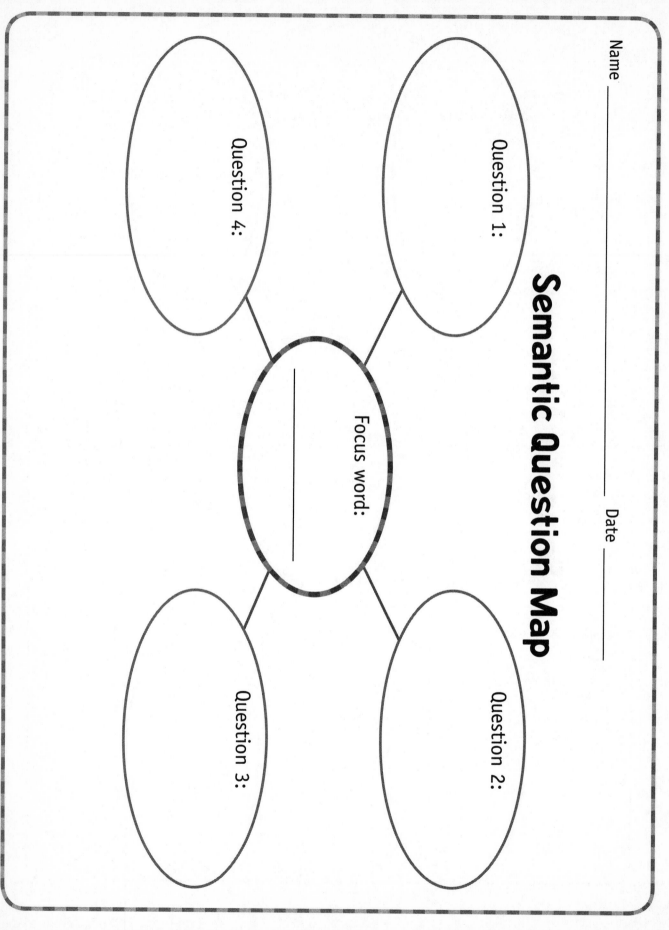

Question 1:

Question 4:

Focus word:
_____

Question 2:

Question 3:

Name _____ Date _____

Semantic Map Summary

Focus Word: _____

Summary:

Vocabulary Bookmark

Name_____

A word I think the whole class needs to talk about is...

I think this word means...

because...

Page_____

Paragraph_____

Vocabulary Bookmark

Name_____

A word I think the whole class needs to talk about is...

I think this word means...

because...

Page_____

Paragraph_____

Appendix D

Comprehension Strategies, Teaching Ideas, and Blacklines

STRATEGY	TEACHING IDEA	PAGE	BLACKLINE
Previewing	Story Impressions	192	198
Self-Questioning	"I Wonder" Statements	193	199
Making Connections	Connection Stems	194	——
Visualizing	Draw and Label Visualizations	195	200
Monitoring	Bookmark Technique	196	201–202
Summarizing	Bio-Pyramid	197	203

(TEACHING IDEA) Story Impressions

Comprehension Strategies: Previewing, Making Connections

(See blackline, page 198.)

TEXT: Narrative

USE: Before reading, to introduce story vocabulary, make predictions, and make connections to the story structure

PROCEDURE:

1. Explain Previewing and Story Impressions.

2. Think aloud while demonstrating writing a Story Impression.

3. Provide students with a list of words that offer clues about the story. Choose words that relate to the narrative elements—characters, setting, problem, events, and solution. Limit the list to ten words, using no more than five words per clue. Present the clues in a list in the order in which they appear in the story following the downward arrows on blackline.

4. Have students read the list of words in order and work in small groups to write a Story Impression, using the words in the order in which they were presented.

5. Have each group share its Story Impression with the class. Discuss each story.

6. Read the original story to the class and engage students in a discussion of comparisons and contrasts.

7. For variety, adapt this technique to Poem Impressions using story poems, or Picture Impressions, in which students sketch in response to the clues provided.

EXAMPLE LESSON: Chapter 5, Lesson 5, pages 152–158

SOURCE: McGinley, W., & Denner, P. (1987). Story impressions: A prereading/prewriting activity. *Journal of Reading, 31,* 248–253.

(TEACHING IDEA) "I Wonder" Statements

Comprehension Strategies: Previewing, Self-Questioning

(See blackline, page 199.)

TEXT: Narrative, expository

USE: Before and during reading to promote Self-Questioning and active thinking

PROCEDURE:

1. Explain Self-Questioning and how to create "I Wonder" Statements and support them with reasoning; provide prompts such as "I wonder . . . because . . ."

2. Think aloud while demonstrating how to wonder orally, in writing, and by sketching.

3. Guide students to wonder about things in everyday life, stories, or ideas presented in texts.

4. Share wonders and discuss with text support, if possible.

5. Encourage students to wonder throughout the reading of a text.

EXAMPLE LESSON: Chapter 5, Lesson 1, pages 131–135

SOURCE: Harvey, S., & Goudvis, A. (2000). *Strategies that work: Teaching comprehension to enhance understanding.* York, ME: Stenhouse.

(TEACHING IDEA) ## Connection Stems
Comprehension Strategies: Making Connections

TEXT: Narrative, expository

USE: After reading to make connections to text

PROCEDURE:

1. Show students a sentence stem and think out loud about the process for completing it.

2. Use text support and personal experiences to explain the connection.

3. Read another text aloud and guide students to complete the stem orally with a partner.

4. Ask students to read a short text in small groups and work together to complete a Connection Stem.

5. Use stems for discussion after a read-aloud, for response journals, or for large- and small-group discussion.

Connection Stems:

- That reminds me of . . .

- I remember when . . .

- I have a connection . . .

- An experience I have had like that . . .

- I felt like that character when . . .

- If I were that character, I would . . .

EXAMPLE LESSON: Chapter 5, Lesson 4, pages 147–152

SOURCE: Adapted from Harvey, S., & Goudvis, A. (2000). *Strategies that work: Teaching comprehension to enhance understanding.* York, ME: Stenhouse.

(TEACHING IDEA) Draw and Label Visualizations

Comprehension Strategies: Visualizing (See blackline, page 200.)

TEXT: Narrative, expository

USE: During and after reading, to visually represent and label mental images created while reading

PROCEDURE:

1. Explain visualizing and how to visualize (create mental pictures while reading).

2. Demonstrate how to use visual representations (pictures, shapes, lines) to communicate mental pictures.

3. Think aloud about what you see in your mind and how you will express it in a drawing. Then think aloud about what you will write to label the drawing (one or more sentences).

4. Have students listen to a selection and then ask them to create a visual representation of their mind pictures and write about it. Ask them to share their drawings in pairs or small groups and explain the images they saw in their minds.

5. Encourage students to visualize while they read.

EXAMPLE LESSON: Chapter 5, Lesson 6, pages 159–165

SOURCE: Adapted from McLaughlin, M., & Allen, M. B. (2002a). *Guided Comprehension: A teaching model for grades 3–8.* Newark, DE: International Reading Association.

(TEACHING IDEA) Bookmark Technique

Comprehension Strategies: Monitoring, Knowing How Words Work

(See blacklines, pages 201–202.)

TEXT: Narrative, expository

USE: During reading, to monitor comprehension and understand how words work

PROCEDURE:

1. Explain Monitoring and the Bookmark Technique. Explain that there are four bookmarks. As students read, they make decisions and record (write or sketch) information on each bookmark. This includes the page and paragraph where their choice is located and the following specific information for each bookmark:

   Bookmark One: Write or sketch the part of the text that was most interesting.

   Bookmark Two: Write or sketch a part of the text that was confusing.

   Bookmark Three: Write a word the whole class should discuss; provide a possible meaning.

   Bookmark Four: Write about an illustration, map, chart, or graph that helped you understand the text.

2. Think aloud while demonstrating how to use the Bookmark Technique.

3. Invite students to complete bookmarks.

4. Use completed bookmarks as the basis of discussion.

EXAMPLE LESSON: Chapter 5, Lesson 2, pages 136–141

SOURCE: McLaughlin, M., & Allen, M. B. (2002a). *Guided Comprehension: A teaching model for grades 3–8.* Newark, DE: International Reading Association.

(TEACHING IDEA) Bio-Pyramid

Comprehension Strategies: Making Connections, Monitoring, Summarizing (See blackline, page 203.)

TEXT: Expository

USE: After reading to summarize important points about a person's life

PROCEDURE:

1. Show students the format for writing Bio-Pyramids:

   Line 1: person's name

   Line 2: two words describing the person

   Line 3: three words describing the person's childhood

   Line 4: four words indicating a problem the person had to overcome

   Line 5: five words stating one of his/her accomplishments

   Line 6: six words stating a second accomplishment

   Line 7: seven words stating a third accomplishment

   Line 8: eight words stating how humankind benefited from his/her accomplishment

2. Create a Bio-Pyramid as a class. Model the format.

3. Have students create individual or group Bio-Pyramids for some famous people they are studying.

EXAMPLE LESSON: Chapter 5, Lesson 3, pages 142–147

SOURCE: Macon, J. M. (1991). *Literature response.* Paper presented at the Annual Literacy Workshop, Anaheim, CA.

Story Impression

Clues

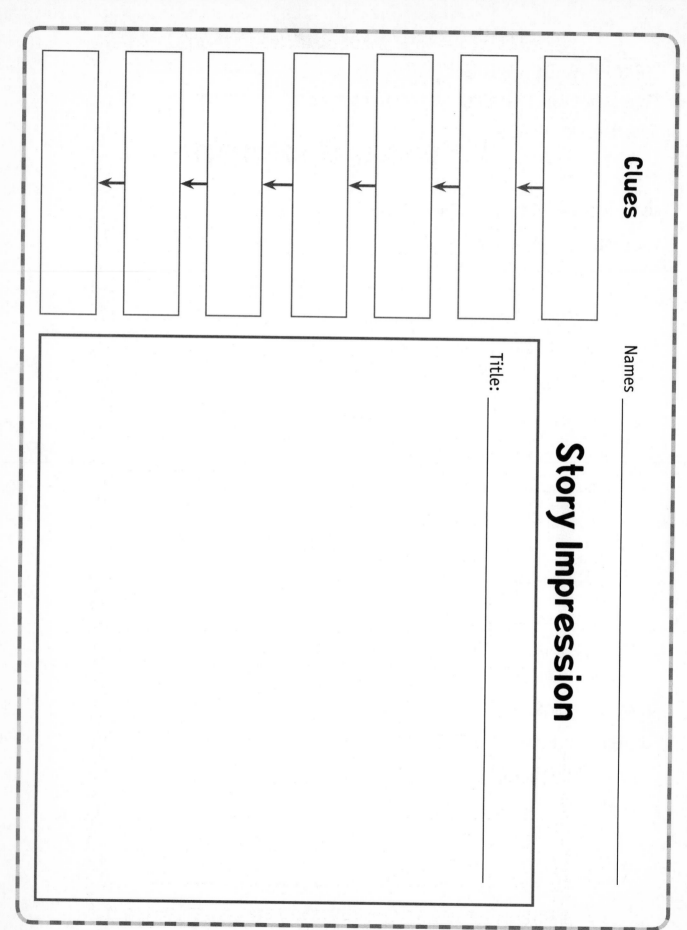

Names _____

Title: _____

Name_____

I Wonder Bookmark

Page_____

I wonder _____

_____

_____

_____

because _____

_____

_____

_____

Page_____

I wonder _____

_____

_____

_____

because _____

_____

_____

_____

Name _____ Date _____

Draw and Label Visualizations

Drawing: Sketch your visualization.

Label: Write a sentence to explain your drawing.

_____

_____

_____

_____

_____

© McLaughlin, Homeyer, & Sassaman. (2006) *Research-Based Reading Lessons: Grades 4–6.* New York: Scholastic. Page 200

Name_____

Bookmark One

The most interesting part was...

Page_____

Paragraph_____

Name_____

Bookmark Two

Something that confused
me was...

Page_____

Paragraph_____

Name_____

Bookmark Three

A word I think the whole class needs to talk about is...

I think the word means...

Page_____

Paragraph_____

Name_____

Bookmark Four

The illustration, chart, map, or graph that helped me understand what I was reading was...

Page_____

Paragraph_____

Name _____

Date _____

Bio-Pyramid

_____
person's name

_____
two words describing the person

_____
three words describing the person's childhood

_____
four words indicating a problem the person had to overcome

_____
five words stating one of his/her accomplishments

_____
six words stating a second accomplishment

_____
seven words stating a third accomplishment

_____
eight words stating how humankind benefited from his/her accomplishments

Ideas for Teaching Centers, Literature Circles, and Cross-Age Reading Experiences

Comprehension Center Student Self-Assessment

Name _____ Date _____

	LOW ⟷ HIGH			
① I used my time wisely.	1	2	3	4
② I followed the directions carefully.	1	2	3	4
③ I used my comprehension strategies.	1	2	3	4
④ I worked well with my partners.	1	2	3	4
⑤ Overall, I give myself a score of	1	2	3	4

Something I did well was _____

_____

_____

_____ .

Next time, I will _____

_____

_____

_____ .

© McLaughlin, Homeyer, & Sassaman. (2006). *Research-Based Reading Lessons: Grades 4–6.* New York: Scholastic. Page 204

Cross-Age Reading Experience
Student Self-Assessment

Name _____ Date _____

		LOW ←————————→ HIGH

① I was prepared to read with my partner.   1   2   3   4

② I listened carefully.   1   2   3   4

③ I used my comprehension strategies.   1   2   3   4

④ I worked well with my partner.   1   2   3   4

⑤ Overall, I give myself a score of   1   2   3   4

I especially enjoyed _____

_____

_____

_____

_____ .

Next time, my CARE partner and I will _____

_____

_____

_____

_____ .

Literature Circle
Student Self-Assessment

Name _____ Date _____

		LOW ⟵⟶ HIGH			
(1)	I was prepared for Literature Circle.	1	2	3	4
(2)	I discussed the assigned pages.	1	2	3	4
(3)	I completed my circle role.	1	2	3	4
(4)	I worked well with circle members.	1	2	3	4
(5)	I listened carefully to others' ideas.	1	2	3	4
(6)	Overall, I give myself a score of	1	2	3	4

To prepare for our next session, I will _____

_____

_____

_____

_____.

Next time, my group will _____

_____

_____

_____

_____.

© McLaughlin, Homeyer, & Sassaman. (2006). Research-Based Reading Lessons: Grades 4–6. New York: Scholastic. Page 206

Literature Circle Extension Project List

There are many ways to extend our thinking about the books we read in Literature Circle. Members of your circle may choose a project from this list or you may create an extension project your group has designed. I will meet with you to discuss your choice.

1. Create a museum exhibit for the book. (Example: Research clothing, music, sports, or transportation of the time in which the book was written.)

2. Create an illustrated time line for the story. Be creative in your design.

3. Design a creative response to the novel (examples: a dramatization, a song, a painting, a project).

4. Create a travel brochure for the setting of the story.

5. Create a book jacket to use in a Book Sell.

6. Retell the book through a series of watercolor paintings.

7. Create a scrapbook from the perspective of one of the characters in the novel. Explain why the artifacts are important to that character.

8. Create an alphabet quilt based upon the novel.

9. Create a cookbook or a menu of the favorite foods of characters in the book.

10. Create a time capsule from the perspective of one of the characters in the novel. Describe the significance of items to be included. Write a newspaper article about opening the time capsule in the present day.

11. Create a children's book—narrative or alphabet—telling the essential story of the novel.

12. Create advertisements—audio, video, or print—depicting characters or events in the book to persuade others to read the novel.

13. Choose background music for a particular scene or chapter in a novel. Explain how the music you chose relates to that section of the book.

14. Develop and market a product that would solve the major conflict in the novel.

15. Use a memorable quote from the novel to create a picture book, repeated phrase poem, or other project.

© McLaughlin, Homeyer, & Sassaman. (2006). Research-Based Reading Lessons: Grades 4–6. New York: Scholastic. Page 207

Appendix F

Theme Resources

MYSTERY

Texts

Abrahams, P. (2005). *Down the rabbit hole.* **New York: HarperCollins.**
Eighth-grader Ingrid Levin-Hall idolizes Sherlock Holmes and uses her head to solve a real-life mystery in her own hometown.

Aiken, J. (2005). *The witch of Clatteringshaws.* **New York: Delacorte.**
In this exciting novel, three friends use their skills to fight bad magic.

Balliet, B. (2005). *Chasing Vermeer.* **New York: Scholastic.**
Two sixth-grade detectives solve the case of a mysterious art theft of a famous Vermeer painting.

Black, H. (2004). *The wrath of Mulgarath (The Spiderwick chronicles, book #5).* **New York: Simon & Schuster.**
Mallory and Jared use a magical stone, which makes visible normally invisible things, in an attempt to rescue Simon from goblins.

DeFelice, C. (2005). *The missing manatee.* **New York: Farrar, Straus and Giroux.**
Eleven-year-old Skeet discovers a manatee shot to death in a Florida river and spends spring break looking for the killer.

Dodds, R. (2005). *The secret of Iguando.* **London: Transworld Publishers.**
Ben and Claire, while traveling with their father as members of a group of zoologists, disturb something supernatural in a remote jungle in Mexico.

Edwards, J. A. (2005). *Dragon: Hound of honor.* **New York: HarperCollins.**
An adaptation of *The Legend of the Dog of Montargis, Dragon* is a story of intrigue, power, loyalty, and friendship set in medieval France.

Gaiman, N. (2003). *Coraline.* **New York: HarperCollins.**
Coraline, after moving into her family's new home, discovers a mysterious door. Upon venturing through the door she discovers a world disturbingly different from her own.

Johnson, A. (2004). *Bird.* **New York: Dial.**
A young girl helps others while trying to find her father.

Schumacher, J. (2005). *Chain letter.* **New York: Random House.**
Livvie doesn't believe in the superstitious idea that breaking a chain letter will bring bad luck—until the day she throws one into the trash.

Shan, D. (2004). *Hunters of the dusk (Cirque du freak, book #7).* **New York: Little, Brown.**
Darren and the team set out to destroy the Vampanese Lord and the other vampires once and for all.

Snicket, L. (2004). *Grim grotto: Book the eleventh: A series of unfortunate events.* **New York: HarperCollins.**
The Baudelaire orphans, still pursued by the evil Count Olaf, travel by submarine to Gorgonian Grotto in an attempt to make a VFD meeting and find the sugar bowl.

Van Draanen, W. (2005). *Sammy Keyes and the art of deception*. New York: Bantam Doubleday Dell.
Sammy Keyes, a seventh-grade sleuth, sets to work on solving a crime at an art gallery.

Yolen, J., & Stemple, H. E. (1999). *The Mary Celeste: An unsolved mystery from history*. New York: Simon & Schuster.
A young girl gives readers the clues to help solve the real-life mystery of the Mary Celeste.

Web sites

The Anybodies
http://theanybodies.com
This is an interactive site that explores the characters and plotline of *The Anybodies*.

Enlighten Me—The Peetnik Mysteries
http://www.superpages.com/enlightenme
A fully interactive mystery-solving program that lets students use a variety of problem-solving skills.

The Hardy Boys unofficial online resource
http://www.geocities.com/Heartland/Hills/5567/?200515
An unofficial site with information on the characters, the history of the series, and background information on the author.

Kids Love a Mystery
http://www.kidsloveamystery.com
This site, which offers a history of mystery, allows students to solve mysteries and discuss Nancy Drew.

King Tut's Mysterious Death—National Geographic
http://www.nationalgeographic.com/ngkids/0508
This site offers an interactive investigation into the mysterious death of King Tut.

Museum of Unnatural Mystery
http://unmuseum.mus.pa.us/unmain.htm
This site has links to information on mysteries of science as well as history.

The Mysterious and Unexplained
http://www.activemind.com/Mysterious
From lost civilizations to UFOs, this Web site has links to all things mysterious.

MysteryNet's Kids Mysteries
http://kids.mysterynet.com
Online mysteries to solve, stories to read, and magic tricks to learn. Plus links to mystery books.

The Nancy Drew unofficial Web site
http://www.nancydrewsleuth.com
This site contains information about the Nancy Drew series as well as links to other Web sites on the topic.

A Series of Unfortunate Events
http://www.lemonysnicket.com/index.cfm
Information on the author, Lemony Snicket, as well as the illustrator, books, and characters of the Series of Unfortunate Events series.

The Spiderwick Chronicles
http://www.spiderwick.com
This site offers news about the author, books, and characters of the *Spiderwick Chronicles*.

SURVIVAL

Texts

Cowley, J. (2004). *Hunter*. New York: Penguin Putnam.
Two stories, 200 years apart; both take place in New Zealand. A Maori warrior from 1805 helps a young girl survive in 2005 in the New Zealand wilderness.

Cushman, K. (2005). *Rodzina*. New York: Random House.
One Polish-American girl's story of being sent west on an orphan train to a life of slavery.

George, J. C. (2004). *Snowboard twist*. New York: Katherine Tegen.
Kelly is nearly caught in an avalanche while snowboarding in the Teton Mountains.

Haycak, C. (2004). *Red palms*. New York: Random House.
Bankrupt due to the Depression, Benita and her family move from city life in Ecuador to a primitive island to start a coconut plantation.

Hobbs, W. (2004). *Beardance*. New York: Simon & Schuster.
In the sequel to *Bearstone*, Cloyd, a Ute Indian boy, attempts to help two orphaned grizzly bear cubs survive the winter.

Morgan, C. (2005). *The boy who spoke dog*. New York: Penguin Putnam.
Jack struggles to survive after being shipwrecked on an island populated by sheep, sheepdogs, and wild dogs, but no people.

Morpurgo, M. (2004). *Kensuke's kingdom*. New York: Scholastic.
Michael struggles to survive after being washed up on what he believes to be a deserted island.

Myers, E. (2004). *Survival of the fittest*. Millburn, NJ: Montemayor Press.
When Rus travels with his uncle and cousins to the rain forests of Peru, their plane crashes into a river and only the children survive.

Neale, J. (2004). *Himalaya*. New York: Houghton Mifflin.
Orrie and her older brother tell the story of their climbing expedition to Island Peak in Nepal with their family.

Neale, J. (2004). *Lost at sea*. New York: Houghton Mifflin.
A brother and sister tell the story of their ocean voyage on a yacht with their mother and her boyfriend.

Scieszka, J. (2001). *Baloney, Henry P.* New York: Penguin.

Van Leeuwen, J. (2004). *Cabin on Trouble Creek*. New York: Penguin.
In 1803 Ohio, a father leaves two brothers to finish building a cabin and protect the family's new land while he goes to fetch their mother and younger siblings.

Whelan, G. (2004). *Burying the sun*. New York: HarperCollins.
Living in Leningrad in 1941, 14-year-old Georgi vows to do something to help his family when Germany turns its forces on Russia.

Web sites

Brief History of the Trail of Tears
http://www.neosoft.com/powersource/cherokee/history.html
This site offers information on the Trail of Tears.

Conscience and the Constitution
http://www.pbs.org/itvs/conscience
This site offers information on the Japanese internment camps of World War II.

CyberHunt: Anne Frank
http://teacher.scholastic.com/products/instructor/May04_cyberteacher.htm
This site takes students on a CyberHunt for information on Anne Frank.

Endangered Cultures—National Geographic
http://www.nationalgeographic.com/ngkids/0409
This site provides information on how endangered cultures all over the world are struggling to preserve their traditions.

Hatchet
http://www.mce.k12tn.net/survival/hatchet/
hatchet.htm
This site contains information on the survival
novel *Hatchet* by Gary Paulsen.

**Incredible Story of Survival
at the South Pole**
http://www.nationwidespeakers.com/
speakers/jerri_nielsen.htm
This site documents the experiences of Jerri
Nielsen, the scientist diagnosed with cancer
while at the South Pole.

Lance Armstrong
http://www.lancearmstrong.com/index.html
This is the official Web site of Lance
Armstrong, the seven-time Tour de France
winner, who also battled cancer.

NOVA Online, *Escape!*
http://www.pbs.org/wgbh/nova/escape
This is a companion Web site to the four-part
NOVA special *Escape!* It contains information
on true-life stories of survival.

Rabbit in the Moon
http://www.pbs.org/pov/pov1999/
rabbitinthemoon/index.html
This is the companion Web site to *Rabbit
in the Moon*, a documentary about the
internment of Japanese Americans during
World War II.

**We Survived September 11th—National
Geographic**
http://www.nationalgeographic.com/
ngkids/0210
This site provides an account of a fourth-
grade classroom four blocks away from the
World Trade Center attacks.

Westward Expansion
http://www.pbs.org/wgbh/aia/part4/
4narr4.html
This site provides information about the
westward expansion, the African American
point of view, and the Trail of Tears.

BIOGRAPHY

Texts

Adler, D. A. (1993). *A picture book
of Anne Frank* (Picture Book Biography
series). New York: Holiday House.
A picture-book biography of Anne Frank.

Christopher, M. (2004). *On the court
with Yao Ming: Matt Christopher's sports
biographies.* New York: Little, Brown.
Biography of Chinese basketball great
Yao Ming.

Faran, J. (2004). *Dr. Seuss.* New York:
Weigl Publishers.
This biography of Theodore Geisel, better
known as Dr. Seuss, tells about his struggles
to become a children's writer. His first book
was rejected 30 times, yet he went on to
become one of the world's most beloved
children's authors.

Gutman, B. (2003). *Lance Armstrong: A
biography.* New York: Simon & Schuster.
The story of cyclist Lance Armstrong's
competitive desire to let nothing get in his
way, not even cancer.

Hill, A. E. (2004). *Michelle Kwan* (Sports
heroes and legends series). Minneapolis:
Lerner Publishing Group.
This biography of figure skater Michelle Kwan
chronicles her dedication to the sport.

Isabouts, J. P. (2001). *Discovering Walt:
The magical life of Walt Disney.* New York:
Roundtable Press.
With rarely seen photographs, this book tells
the story of the man behind the mouse.

Kallen, P. M., & Kallen, S. A. (2004).
Ben and Jerry (Inventors and creators
series). Farmington Hills, MI: Kid Haven
Press.
The biography of the creators of Ben and
Jerry's ice cream.

King-Farris, C. (2003). *My brother Martin: A sister remembers growing up with Rev. Dr. Martin Luther King, Jr.* New York: Simon & Schuster.

Dr. Martin Luther King, Jr.'s older sister recalls her memories of growing up with her younger brother.

Krull, K. (2000). *Lives of extraordinary women: Rulers, rebels (and what the neighbors thought)*. San Diego: Harcourt.

Interesting women throughout history are celebrated in this collection by Kathleen Krull.

McDonough, Y. Z. (1997). *Anne Frank.* New York: Henry Holt.

The familiar story of Anne Frank told with colorful and thought-provoking illustrations and text.

Paulsen, G. (1993). *Eastern sun, winter moon.* New York: Harcourt Brace Jovanovich.

An autobiography of Gary Paulsen as a young boy in a time of war.

Paulsen, G. (2001). *Guts.* New York: Delacorte.

An autobiography of author Gary Paulsen and the times in his life that inspired some of his best-known works, including *Hatchet*.

Shores, E. L. (2005). *Rosa Parks* (Fact finders series). Mankato, MN: Capstone Press.

This biography introduces us to the woman who refused to give up her bus seat, describing what led up to that moment and the far-reaching results of her actions.

Woog, A. (2004). *Roald Dahl* (Inventors and creators series). Farmington Hills, MI: Thompson Gale.

This well-designed biography for young readers introduces us to the author of such books as *Charlie and the Chocolate Factory*, *Matilda*, and *Witches*.

Web sites

AandE.com
http://www.aande.com
Biography and *Biography for Kids*, resources focused on the lives of numerous people from varied professions, can be found on this site.

The American Presidency
http://ap.grolier.com/splash
This thorough Web site contains information on all the American presidents to date, each available in multiple grade levels.

Betsy Ross: Her Life
http://www.ushistory.org/betsy/flaglife.html
This site contains information on the life of Betsy Ross and the historical events of the time.

Commodore John Barry
http://www.ushistory.org/more/commodorebarry.html
Students come for insight into the life of Commodore John Barry, who is often called "The Father of the American Navy."

Current Biography Excerpts
http://www.hwwilson.com/currentbio/cbonline.html
An extensive collection of biographies of famous athletes, from sports that range from auto racing to track and field.

CyberHunt: Benjamin Franklin
http://teacher.scholastic.com/products/instructor/Jan04_cyberteacher.htm
This site sends students on a hunt through various Web sites for information on the life and many inventions of Benjamin Franklin.

Deborah Sampson
http://teacherlink.ed.usu.edu/tlresources/units/Byrnes-famous/sampson.htm
This site includes a biography and lesson plans about Deborah Sampson, a female soldier in the American Revolution.

Distinguished Women of Past and Present
http://www.distinguishedwomen.com
This site has links to biographical information on famous women, from writers and educators to athletes and heads of state, past and present.

The Electric Ben Franklin
http://www.ushistory.org/franklin
An extensive Web site with information on all aspects of Ben Franklin's life.

The Nobel Prize Internet Archive—Nelson Mandela
http://almaz.com/nobel/peace/1993a.html
This Web site displays a brief biography of Nelson Mandela along with links to books and other Web sites.

PAL: Perspectives in American Literature—A Research and Reference Guide—An Ongoing Project
http://www.csustan.edu/english/reuben/pal/chap2/wheatley.html
This site displays biographies and works on Phyllis Wheatley, a black American poet.

Spotlight: Biography
http://www.smithsonianeducation.org/spotlight/start.html
This Web site offers biographical information compiled by the Smithsonian Institution on a wide variety of people, from American Indians to jazz and blues musicians.

Thomas Paine
http://www.ushistory.org/paine/index.htm
Information on the life of Thomas Paine as well as links to sites on his writings are available here.

FANTASY

Texts

Curley, M. (2002). *The named.* **New York: Bloomsbury.**
By traveling through time, Ethan, one of the Named, fights the Order of Chaos and its destruction.

Curley, M. (2003). *The dark.* **New York: Bloomsbury.**
In this sequel to *The Named*, Ma Arkarian, the ageless mentor to Ethan and Isabel, is kidnapped and sent to a frightening underworld filled with strange creatures.

Haddix, M. P. (2004). *Shadow children.* **New York: Simon & Schuster.**
In world where families are allowed only two children, illegal third children must live in hiding. If these "shadow children" are discovered, the punishment is death.

Hobbs, W. (2005). *Kokopelli's flute.* **New York: Simon & Schuster.**
Thirteen-year-old Tepary discovers an old flute in a cliff dwelling in New Mexico, and through it he learns about ancient Native American magic.

La Fevers, R. L. (2005). *The true blade of power* (Lowthar's blade trilogy, book 3). **New York: Penguin Putnam.**
The young Kenric and his Fey and goblin friends reunite in their ongoing attempt to destroy the power-hungry Lord Mordig and bring peace to the kingdom of Lowthar.

Moredun, P. R. (2005). *The world of Eldaterra: The dragon conspiracy.* **New York: HarperCollins.**
As a police inspector in 1895 and a 15-year-old boy in 1910 work together to stop an evil plot that began in a world of magic, they find their fates intertwined.

Nix, G. (2005). *Drowned Wednesday* (The keys to the kingdom series, book 3). New York: Scholastic.
Strange pirates, shadowy creatures, and Drowned Wednesday—whose gluttony threatens both her world and Arthur's—are after Arthur Penhaligon. Garth Nix, with his unlimited imagination and storytelling powers, has created a character and a world that become even more compelling in this installment.

Osborne, M. P. (2005). *Season of the sandstorms* (Magic tree house #34). New York: Random House.
Jack and Annie travel back in time at Merlin's request to the Middle Eastern desert with only a rhyme to help them in their mission.

Paolini, C. (2005). *Eragon* (Inheritance, book 1). New York: Random House.
Eragon, a 15-year-old boy of unknown lineage living in Aagaesia, discovers a strange blue stone that brings a dragon and changes his life.

Rowling, J. K. (1998). *Harry Potter and the sorcerer's stone.* New York: Scholastic.
In Book One, Harry Potter is enrolled at Hogwarts School of Witchcraft and Wizardry after learning he is a wizard.

Rowling, J. K. (1999). *Harry Potter and the chamber of secrets.* New York: Scholastic.
In Book Two, Harry Potter defends Hogwarts against a basilisk in the Chamber of Secrets.

Rowling, J. K. (1999). *Harry Potter and the prisoner of Azkaban.* New York: Scholastic.
In Book Three, Harry Potter looks for the Prisoner of Azkaban and discovers more about his parents.

Rowling, J. K. (2000). *Harry Potter and the goblet of fire.* New York: Scholastic.
Book Four invites us to watch Harry Potter compete in the Tri-Wizard Tournament.

Rowling, J. K. (2003). *Harry Potter and the order of the phoenix.* New York: Scholastic.
In Book Five, Dumbledore and his followers create the Order of the Phoenix to stand against Voldemort.

Rowling, J. K. (2005). *Harry Potter and the half-blood prince.* New York: Scholastic.
The sixth book in this best-selling series picks up the story of good versus evil in Harry's sixth year at Hogwarts School of Witchcraft and Wizardry.

Stewart, P. (2005). *The last of the sky pirates.* London: David Fickling Books.
Apprentice Rook Barkwater joins sky pirate Captain Twig on a dangerous journey in time to fight against the Guardians of the Night.

Zahn, T. (2005). *Dragon and slave.* New York: Starscape.
Fourteen-year-old Jack was orphaned years ago and raised by his Uncle Virgil. Since his uncle was killed, Jack has been alone except for one friend, Draycos, a draconic K'da poet-warrior.

Web sites

The Book on Jane Yolen
http://www.janeyolen.com
This site offers interviews with the author of *The Young Merlin Trilogy*, as well as teaching materials and links to additional sites.

Fantasy a Success for a Young Novelist
http://teacher.scholastic.com/ scholasticnews/indepth/eragon.asp
A Scholastic Web site that offers information on the teen author Christopher Paolini and his first published novel, *Eragon*.

The Finding of Lokan
http://lokan.everywebhost.com
Learn about the authors, explore the book, and learn about the characters of the novel *The Finding of Lokan* on this interactive site.

Hans Christian Andersen
http://hca.gilead.org.il
A Web site of Hans Christian Andersen stories that provides links to most of his tales, this site also offers an audio version of the song "I'm Hans Christian Andersen."

Harry Potter
http://www.scholastic.com//harrypotter
This site offers information on the Harry Potter series, interactive activities based on the novels, and links to other Harry Potter Web sites.

Magic Tree House
http://www.randomhouse.com/kids/magictreehouse
An interactive Web site on the Magic Tree House series with information on the many books and reference guides from the series.

Philip Pullman—Kidsreads
http://www.kidsreads.com/authors/au-pullman-philip.asp
This Web site offers a short biography, interview, and insight into Philip Pullman's trilogy His Dark Materials.

The Seventh Tower
http://www.scholastic.com/titles/seventhtower/index2.htm
This site provides information on the books, characters, and author of the Seventh Tower series.

Tamora Pierce
http://www.tamora-pierce.com
This Web site provides information on Tamora Pierce, her fantasy-based books, and links to further suggested readings.

Wands and Worlds
http://www.wandsandworlds.com
On this site, find links to lists of fantasy texts on subjects that range from alchemy and giants to King Arthur and unicorns.

THE HOLOCAUST

Texts

Bartoletti, S. (2005). *Hitler youth: Growing up in Hitler's shadow.* **New York: Scholastic.**
The Hitler Youth were the largest youth group in history. The author explores how Hitler gained the following of Germany's young.

Hillman, L. (2005). *I will plant you a lilac tree: A memoir of a Schindler's List survivor.* **New York: Simon & Schuster.**
An amazing true story of one woman's coming of age during a nightmarish time in history.

Kacer, K. (2005). *The underground reporters.* **Toronto: Second Story Press.**
A true story of a group of Jewish teenagers living in the Czech Republic during the Nazi occupation who created a community-based newspaper that became a symbol of resistance.

Nicholson, D. M. (2005). *Remember World War II: Kids who survived tell their stories.* **Washington, DC: National Geographic Children's.**
The third in a series, this historical narrative makes the events of World War II real for young readers.

Pressler, M. (2005). *Malka.* **New York: Penguin Putnam.**
The story of a seven-year-old Jewish girl who is separated from her mother and sister as they attempt to flee Poland during the Nazi invasion.

Rubin, S. G. (2001). *Fireflies in the dark: The story of Freidl Dicker-Brandeis and the children of Terezin.* **New York: Holiday House.**
Stories and art from children who lived in the Terezin concentration camp.

Rubin, S. G. (2005). *The flag with fifty-six stars: A gift from the survivors of Mauthausen.* **New York: Holiday House.**
The story about the handmade American flag created by detainees of the Mauthausen concentration camp and given to the American troops that liberated them.

Russo, M. (2005). *Always remember me: How one family survived World War II.* **New York: Simon & Schuster.**
The author retells her family's story of Holocaust survival in a fictionalized way that young children can understand.

Sachs, M. (2005). *Lost in America.* **New York: Roaring Brook Press.**
Nicole, a 17-year-old, struggles to fit in in America but is haunted by the memories of her family, killed by the Nazis at Auschwitz.

Spinelli, J. (2003). *Milkweed.* **New York: Random House.**
The story of a young Jewish orphan's struggle for survival on the streets of Warsaw.

Van Maarsen, J. (2005). *Friend called Anne: One girl's story of war, peace and a unique friendship with Anne Frank.* **New York: Viking Penguin.**
Anne Frank's best friend tells the story of Frank's life before she went into hiding from the Nazis.

Volavkova H. (1993). *I never saw another butterfly: Children's drawings and poems from Terezin Concentration Camp, 1942–1944.* **New York: Schocken.**
A collection of poems and drawings by young inmates of the Terezin concentration camp during World War II.

Yolen, J. (2005). *Devil's arithmetic.* **New York: Penguin Putnam.**
A young Polish girl learns to value her Jewish heritage during the Nazi occupation of her village.

Zullo, A. (2005). *Survivors: True stories of children in the Holocaust.* **New York: Scholastic.**
True accounts of how nine Jewish children survived the Holocaust.

Web sites

Abe's Story: A Holocaust Memoir
http://www.remember.org/abe/index.html
This site contains excerpts from the book, a biography of the editor, and an interactive map that follows the story.

About Simon Wiesenthal
http://www.wiesenthal.com
This Web site provides information on Simon Wiesenthal, a survivor of the death camps of World War II, and offers links to other information on the Holocaust.

Candles Holocaust Museum
http://www.candlesholocaustmuseum.org
At this online museum there is information on the Mengele Twins experiments and other links to information about the Holocaust.

Daring to Resist: 3 Women Face the Holocaust
http://www.pbs.org/daringtoresist/
A PBS Web site offers information on a television documentary about three women who defied the odds and took great risks as teenagers during World War II.

The Holocaust Memorial Center
http://holocaustcenter.org
The Holocaust Memorial Center Web site offers links to historical information, oral history collections, and a virtual tour of the museum.

Korczak International School
http://www.korczak-school.org.il/eng
This site offers information on the lessons learned from the Holocaust and how it continues to affect people today.

**Memories of My Childhood
in the Holocaust**
http://www.remember.org/witness/
jagermann.html
A firsthand account of a young adult's
experience during the Holocaust.

A Teacher's Guide to the Holocaust
http://fcit.coedu.usf.edu/holocaust/activity/
Intermed.htm
This site for teachers offers a number of
lesson plans to help introduce younger
students to the Holocaust.

**United States Holocaust Memorial Museum:
For Students Learning About the Holocaust**
http://www.ushmm.org/education/
forstudents
The United States Holocaust Memorial
Museum offers information on the Holocaust
geared toward students.

**Voice/Vision Holocaust Survivor Oral
History Archive**
http://holocaust.umd.umich.edu
Interviews with Holocaust survivors by
Dr. Sidney Bolkosky, professor of history at
the University of Michigan–Dearborn.

POETRY

Texts

Borden, L. (2005). *America is . . .*
New York: Aladdin.
A salute to our country in words and pictures.

Clinton, C. (1998). *I, too, sing, America:
Three centuries of African American poetry.*
Boston: Houghton Mifflin.
A collection of poems that spans the history
of African American poetry in America.

Dakos, D. (1990). *If you're not here, please
raise your hand.* **New York: Macmillan.**
Thirty-eight poems about the lives of students
and teachers.

Fleischman, P. (2000). *Big talk: Poems for
four voices.* **Cambridge, MA: Candlewick.**
An interactive book that allows four readers
to share the spotlight of poetry reading.

Fletcher, R. J. (2002). *Poetry matters:
Writing a poem from the inside out.*
New York: HarperCollins.
A guide for children on the how-to of writing
poetry that includes poems and interviews
with poets to inspire young writers.

Gillooly, E. (Ed.). (2001). *Poetry for
young people: Robert Browning.* **New York:
Sterling.**
A collection of Victorian poetry that includes
a biography of Browning.

Hudson, W. (1993). *Pass it on: African
American poetry for children.* **New York:
Scholastic.**
African American poetry that inspires
intergenerational dialogue.

**Kasten, D. S., & Kasten, M. (Eds.).
(2000).** *Poetry for young people: William
Shakespeare.* **New York: Sterling.**
Excerpts of sonnets and plays to introduce
children to the writings of William
Shakespeare.

Koontz, D. (2001). *The paper doorway.*
New York: HarperCollins.
Funny poems, scary poems, and everything
in between from Dean Koontz.

Lewis, J. P. (2005). *Heroes and she-roes:
Poems of amazing and everyday heroes.*
New York: Dial.
Twenty-one poems celebrating real-life heroes.

Longfellow, H. W. (2001). *The children's
own Longfellow.* **Boston: Houghton Mifflin.**
A collection of eight of Longfellow's most
popular children's poems.

Mendelson, E. (Ed.). (2000). *Poetry for
young people: Lewis Carroll.* **New York:
Sterling.**
A selection of 26 classic Carroll poems.

Paschen, E., & Mosby, R. P. (Eds.). (2001). *Poetry speaks.* Naperville, IL: Sourcebooks. Hear the poets read their own work in this large collection of important poems, which comes with three audio CDs.

Soto, G. (2005). *Neighborhood odes.* New York: Harcourt. Twenty-one poems about growing up in a Hispanic neighborhood.

Web sites

Favorite Poem Project
http://www.favoritepoem.org/thevideos/index.html
This site has video images of everyday people reading their favorite poems and expressing how the poems have affected them.

Fizzy Funny Fuzzy: Fun Poetry for Kids!
http://www.fizzyfunnyfuzzy.com
This site contains child-friendly poetry.

Giggle Poetry
http://www.gigglepoetry.com/index.aspx
This site has various poetry activities, from fill-in-the-blanks to producing poetry plays.

Inki and Taz's Poetry Corner
http://library.thinkquest.org/11883
This site contains a variety of poems of different styles.

Instant Poetry Forms
http://ettcweb.lr.k12.nj.us/forms/newpoem.htm
This site contains various poetry forms and examples.

KidLit—Poetry Gallery
http://mgfx.com/kidlit/kids/artlit/poetry
This site contains a gallery of poetry written by children.

KidzPage!
http://gardenofsong.com/kidzpage
Fun children's poems and links are featured here.

Magnetic Poetry
http://home.freeuk.net/elloughton13/scramble.htm
This site offers students an opportunity to manipulate and create poetry online.

Poetry4Kids.com
http://www.poetry4kids.com/index.php
Author Kenn Nesbitt presents poetry lessons and fun poetry games.

Poetry for Kids
http://www.kathimitchell.com/poemtypes.html
This site demonstrates how to write different forms of poetry.

Poetry for Kids: Giggle Poetry
http://www.gigglepotz.com/kidspoetry.htm
This site displays poems and offers instruction on how to write poems and how to teach poem writing.

References

Alvermann, D. (1991). The discussion web: A graphic aid for learning across the curriculum. *The Reading Teacher*, 45, 92–99.

Anderson, R. C. (1994). Role of reader's schema in comprehension, learning, and memory. In R. B. Ruddell, M. R. Ruddell, & H. Singer (Eds.), *Theoretical models and processes of reading* (4th ed., pp. 469–482). Newark, DE: International Reading Association.

Anderson, R. C., & Pearson, P. D. (1984). A schema-theoretic view of basic processes in reading comprehension. In P. D. Pearson, R. Barr, M. L. Kamil, & P. Mosenthal (Eds.), *Handbook of reading research* (Vol. 1, pp. 225–253). New York: Longman.

Askew, B.J., & Fountas, I. (1998). Building an early reading process: Active from the start! *The Reading Teacher*, 52(2), 126–134.

Asselin, M. (2002). Vocabulary instruction. *Teacher Librarian*, 29(3), 57–59.

Bear, D. R., Invernizzi, M., Templeton, S., & Johnston, F. (2003). *Words their way: Word study for phonics, vocabulary, and spelling* (3rd ed.). Upper Saddle River, NJ: Merrill/ Prentice Hall. (Videotape: *Words their way*, ISBN: 013022183X.)

Blachowicz, C. L., & Fisher, P. (2000). Vocabulary instruction. In M. L. Kamil, P. Mosenthal, P. D. Pearson, & R. Barr (Eds.), *Handbook of reading research* (Vol. 3, pp. 503–523). Mahwah, NJ: Lawrence Erlbaum Associates.

Blevins, W. (2003). *Teaching phonics and word study in the intermediate grades*. New York: Scholastic.

Bloodgood, J. W., & Pacifici, L. C. (2004). Bringing word study into intermediate classrooms. *The Reading Teacher*, 58(3), 250–263.

Brabham, E. G., & Villaume, S. K. (2000). Continuing conversations about literature circles. *The Reading Teacher*, 54(3), 278-281.

Buehl, D. (2001). *Classroom strategies for interactive learning* (2nd ed.). Newark, DE: International Reading Association.

Cambourne, B. (2002). Holistic, integrated approaches to reading and language arts instruction: The constructivist framework of an instructional theory. In A. Farstrup & S. Samuels (Eds.), *What research has to say about reading instruction* (3rd ed., pp. 25–47). Newark, DE: International Reading Association.

Clark, K. F., & Graves, M. F. (2004). Scaffolding students' comprehension of text. *The Reading Teacher*, 58(6), 570–580.

Cunningham, P. (2000). *Phonics they use: Words for reading and writing* (3rd ed.). New York: HarperCollins.

Daneman, M. (1991). Individual differences in reading skills. In R. Barr, M. L. Kamil, P. B. Mosenthal, & P. D. Pearson (Eds.), *Handbook of reading research* (Vol. 2, pp. 518–538). White Plains, NY: Longman.

Daniels, H. (1994). *Literature circles: Voice and choice in the student-centered classroom*. York, ME: Stenhouse.

Day, J. P., Spiegel, D. L., McLellan, J., & Brown, V. B. (2002). *Moving forward with literature circles*. New York: Scholastic.

Drucker, M. J. (2003). What reading teachers should know about ESL learners. *The Reading Teacher*, 57(1), 22–29.

Duke, N., & Pearson, P. D. (2002). Effective practices for developing comprehension. In A. Farstrup & S. Samuels (Eds.), *What research has to say about reading instruction* (3rd ed., pp. 205–242). Newark, DE: International Reading Association.

Ehri, L. C., & Nunes, S. R. (2002). The role of phonemic awareness in learning to read. In A. Farstrup, & S. Samuels (Eds.), *What research has to say about reading instruction* (3rd ed., pp. 110–139). Newark, DE: International Reading Association.

Fang, Z. (Ed.). (2005). *Literacy teaching and learning: Current issues and trends*. Upper Saddle River, NJ: Merrill/ Prentice Hall.

Farstrup, A., & Samuels, S. (Eds.). (2002). *What research has to say about reading instruction* (3rd ed.). Newark, DE: International Reading Association.

Flynn, R. M. (2004). Curriculum-based Readers Theater: Setting the stage for reading and retention. *The Reading Teacher*, 58(4), 360–365.

Ford, M. P., & Opitz, M. F. (2002). Using centers to engage children during guided reading time: Intensifying learning experiences away from the teacher. *The Reading Teacher*, 55, 710–717.

Fountas, I. C., & Pinnell, G. S. (1996). *Guided reading: Good first teaching for all children*. Portsmouth, NH: Heinemann.

Fountas, I. C., & Pinnell, G. S. (1999). *Matching books to readers: Using leveled books in guided reading, K–3*. Portsmouth, NH: Heinemann.

Fredericks, A. (2001). *The complete phonemic awareness handbook*. Orlando, FL: Rigby Press.

Gambrell, L. B. (1996). Creating classroom cultures that foster reading motivation. *The Reading Teacher, 50*(1), 14–25.

Graves, M., & Watts-Taffe, S. (2002). The place of word consciousness in a research-based vocabulary program. In A. Farstrup & S. Samuels (Eds.), *What research has to say about reading instruction* (3rd ed., pp. 140–165). Newark, DE: International Reading Association.

Griffith, L. W., & Rasinski, T. V. (2004). A focus on fluency: How one teacher incorporated fluency with her reading curriculum. *The Reading Teacher, 58*, 126–137.

Guthrie, J. T., & Wigfield, A. (2000). Engagement and motivation in reading. In M. L. Kamil, P. Mosenthal, P. D. Pearson, & R. Barr (Eds.), *Handbook of reading research* (Vol. 3, pp. 403–422). Mahwah, NJ: Lawrence Erlbaum Associates.

Harris, T. L., & Hodges, R. E. (Eds.). (1995). *The literacy dictionary: The vocabulary of reading and writing*. Newark, DE: International Reading Association.

Harvey, S., & Goudvis, A. (2000). *Strategies that work: Teaching comprehension to enhance understanding*. York, ME: Stenhouse.

Herman, P. A., & Dole, J. (2005). Theory and practice in vocabulary learning and instruction. In Z. Fang (Ed.), *Literacy teaching and learning: Current issues and trends* (pp. 112–120). Upper Saddle River, NJ: Merrill/Prentice Hall.

Hickman, P., Pollard-Durodola, S. & Vaughn, S. (2004). Storybook reading: Improving vocabulary and comprehension for English-language learners. *The Reading Teacher, 57*(8), 720–730.

Hilden, K., & Pressley, M. (2002). *Can teachers become comprehension strategy teachers given a small amount of training?* Paper presented at the 52nd Annual Meeting of the National Reading Conference, Miami, FL.

Hudson, R. F., Lane, H. B., & Pullen, P. C. (2005). Reading fluency assessment and instruction: What, why, and how? *The Reading Teacher, 58*(8), 702–714.

International Reading Association. (2000). *Excellent reading teachers: A position statement of the International Reading Association*. Newark, DE: International Reading Association.

International Reading Association. (2002). *IRA Literacy Study Groups vocabulary module*. Newark, DE: International Reading Association.

Johnson, D. D., & Pearson, P. D. (1984). *Teaching reading vocabulary* (2nd ed.). New York: Holt, Rinehart and Winston.

Kamil, M. L., Mosenthal, P. B., Pearson, P. D., & Barr, R. (Eds.). (2000). *Handbook of reading research* (Vol. 3). Mahwah, NJ: Lawrence Erlbaum Associates.

Lubliner, S. (2004). Help for struggling upper-grade elementary readers. *The Reading Teacher, 57*(5), 430–438.

Macon, J. M. (1991). *Literature response*. Paper presented at the Annual Literacy Workshop, Anaheim, CA.

McGinley, W., & Denner, P. (1987). Story impressions: A prereading/prewriting activity. *Journal of Reading, 31,* 248–253.

McLaughlin, M. (2003). *Guided comprehension in the primary grades*. Newark, DE: International Reading Association.

McLaughlin, M. (2005). *Vocabulary Bookmark Technique: Examining students' word choices*. Paper presented at the 52nd Annual Meeting of the National Reading Conference, Miami, FL.

McLaughlin, M., & Allen, M. B. (2002a). *Guided comprehension: A teaching model for grades 3–8*. Newark, DE: International Reading Association.

McLaughlin, M., & Allen, M. B. (2002b). *Guided Comprehension in action: Lessons for grades 3–8*. Newark, DE: International Reading Association.

McLaughlin, M., & Fisher, L. (2005). *Research-based lessons for K–3: Phonemic awareness, phonics, fluency, vocabulary, and comprehension*. New York: Scholastic.

Morrow, L. M. (1985). Retelling stories: A strategy for improving children's comprehension, concept of story, and oral language complexity. *Elementary School Journal, 85*(5), 647–661.

Nathan, R., & Stanovich, K. (1991). The causes and consequences of differences in reading fluency. *Theory into Practice, 30,* 176–184.

National Commission on Teaching and America's Future. (1997). *Doing what matters most: Investing in quality teaching*. Available at http://www.tc.columbia.edu/teachingcomm.

National Reading Panel. (2000). *Teaching children to read: An evidence-based assessment of the scientific research literature on reading and its implications for reading instruction.* Washington, DC: National Institutes of Health.

Oakley, G. (2003). Improving oral reading fluency (and comprehension) through the creation of talking books. *Reading Online, 6*(7). Retrieved from http://readingonline.org/articles/Oakley

Pearson, P. D. (2001). *Comprehension strategy instruction: An idea whose time has come again.* Paper presented at the Annual Meeting of the Colorado Council of the International Reading Association, Denver, CO.

Pikulski, J. J., & Chard, D. J. (2005). Fluency: Bridge between decoding and reading comprehension. *The Reading Teacher, 58*(6), 510–519.

Pressley, M. (2000). What should comprehension instruction be the instruction of? In M. Kamil, P. Mosenthal, P. D. Pearson, & R. Barr (Eds.), *Handbook of reading research* (Vol. 3, pp. 545–561). Mahwah, NJ: Lawrence Erlbaum Associates.

Rasinski, T. V. (1999a). Making and writing words. *Reading Online.* Retrieved from http://www.readingonline.org/articles/words/rasinski.index.html

Rasinski, T. V. (1999b). Making and writing words using letter patterns. *Reading Online.* Retrieved from http://www.readingonline.org/articles/words/rasinski_index.html

Rasinski, T. V. (2003). *The fluent reader.* New York: Scholastic.

Rasinski, T. V. (2004). Creating fluent readers. *Educational Leadership, 61*(6), 46–51.

Rasinski, T. V., & Padak, N. (2000). *Effective reading strategies: Children who find reading difficult* (2nd ed.). Columbus, OH: Merrill/Prentice Hall.

Richards, M. (2000). Be a good detective: Solve the case of oral reading fluency. *The Reading Teacher, 53*(7), 534–539.

Richek, M. A. (2005). Words are wonderful: Interactive, time-efficient strategies to teach meaning vocabulary. *The Reading Teacher, 58*(5), 414–423.

Ruddell, R. B. (2004). Researching the influential literacy teacher: Characteristics, beliefs, strategies, and new research directions. In R. B. Ruddell & N. J. Unrau (Eds.), *Theoretical models and processes of reading* (5th ed., pp. 979–997). Newark, DE: International Reading Association.

Ruddell, R. B., Ruddell, M. R., & Singer, H. (Eds.). (1994). *Theoretical models and processes of reading* (4th ed.). Newark, DE: International Reading Association.

Ruddell, R. B., & Unrav, N. J. (Eds.). (2004). *Theoretical models of processes of reading* (5th ed.). Newark, DE: International Reading Association.

Samuels, S. J. (1979). The method of repeated readings. *The Reading Teacher, 32,* 403–408.

Samuels, S. J. (2002). Reading fluency: Its development and assessment. In A. Farstrup & S. Samuels (Eds.), *What research has to say about reading instruction* (3rd ed., pp.166–183). Newark, DE: International Reading Association.

Schwartz, R., & Raphael, T. (1985). Concept of definition: A key to improving students' vocabulary. *The Reading Teacher, 39*(2), 198–205.

Shanahan, T. (1997). Reading-writing relationships, thematic units, inquiry-learning . . . in pursuit of effective integrated literacy instruction. *The Reading Teacher, 51*(1), 12–19.

Snow, C. E., Burns, M. S., & Griffin, P. G. (Eds.). (1998). *Preventing reading difficulties in young children.* Washington, DC: National Academy Press.

Stahl, S. A., & Heubach, K. M. (2005). Fluency-oriented reading instruction. *Journal of Literacy Research, 37*(1), 25–60.

Strecker, S. K., & Roser, N. L. (2005). Toward understanding oral reading fluency. In Z. Fang (Ed.), *Literacy teaching and learning: Current issues and trends* (pp. 102–111). Upper Saddle River, NJ: Merrill/Prentice Hall.

Tompkins, G. (2001). *Literacy for the 21st century: A balanced approach* (2nd ed.). Saddle Brook, NJ: Prentice Hall.

Vacca, R.T., & Vacca, J. L. (2002). *Content area reading: Literacy and learning across the curriculum* (7th ed.). New York: Longman.

Walker, B. J. (2005). Thinking aloud: Struggling readers often require more than a model. *The Reading Teacher, 58*(7), 688–692.

Wood, K. (1984). Probable Passages: A writing strategy. *The Reading Teacher, 37,* 496-499.

Young Adult Novels, Picture Books, and Poems Featured in the Lessons in This Book

Babbitt, N. (1975). *Tuck everlasting*. New York: Farrar, Straus, and Giroux.

Bates, K. L., & Gall, C. (2004). *America the beautiful*. New York: Little, Brown.

Bishop, C. H. (1952). *Twenty and ten*. New York: Viking.

Deedy, C. A. (2000). *The yellow star: The legend of King Christian X of Denmark*. Atlanta: Peachtree.

Driscoll, M. (2003). *A child's introduction to poetry*. New York: Blackdog and Leventhal.

Fritz, J. (1976). *What's the big idea, Ben Franklin?* New York: Paperstar.

Fritz, J. (1995). *You want women to vote, Lizzie Stanton?* New York: Paperstar.

George, J. C. (1972). *Julie of the wolves*. New York: HarperTrophy.

Giff, P. R. (1997). *Lily's crossing*. New York: Bantam Doubleday Dell.

Hopkins, L. B. (2000). *My America: A poetry atlas of the United States*. New York: Simon & Schuster.

Keene, C. (1995). *The soccer shoe clue*. New York: Aladdin.

Konigsburg, E. L. (1967). *From the mixed-up files of Mrs. Basil E. Frankweiler*. New York: Aladdin.

Lewis, C. S. (1994). *The lion, the witch, and the wardrobe*. New York: HarperCollins.

Lowry, L. (1989). *Number the stars*. New York: Houghton Mifflin.

Nichol, B. (1994). *Beethoven lives upstairs*. New York: Orchard.

O'Dell, S. (1960). *Island of the blue dolphins*. New York: Dell Yearling.

Paulsen, G. (1987). *Hatchet*. New York: Simon & Schuster.

Paulsen, G. (1996). *Brian's winter*. New York: Delacorte.

Pinkney, A. D. (1994). *Dear Benjamin Banneker*. San Diego: Harcourt.

Polacco, P. (2000). *The butterfly*. New York: Philomel.

Prelutsky, J. (1984). *The new kid on the block*. New York: Greenwillow.

Raskin, E. (1978). *The Westing game*. New York: Dutton.

Rogasky, B. (1994). *Winter poems*. New York: Scholastic.

Rowling, J. K. (1997). *Harry Potter and the sorcerer's stone*. New York: Scholastic.

Rowling, J. K. (1999). *Harry Potter and the chamber of secrets*. New York: Scholastic.

Rowling, J. K. (1999). *Harry Potter and the prisoner of Azkaban*. New York: Scholastic.

Sobol, D. J. (1982). *Encyclopedia Brown takes the cake*. New York: Scholastic.

Sonek, B. (1995). Retrieved from www.auschwitz.dk/id6.htm.

Sperry, A. (1940). *Call it courage*. New York: Simon & Schuster.

Weidt, M. N. (2002). *Rosa Parks*. Minneapolis: Lerner Publications.

Woodruff, E. (1999). *The Ghost of Lizard Light*. New York: Knopf.

World's best-loved poetry. (2002). New York: Troll. (This is a collection of poems. No author or editor is listed. "Stopping by Woods on a Snowy Evening" is a poem in this volume.)

Yolen, J. (1988). *The devil's arithmetic*. New York: Viking.

Index